FROM
KINSHASA
TO
KANDAHAR

Beyond Boundaries:
Canadian Defence and Strategic Studies Series
Rob Huebert, Series Editor
ISSN 1716-2645 (PRINT) ISSN 1925-2919 (ONLINE)

Canada's role in international military and strategic studies ranges from peacebuilding and Arctic sovereignty to unconventional warfare and domestic security. This series provides narratives and analyses of the Canadian military from both an historical and a contemporary perspective.

No. 1· **The Generals: The Canadian Army's Senior Commanders in the Second World War** J.L. Granatstein

No. 2· **Art and Memorial: The Forgotten History of Canada's War Art** Laura Brandon

No. 3· **In the National Interest: Canadian Foreign Policy and the Department of Foreign Affairs and International Trade, 1909–2009** Edited by Greg Donaghy and Michael K. Carroll

No. 4· **Long Night of the Tankers: Hitler's War Against Caribbean Oil** David J. Bercuson and Holger H. Herwig

No. 5· **Fishing for a Solution: Canada's Fisheries Relations with the European Union, 1977–2013** Donald Barry, Bob Applebaum, and Earl Wiseman

No. 6· **From Kinshasa to Kandahar: Canada and Fragile States in Historical Perspective** Edited by Michael K. Carroll and Greg Donaghy

UNIVERSITY OF CALGARY
Press

FROM KINSHASA TO KANDAHAR

Canada and Fragile States in Historical Perspective

Edited by Michael K. Carroll and Greg Donaghy

Beyond Boundaries: Canadian
Defence and Strategic Studies Series

ISSN 1716-2645 (Print) ISSN 1925-2919 (Online)

© 2016 Michael K. Carroll and Greg Donaghy

University of Calgary Press
2500 University Drive NW
Calgary, Alberta
Canada T2N 1N4

press.ucalgary.ca

This book is available as an ebook which is licensed under a Creative Commons license. The publisher should be contacted for any commercial use which falls outside the terms of that license.

LIBRARY AND ARCHIVES CANADA CATALOGUING IN PUBLICATION

From Kinshasha to Kandahar : Canada and fragile states in historical perspective / edited by Michael K. Carroll and Greg Donaghy.

(Beyond boundaries : Canadian defence and strategic studies series, 1716-2645 ; no. 6)
Includes bibliographical references and index.
Issued in print and electronic formats.
ISBN 978-1-55238-844-0 (paperback).–ISBN 978-1-55238-845-7 (Open access pdf).–
ISBN 978-1-55238-846-4 (pdf).–ISBN 978-1-55238-847-1 (epub).–
ISBN 978-1-55238-848-8 (mobi)

1. Failed states–History–20th century. 2. Failed states–History–21st century.
3. Canada–Foreign relations–1945-. I. Donaghy, Greg, 1961-, editor
II. Carroll, Michael K. (Michael Kiernan), editor III. Series: Beyond boundaries series ; no. 6

FC242.F76 2016   327.7109'045   C2016-900360-4
                                                       C2016-900361-2

This book has been published with the help of a grant from the Federation for the Humanities and Social Sciences, through the Awards to Scholarly Publications Program, using funds provided by the Social Sciences and Humanities Research Council of Canada.

The University of Calgary Press acknowledges the support of the Government of Alberta through the Alberta Media Fund for our publications. We acknowledge the financial support of the Government of Canada through the Canada Book Fund for our publishing activities. We acknowledge the financial support of the Canada Council for the Arts for our publishing program.

 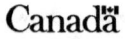   

Cover image: Canadian Master Bombardier Clint Godsoe, Kandahar Provincial Reconstruction Team (PRT) (Credit: ISAF Photo by Staff Sgt. Jeffrey Duran)
Cover design, page design, and typesetting by Melina Cusano
Copy editing by Edwin Janzen

For our mentors and friends:

Robert Bothwell, John English, and Norman Hillmer

Contents

	List of Acronyms	ix
	Michael K. Carroll and Greg Donaghy Introduction	1
1	*Tom Keating* Responding to Failed and Fragile States: The Evolution of Canadian Policy	9
2	*Kevin A. Spooner* Present at the Creation? Canada, United Nations Intervention, and the Congo as a Failed State, 1960–64	33
3	*Stephanie Bangarth* The Politics of African Intervention: Canada and Biafra, 1967–70	53
4	*David Webster* Failing Fragile States: Canada and East Timor	73
5	*Andrew S. Thompson* Entangled: Canadian Engagement in Haiti, 1968–2010	97
6	*Julian Schofield* Diagnostic Confusion and Missed Opportunities: Canada and Pakistan's "Failed State"	121

7	*Duane Bratt* Bosnia: From Failed State to Functioning State	*143*
8	*Stephen M. Saideman* Six Years in Kandahar: Understanding Canada's Multidimensional Effort to Build a Sustainable Afghan State	*165*
9	*Jean Daudelin* Canada and Fragile States in the Americas	*185*
10	*Hevina S. Dashwood* Corporate Social Responsibility in Fragile and Stable States: Dilemmas and Opportunities in South Sudan and Ghana	*207*
11	*Darren Brunk* Conclusion	*237*

Contributors	*251*
Bibliography	*253*
Index	*279*

List of Acronyms

AI	Amnesty International
ANA	Afghan National Army
ANC	Armée nationale congolaise (Congolese National Army)
ANP	Afghan National Police
APEC	Asia-Pacific Economic Cooperation
ASEAN	Association of Southeast Asian Nations
AU	African Union
CCODP	Canadian Catholic Organization for Development and Peace
CF	Canadian Forces
CIDA	Canadian International Development Agency
CIIEID	Canadian International Institute for Extractive Industries and Development
CNG	Conseil National de Gouvernement (Haiti)
CSR	Corporate social responsibility
CUSO	Canadian University Service Overseas
DEA	Department of External Affairs
DFAIT	Department of Foreign Affairs and International Trade
DFATD	Department of Foreign Affairs, Trade and Development
DND	Department of National Defence
DRC	Democratic Republic of the Congo

ECOSOC	Economic and Social Council (United Nations)
EITI	Extractive Industries Transparency Initiative
ETAN	East Timor Alert Network
EU	European Union
FFP	Fund for Peace
FMG	Federal Military Government (Nigeria)
FRAPH	Front pour l'Avancement et le Progrès Haitien
GDP	Gross Domestic Product
GRI	Global Reporting Initiative
ICISS	International Commission on Intervention and State Sovereignty
IDB	Inter-American Development Bank
IFC	International Finance Corporation
IFOR	NATO Implementation Force
IMOT	International Military Observer Team
INCAF	International Network on Conflict and Fragility (OECD)
JNA	Yugoslav National Army
KANUPP	Karachi Nuclear Power Plant
LAC	Library and Archives Canada
LDC	Least developed countries
MICIVIH	Mission Civile Internationale en Haïti (United Nations Civilian Mission in Haiti)
MIF	Multinational Interim Force
MINUSTAH	United Nations Stabilization Mission in Haiti
MNC	Multinational corporation
MNF	Multinational force
NATO	North Atlantic Treaty Organization
NDP	New Democratic Party
NGO	Non-governmental organization

NLC	National Labor Committee
NPT	Non-Proliferation Treaty
PRT	Provincial Reconstruction Team
OAS	Organization of American States
OAU	Organization of African Unity
ODA	Official development assistance
OECD	Organization for Economic Co-operation and Development
ONUC	Opération des Nations Unies au Congo
PAHO	Pan American Health Organization
PMO	Prime Minister's Office
PRT	Provincial Reconstruction Team (Kandahar)
RCMP	Royal Canadian Mounted Police
RoCK	Representative of Canada in Kandahar
SCFAID	Standing Committee on Foreign Affairs and International Development
SCFAIT	Standing Committee on Foreign Affairs and International Trade
START	Stabilization and Reconstruction Task Force
UN	United Nations
UNGA	United Nations General Assembly
UNMIH	United Nations Mission in Haiti
UNSC	United Nations Security Council
UNAMIR	United Nations Assistance Mission for Rwanda
UNHRC	United Nations Human Rights Council
UNMOGIP	United Nations Military Observer Group in India and Pakistan
UNODOC	United Nations Office on Drugs and Crime
UNOSOM	United Nations Operation in Somalia
UNPROFOR	United Nations Protection Force
USAID	United States Agency for International Development

INTRODUCTION

Michael K. Carroll and Greg Donaghy

The world is a dangerous and fragile place. Nation states, the rock-solid foundation of the post-1945 international system, quake before surging Islamic fundamentalists in the Middle East and Asia, narco-terrorists in Latin America, and the deadly Ebola virus in West Africa. Of the world's seven billion people, almost a quarter live in "fragile states," where one-third survive on less than $1.25 per day and half the children die before the age of five.[1]

For decades, the Cold War confrontation between the US-led liberal democracies and the Communist Soviet Bloc obscured the precarious status of the world's weakest nations. Recruited by one side or the other, weak states, especially those that emerged in the Global South during the 1950s and 1960s from the rubble of European empire, were safely frozen into place by the international system's rigid, bipolar structure. Often buttressed by military advisors and offshore bases, or development specialists and agricultural advisors, corrupt presidents and rotten governments stayed afloat atop a vast pool of dollars and rubles.

The collapse of the Soviet Union in 1991 and the end of the Cold War began to reveal the extent of the rot. Though some countries successfully managed the transition from Cold War client to independent state, most did not, confronting the developed West with almost one hundred states, representing almost two billion people, that were "at risk" of imploding.[2]

As the likelihood of Cold War–style interstate conflict was replaced in the 1990s by fears over intrastate conflict in Eastern Europe and Africa, diplomats and policymakers the world over grappled with the implications for international security. Sexy systemic threats—climate change and drought, organized crime and terrorism, pandemic disease—drew lavish attention, undermining established notions of sovereignty.

Canada willingly joined in the search for expansive definitions of sovereignty. As early as September 1991, for instance, Conservative prime minister Brian Mulroney called on states "to re-think the limits of national sovereignty in a world where problems respect no borders."[3] His Liberal successor, Jean Chrétien, picked up these themes. Chrétien's 1995 foreign policy white paper, *Canada and the World*, and his activist foreign minister, Lloyd Axworthy, championed a novel "human security" agenda that favoured the welfare and security of the individual over that of the state.[4]

The 2001 terrorist attacks on the United States by Islamic fundamentalists—hidden amid the ruins of the shattered Afghan state—drove home to the West the direct threat posed by distant fragile states. "The events of September 11, 2001, taught us," the White House declared in 2002, "that weak states, like Afghanistan, can pose as great a danger to our national interests as strong states."[5] Canada learned this lesson too. Liberal prime minister Paul Martin signalled a shift in Canadian policy in his 2005 International Policy Statement. Acknowledging the dangers created by "weak, ineffectually governed states," he edged away from the humanitarian preoccupations associated with Axworthy's human security agenda and embraced a series of measures to enhance global security.[6] He backed the UN's emerging doctrine of Responsibility to Protect (R2P), explicitly aimed at preventing civilian casualties in failing states, and took steps to give Ottawa the capacity to respond quickly to international crises in a coordinated fashion. In 2005, the Department of Foreign Affairs created a Stabilization and Reconstruction Task Force (START), committing $100 million annually to the Global Peace and Security Fund for the next five years. "The 'failed states' agenda," observed Erin Simpson of the Canadian International Council, "represents a return to a more traditional, state-centric view of security threats and their solutions."[7]

But state fragility is difficult to define. Gerald Helman and Steven Ratner, former US State Department officials who coined the term "failed states" in the early 1990s, imprecisely label as "failed" any state "utterly incapable of sustaining itself as a member of the international community."[8] Others have tried to be more precise. Canadian aid officials, for instance, equate state fragility with "weak institutional capacity, poor governance, political instability, and ongoing violence or a legacy of past conflict."[9] The Fund for Peace's Fragile State Index, the most widely used research tool on weak states, is even more exact, employing twelve economic, political, military, and social indicators to assess national stability.[10] Among these definitions, some common themes emerge: sustained conflict, poor governance, widespread corruption, and poverty. In short, concluded Australian anti-slavery activist Nick Grono, "they all describe some type of significant state failure or dysfunction."[11]

Definitional problems arise almost immediately. Assessments of state fragility and failure are often in the eyes of the beholder, and are sometimes deployed for nefarious purposes. Tom Keating hints at this in the chapter that opens this book, pointing out how the emphasis on liberal democratic norms of state behaviour allows Western governments to regulate access to the international community and its resources. Jean Daudelin, in his chapter on fragility in the Americas, challenges the perception that Colombia is the most fragile state in the Americas, save Haiti. Similarly, Julian Schofield's essay on Pakistan questions the country's high ranking among at-risk states, insisting that it is neither "failed, fragile, nor weak." Rather, the label is used to mobilize public opinion in Canada behind Western anti-terrorist strategies in Afghanistan, while simultaneously encouraging policymakers to adopt inappropriate strategies for Pakistan. David Webster is even more explicit in tackling the rhetorical uses of "failed state" language, exploring how it was used for decades to delegitimize East Timor's demand for independence following the Indonesian invasion in 1975. He shows, too, how challenging that rhetoric made independence possible, and how just a shift from "failed" to "fragile" makes it possible to imagine new ways of engaging the world's weaker states.

Though problems of state fragility seem to loom especially large today, this collection reminds us that Canada's stake in fragile and failed states stretches back into the early post–Second World War era. As Keating demonstrates, the notion of state fragility was implicit in the military help that Prime Minister Louis St. Laurent's government dispatched to the shaky postwar states of Western Europe, which cowered before the Soviet Union's aggressive communism. It was implicit, too, in the

Commonwealth's Colombo Plan, conceived in 1950, to send financial and technical aid to uncertain postcolonial nations of South and Southeast Asia. "These new Governments are highly precarious," Foreign Minister Lester B. Pearson wrote a cabinet colleague in early 1951 to plead for help. "They need external financial assistance if they are to have a chance of making some improvement in the appallingly low standard of living of their people and so of sheltering them from the attractions of Communist propaganda. We must try, I believe, to strengthen the will and the capacity of these countries to assist in the struggle against Communist imperialism; and one of the very few ways we can do so is by showing a practical interest in their economic welfare."[12] Then, as now, Canadian policymakers recognized that Canada's security and its national interests were best served by a world order composed of stable and secure states.

For Canada, Keating continues, tackling fragile states in search of global order was usually a multilateral effort tied to NATO and its Anglo-American leadership, the Commonwealth, and the United Nations. This is a theme picked up and elaborated in several chapters. Alliances motivate Canadian intervention, provide the means to act, and ultimately limit and constrain Canadian action. Canada was rarely ready to confront the consequences of state fragility alone, a point that is made clear in Kevin Spooner's chapter on Canada's struggle to help Congolese leaders build a professional, non-political military in the midst of the civil war that tore apart their country in the early 1960s. Canadian diplomats and soldiers were certainly aware that strong governing institutions were key to state stability, but they repeatedly declined to act without the UN's multilateral blessing. "Canada may well have been witness, and even unwittingly contributed," Spooner grimly concludes, "to a critical moment when the seeds of a failing state were sown."

Alliances have similarly defined Canada's long engagement with the impoverished Caribbean nation of Haiti. Beset in equal measure by natural disasters and unnatural dictators, Haiti has lurched along from crisis to crisis for decades. Despite billions of dollars in aid, much of it from Canada, progress has been glacial. Yet, as Andrew Thompson points out, Canada persists. His chapter shows why: Though Canada's domestic stake in Haiti is small and the island poses no direct danger to Canada, the same cannot be said of the United States. The thought of an unsettled Haiti, driving boatloads of refugees to nearby Florida, is a genuine worry for

Washington. In Thompson's view, the ebb and flow of US-Haitian relations determines Canada's uneven commitment to the island's fate. Saving Haiti often takes a backseat to saving Washington.

Though national interest and alliances were doubtless foremost, they have not been the only influences on Canadian policy. The challenges of addressing state fragility after the terrorist attacks on the United States of 11 September 2001 renewed debate between realists and idealists over why and when to intervene. Keating's overview dissects this recent discussion, while historian Stephanie Bangarth locates the same tensions in Canada's response to the Nigerian civil war of the late 1960s. The war between the Federal Military Government and the breakaway state of Biafra pitted Canadian humanitarians against the early realist inclinations of their prime minister, Pierre Trudeau. Humanitarian members of Parliament David MacDonald and Andrew Brewin campaigned hard for direct aid to civilians in Biafra, but were denied by Trudeau, who feared that support for a secessionist state might establish a useful precedent for Quebec separatists. The uneasy compromises that eventually permitted a trickle of NGO aid to flow into Biafra in 1970 highlight the range and mix of motives driving Canadians toward intervention.

Fragile states are not for the fainthearted. Keating's opening catalogue of Canadian engagement records few victories. Accounts of Canadian efforts in the Congo, Haiti, and Pakistan emphasize the constraints on success. Yet, there are grounds for a careful optimism, especially when will and resources are mobilized. Duane Bratt's account of Canada's engagement in Bosnia, alongside its UN and NATO partners, is clear: though far from perfect, forceful and sustained international intervention turned a "failed state into a functioning state," and helped reestablish stability in the Balkans. Jean Daudelin's rigorous examination of the data on Canadian aid to fragile states in the Americas strikes a similar, balanced note: too much aid to Haiti, not enough help in Central America, just right across the Caribbean, where Canada has historically been active. Practice and commitment make perfect.

Even in Afghanistan, perhaps the most complex and difficult environment addressed in this collection, progress is still possible, concludes Stephen Saideman. Backed by real force and a strong political commitment, Canada made a difference in rural Kandahar, though the cost was high and the effect fleeting. For Saideman, the costly commitment and the lessons hard-learned presage other, better-managed, more realistic campaigns to come.

Africanist Hevina Dashwood is more hopeful still, as she traces the growing international willingness to tackle some of the underlying challenges that give rise to fragile states and weak governments. Combining natural resource riches—oil, gas, and minerals—and corporate greed often produces the kind of systemic corruption and factional violence that can compromise a weak state. But this is changing. Dashwood's chapter examines the successful global campaign by liberal states, the UN and its many civil society backers, and multinational corporate stakeholders to create guidelines to reinforce the state's capacity to govern. Recent Canadian governments, both Liberal and Conservative, have championed notions of Corporate Social Responsibility (CSR), voluntary commitments to act in "an economic, social and environmentally sustainable manner," as a key part of the resolution of state fragility.

The lessons of these chapters on the history of Canada and fragile states are modest but worth retaining. First, Canadian foreign policy, this collection shouts, "does" state fragility, having a long record of recurring engagements in fragile states. Ottawa's efforts were not always perfect and did not always spring from the purest of motives. Indeed, Canadians were rarely the disinterested participants that they—and their governments—imagined themselves to be. Rather, as this volume shows time and again, Canada's policies have been driven by a complex range of motives: humanitarian, electoral and geopolitical, national security, and economic. Policymakers who ignored these broad motivations were likely to find themselves in real trouble, both at home with voters and in the field abroad.

Second, Canada mattered. *Kinshasa to Kandahar* sometimes makes for grim and discouraging reading. Despite fifty years of effort, the landscape of fragility seems sadly familiar: Congo, Haiti, Afghanistan. Yet this collection reminds readers that Canada has made a difference, however incremental and imperfect. And over time, Canada, like the UN and NATO, has learned to address state fragility, developing better tools to reinforce weak states and better techniques for intervening.

Finally, this volume underlines the enduring challenge of getting Canadian engagement right, striking a balance between competing interests, and finding the will to support sustainable commitments. Policymaker Darren Brunk's concluding reflections address this point forcefully, asking: when are Canada's efforts "good enough"? It's a tough question, one which demands that government and all sectors of civil society interrogate frankly the motives prompting and constraining engagement with fragile states, as well as the uncertain prospects for success.

This discussion is already under way. Perhaps, as former Supreme Court justice Louise Arbour has argued recently, there are no obvious answers to the problems of state fragility. After working on improving global governance, R2P, and international criminal justice issues since the mid-1990s, she has become increasingly skeptical of Western intervention, wondering if the simultaneous pursuit of peace, justice, and human rights might be impossible. "What I'm trying to promote," she explains, "is the idea of a kind of political empathy as a strategic advantage ... a blueprint for understanding before you act, as opposed to rushing into things."[13] Former Canadian foreign minister Lloyd Axworthy, who champions intervening in fragile states to protect the vulnerable, sharply dismisses this view as "ill-founded, based on faulty information and questionable assessments."[14] R2P and international criminal law, he insists, remain part of a broader process of developing enforceable global norms of behaviour, reinforcing the rule of law and promoting a humane world.

We hope this book represents a contribution to this vital national discussion.

Notes

1 Organization for Economic Co-operation and Development (OECD), *Fragile States: Resource Flows and Trends* (Paris, 2013); USAID, "Getting to Zero: A discussion paper on ending extreme poverty," 21 November 2013, http://www.usaid.gov/sites/default/files/documents/1870/USAID-Extreme-Poverty-Discussion-Paper.pdf; Save the Children UK, *Unlocking Progress in Fragile States: Optimising high-impact maternal and child survival interventions*, http://www.savethechildren.org.uk/sites/default/files/docs/Unlocking_Progress_in_Fragile_States_low_res_1.pdf (accessed 11 November 2014).

2 See Lothar Brock, Hans-Henrik Holm, Georg Sørensen, and Michael Stohl, *Fragile States* (Cambridge, UK: Polity Press, 2012).

3 Canada, Office of the Prime Minister, Notes for an address by Prime Minister Brian Mulroney on the occasion of the centennial anniversary convocation, Stanford University, 29 September 1991.

4 Greg Donaghy, "All God's Children: Lloyd Axworthy, Human

Security, and Canadian Foreign Policy, 1996–2000," *Canadian Foreign Policy*, 10, no. 2 (Winter 2003): 39–58.

5   President, *The National Security Strategy of the United States*, 17 September 2002, http://www.state.gov/documents/organization/63562.pdf (accessed 10 October 2014).

6   Canada, Department of Foreign Affairs and International Trade, *Canada's International Policy Statement: A Role of Pride and Influence in the World—Diplomacy*, 2005, http://publications.gc.ca/collections/Collection/FR4-4-2005E.pdf (accessed July 10, 2014).

7   Erin Simpson, "Who Failed the World's 'Failed States'?," *Peace Magazine* (Apr–June 2007): 6, http://peacemagazine.org/archive/v23n2p06.htm (accessed 8 July 2014).

8   Gerald B. Helman and Steven R. Ratner, "Saving Failed States," *Foreign Policy* 89 (Winter 1992–93): 3.

9   Foreign Affairs, Trade and Development Canada, "CIDA's Strategic Overview," http://www.acdi-cida.gc.ca/acdi-cida/acdi-cida.nsf/eng/NAT-911133132-NK9 (accessed 11 July 2014).

10 While perhaps the most widely recognized, the Fund for Peace (FFP) is by no means the only index available for the ranking of fragile states. The Country Indicators for Foreign Policy (CIFP) program, headed by David Carment at Carleton University in Ottawa, is excellent, and is designed to assist the Canadian International Development Agency (CIDA) in prioritizing Canada's Official Development Assistance (ODA).

11 Nick Grono, "Fragile States, Searching for Effective Approaches and the Right Mix of Instruments," 29 January 2007, http://www.crisisgroup.org/en/publication-type/speeches/2007/grono-fragile-states-searching-for-effective-approaches-and-the-right-mix-of-instruments.aspx (accessed 14 June 2014).

12 Secretary of State for External Affairs to Minister of Finance, 17 January 1951, reprinted in Greg Donaghy, ed., *Documents on Canadian External Relations, Volume 17: 1951* (Ottawa: Canadian Government Publishing, 1996), 1042.

13 Doug Saunders, "Why Louise Arbour is thinking twice," *Globe and Mail*, 28 March 2015, online edition (accessed 18 June 2015). See also Lysiane Gagnon, "The suspension of intervention," *Globe and Mail*, 8 April 2015, online edition (accessed 18 June 2015).

14 Lloyd Axworthy, "Louise Arbour has it wrong," *Globe and Mail*, 13 April 2015, online edition (accessed 18 June 2015).

CHAPTER 1

RESPONDING TO FAILED AND FRAGILE STATES:
The Evolution of Canadian Policy

Tom Keating

Introduction

In February 2008, the Kosovo parliament issued a unilateral declaration of independence from the Federated Republic of Serbia. Within hours, the independence of Kosovo was recognized by the United States. Six weeks later, the Canadian government joined the Americans and a few dozen other states in announcing its own recognition of the independence of Kosovo. The Canadian government stated that Kosovo was a "very unique" situation that carried no implications for other separatist movements at home or abroad, but Dragan Ciric of the Canadian Serbian League expressed a different concern: "My only thought is that by this decision, Canada just supported one more failed state, and I didn't think that that's a goal of Canadian foreign policy."[1] The Canadian government's recognition of Kosovo was perhaps inevitable, given Ottawa's participation in the 1999 air war against Serbia and its support for the subsequent joint United Nations–North Atlantic Treaty Organization (UN–NATO) occupation of Kosovo established in June 1999. The government had long since decided that the sovereignty of the former Republic of Yugoslavia had to be violated as the state had failed to protect vulnerable segments of its population. The initial intervention against Serbia in March 1999 also demonstrated a willingness to use NATO as the institutional authority to legitimize the intervention, confirming Canada's new willingness to use military force to intervene in failed states. The effort in Kosovo had been foreshadowed by practices in places such as Iraq, Somalia, and Haiti, and has been followed by interventions in Afghanistan and, more recently, Libya, where outside agents, sometimes at the expense of local authorities, have been empowered to take on the country's administration and security needs. These interventions have been part of a long-term, post–Second World War policy of support for more intrusive international rules and practices that constrain the authority of sovereign states that have failed to meet standards of practice defined by the international community.

The discourse on "failed states" within both the academic community and policy circles is a recent one.[2] While there is clearly a long history to what we now call failed states, it would seem that the concept entered into policy discourses in an explicit and significant manner only since the end of the Cold War, and even more dramatically after the terrorist attacks on the United States in September 2001. A quick scan of the Factiva database is revealing in this respect. The notion is not found in databases prior to 1990, but appears with increased frequency as one moves through the 1990s (122 times between 1990 and 1995 and 373 mentions between 1996 and 2000), and then increases exponentially in the 2000s (3,401 mentions between 2001 and 2005 and more than 8,000 between 2006 and 2012.) The term has become ubiquitous in many discussions on development, civil conflict, and terrorism. It might appear from this that failed states are unique to the post–Cold War period and have not existed in the past. Perhaps, however, the circumstances that have given rise to the contemporary policy concern for failed states are also a reflection of the broader international context in which these states have emerged. Instead of being a mere backdrop, failed states have moved to the foreign policy centre, a shift that may help to account for the policy responses that have been taken by the Canadian and other governments in response to the phenomenon. The intense attention given to failed states in recent years suggests that factors other than those existing within particular states may be driving Canadian government policy. Indeed, it will be argued here, and elsewhere throughout this collection, that Canadian governments have had a long-standing interest in "failed states" and that policy in response to these states has been influenced more by the broader international environment than by the specific conditions that exist within particular failed states.

This chapter examines the evolution of successive Canadian governments' policies toward failed states in an effort to understand how and why such states have emerged as a significant focus of attention for Canadian foreign policy, attracting the attention of diplomats, development experts, and defence analysts alike. It also explores the mix of domestic and external factors that have shaped Canadian policy in this area and suggests that shifting concerns related both to matters of international security and to international order have largely accounted for the shifts in Canadian policy in this area. In the end, the particular conditions that have given rise to failed states seem to be of less significance and thus might account for the very limited commitments that the government has been willing to undertake in order to redress the conditions that foster failed states in the contemporary system.

It is useful to consider failed states in a broader historical context because it can help better to define both the nature of failed states and how the range of policy responses that have been adopted have varied over time. Scholarly and media attention since the late 1990s aside, it is worth noting that failed states are best viewed as a phenomenon of the late twentieth century. This view is based on Robert Jackson's arguments about the rise of quasi-states in the post–Second World War wave of decolonization.[3] It would appear that for much of the eighteenth and nineteenth centuries, sovereignty was seldom granted to states that failed to demonstrate their effectiveness, their capacity to govern domestically through whatever means employed, and their ability to defend their territory with varying degrees of success over time. One could, for example, consider Canada's own difficult and incremental road to gaining international recognition for its sovereignty. A prominent issue for much of the nineteenth century was the effort of dominant European states to establish "standards of civilization" to control which political entities would gain access to international forums and equal treatment under international law. Statehood was something to be earned, both at home and in the eyes of European powers. The Russo-Japanese War of 1904–5 provided one of the early breakthroughs against the stranglehold that European powers held over defining these international norms.[4]

These practices were challenged in dramatic fashion with the attempt to establish the principle of self-determination as part of the settlement at Versailles in 1919, and more significantly with the wave of decolonization that swept the Global South after the Second World War. Particularly noteworthy in this regard was the UN General Assembly's 1960 Declaration on the Granting of Independence to Colonial Countries and Peoples (Resolution 1514), which stated that "inadequacy of political, economic, social or educational preparedness should never serve as a pretext for delaying independence."[5] The resolution received widespread support and set the stage for the acceleration of decolonization and the establishment of new sovereign states, some of which lacked the capacity to provide the range of functions generally associated with state sovereignty. Contemporary definitions of failed or fragile states stand in glaring contrast to the sentiments of UNGA Resolution 1514. For example, the Canadian International Development Agency (CIDA) offers the following assessment:

> Though no universal definition of "fragile state" exists, states are perceived as fragile when the government does not demonstrate the will and/or capacity to deliver on core state functions such as the enforcement of legitimate security and authority, *the protection, promotion and implementation of human rights and gender equality, the rule of law, and even the most basic provision of services (e.g., in health and education, in enabling the private sector, and in environmental protection)*. When these core state functions are unreliable or inaccessible, the legitimacy of the state erodes and is likely to result in a breakdown in the social "pact" of trust and cooperation within civil society and between civil society and the state.[6] [Emphasis added.]

Two aspects of this definition are worth noting. First, a comparison with the words of Resolution 1514 indicates that those characteristics which place a state in the failed or fragile category would now prevent it from securing its independence, sovereignty, and the recognition and diplomatic support of the international community. Yet just a few decades ago such "trivial" concerns as providing basic services to the population were not considered important enough to delay the granting of statehood to colonial territories. Second, the italicized passage demonstrates the degree to which liberal values have now entered into the characteristics considered necessary for a state to be considered legitimate. Such requirements are reminiscent of those employed by European powers as "standards of civilization" in the nineteenth century.

These are points worth returning to, but for the moment it is important to keep in mind that the characteristics of statehood were redefined as a result of pressures for decolonization in the post–World War II period. As such, the current preoccupation with failed states may suggest that the global community is in the midst of another redefinition of statehood and state sovereignty. If so, then perhaps the issue is not one of failed states as much as how the characteristics of statehood and state sovereignty are to be determined, and once determined, how they are to be applied to all of those entities that already have been granted sovereign statehood. If this is what surrounds the various practices and discourses of failed states, then this needs to be part of the conversation to demonstrate why a state that met the standards for sovereignty—and hence non-intervention—that were set out and adopted fifty years ago, is today subject to intervention.

A Survey of Canadian Policy

Adopting a broader view of failed states than is usually found in the literature, one can find evidence that Canadian officials have been concerned about failed or failing states since long before the term came into vogue in the 1990s. There have been four phases of heightened concern on the part of Canadian officials for what we now call failed states, reflecting, at least in part, different international and institutional environments and, to a lesser degree, different domestic ones, as well. These phases do not appear to be distinctive or exclusive, as there are some important and interesting commonalities across them. Nor are they completely time-bound, though that is the initial distinction made here.

The first phase can be seen in the immediate aftermath of the Second World War and applied as much to Western Europe as it did to the states rising out of colonialism in the Global South. In this phase, the Canadian government's policy was shaped by its alliance commitments and Cold War fears. States made fragile by the effects of the war, or states in the early stages of independence and confronting domestic unrest and economic instability, might not only fail, but, more alarmingly in the context of the times, fall prey to Communist governments and align with the Soviet bloc. It was essentially a concern that states might "fail" to remain both economically and politically secure and within the Western camp. The critical point, for this discussion, was the concern displayed for the capacity of these governments to govern. The primary source of this capacity gap was assumed to be economic, but the support of Western states was also seen as necessary to provide an important element of moral support to governments confronting domestic or external unrest. The response was rather straightforward. It involved giving financial and technical assistance to national governments so that they could withstand the economic and political turmoil created by the war's end and the first stages of independence. Participation in the Marshall Plan and the Colombo Plan are illustrative of Canadian policy in this period. The degree to which this was accompanied by more overt forms of intervention tended to vary. The US-led Marshall Plan, for instance, attached conditions to its support for the European countries, designed to encourage both liberalization and internal cooperation. Such conditions were not explicitly imposed as part of the Colombo Plan, though forms of technical assistance in areas such as governance, public order, and military training constituted more interventionist practices than is usually acknowledged.[7]

Canadian policy during this period was influenced more by Canada's position in the Western alliance and the British Commonwealth than by concerns about any specific state, let alone a humanitarian concern for individuals living within these states. In retirement, former secretary of state for external affairs and prime minister Lester Pearson lamented the fact that Cold War security concerns had led the Canadian government to adopt a development assistance policy that it should have adopted for other—more humanitarian—reasons. "It is a sorry commentary on the postwar period that without them [the Soviets and Chinese] and the threat which they represent we might not so readily have done what we should have been doing anyway."⁸ Such concerns continued to play a role in Canadian development assistance policy to the point where aid was sometimes considered an extension of national security policy and development assistance as something akin to defence contributions to NATO.

By the late 1950s and early 1960s, there is evidence of a second phase in Canadian policy in response to the emergence of new states in the Global South as decolonization accelerated. The end of the European empires posed a significant challenge to regional and international peace and security. The armed conflicts in Cyprus, the Congo, Vietnam, and Nigeria are examples of this, as a combination of nationalist aspirations, economic uncertainty and inequality, and ethnic differences became the source of intra- and inter-state conflict, the latter largely involving Western colonial powers. These conflicts also created instability between the superpowers as they jockeyed for influence over these new states. Much of Canada's policy response to decolonization at this time was influenced by, and conducted through, the UN and the Commonwealth in the form of participation in UN peacekeeping operations, economic assistance programs, and the politics of recognition. Indeed, the Canadian government orchestrated a reform of UN admission practices in 1955 that eased the way for newly independent states to join the organization. There was a good deal of concern for facilitating the integration of these newly independent states into the UN framework and, where appropriate, the Commonwealth.

Another important consideration shaping Canadian policy was domestic in nature. By the 1960s, the postwar consensus on foreign policy had begun to collapse, as the public debated Canada's role in the world and the independence of Canadian diplomacy. The growing influence of the media interest in foreign policy created expectations for action that Ottawa felt compelled to meet. This was evident, for example, in the government's reaction to the crisis over Biafra in Nigeria.⁹

While Canada's response to decolonization was heavily influenced by its alliance membership and corresponding connections with colonial powers—Britain, France, Belgium, and Portugal—its specific concern over the possibility of failed states resulting from such a process was reflected in its position on Resolution 1514, the Declaration on the Granting of Independence to Colonial Countries and Peoples. Unlike its principal allies, and despite their pressure to abstain on the resolution, the Canadian delegation at the UN supported Resolution 1514. Canadian support was not

Figure 1: Secretary of State for External Affairs Howard Green broke with Canada's Western allies to support strongly Afro-Asian decolonization and UN Resolution 1514 in the early 1960s. (Credit: UN 62975)

an indication that they were ignorant of the looming problems that these newly independent states might encounter or pose to regional and international order. Indeed, the Congo had already clearly demonstrated the potential pitfalls, and these fears were duly noted by government officials.

Howard Green, Progressive Conservative secretary of state for external affairs from 1959 to 1963, however, recognized that the weight of opinion had shifted to ending colonialism in a manner that would solidify the majority position of African and other former colonies in both the UN and the Commonwealth. Green took the view "that on colonial questions the newly independent states often viewed an abstention as the same as a vote against." Additionally, if Canadians were "to have any influence, then, it would be best to vote in favour of certain resolutions, even if they were somewhat unpalatable. Then, from this 'position of seeming alignment' with the Afro-Asians, Canada would be in a position 'to demonstrate sympathy with those countries with whom we do in fact sympathize, and to give encouragement to those elements we wish to encourage.'"[10] It is doubtful that this influence ever amounted to a great deal, but on balance the desire to avoid being on the wrong side of history by resisting resolutions strongly supported by these newly independent states convinced the government to abandon its principal allies and back the resolution.

Once it accepted the principle that decolonization should lead directly to sovereignty, the Canadian government applied the principle of non-intervention, even in instances where the legitimacy of the state had been called into question. This was certainly a consideration in the reaction of Liberal prime minister Pierre Trudeau's government to the conflict in Nigeria in the late 1960s. It remained important throughout the 1970s and was a consideration in shaping the Trudeau government's policy toward liberation movements in southern Africa. Domestic fears about rising Quebec nationalism and resulting pressures for separatism reinforced the government's support for the principle of non-intervention. Trudeau was especially determined to avoid precedents that could be used to undermine Canadian sovereignty. Failing or failed states could rely on the Canadian government's formal recognition and adherence to a policy of non-intervention. There was also the continued support of development assistance programs, which were still generally funnelled through national governments, adding further legitimacy to these regimes.

A shift in Canadian policy and a third phase began in the waning days of the Cold War, when Trudeau's successor, Progressive Conservative prime minister Brian Mulroney, adopted a good governance policy and sought to export this policy through its development assistance programs, its efforts at standard-setting in international institutions, and its support for interventions under the auspices of these bodies. This change in Canadian policy pre-dated, but overlapped with and was reinforced by, the new wave of state creation and democratization that occurred at the end of the Cold War; the former Yugoslavia became a significant starting point for Canada's new policy. The rapid end of the Cold War facilitated the pursuit of these policy shifts within multilateral institutions. The approach was overtly and explicitly interventionist, and, while initially limited to diplomatic and development assistance policy, it soon took the form of military interventions operating under the authority and auspices of the UN, NATO, and the Organization of American States, as the failing states of Yugoslavia, Somalia, and Haiti respectively slipped into disarray. Each

Figure 2: By the early 1990s, Prime Minister Brian Mulroney had explicitly embraced the promotion of good governance and human rights as key elements in an interventionist response to state fragility. (Credit: Peter Bregg)

of these interventions carried with it a different rationale and mandate, but they collectively helped shape a conditional approach toward sovereignty and a growing acceptance of the legitimacy of intervention, including the use of armed force.

Prime Minister Mulroney's interventionist approach had some precursors in the practice of conditionality that had been integrated into Canadian development assistance policy in the 1980s, which was designed to influence economic and political practices in the recipient state. The human rights movement of the 1960s and 1970s, the successful Conference on Security and Co-operation in Europe, US president Jimmy Carter's support for human rights, and the discourse of rights associated with Trudeau's constitutional changes in the 1980s generated popular support for this interventionist policy. The international context was, of course, vitally important, as the end of the Cold War and the accompanying democratic consensus influenced many into thinking that democracy, the rule of law, human rights, and free markets would prevail around the globe, and should be encouraged with more overt forms of support.[11]

It was at this time that explicit references to failed states begin to appear in both academic and policy discourse alongside human security as a guiding principle for how to respond to these failed states. The increased attention directed toward human rights and the protection of civilians, integral to the notion of human security, made the conditions within failed states that much more of a concern to policymakers and an interested public. The term "failed states" appears, for example, in the Liberal government's 1994 White Paper on defence. In describing "failed states," this document observes that "the breakdown of authority in certain states is another source of instability. It is characterized by chaos, violence and the inability of political leaders to provide the population with the most basic of services." The White Paper turns almost immediately to a discussion of regional conflict along more traditional inter-state lines, but the flag had been raised over failed states. Moreover, the defence white paper made it clear that this was not simply, or primarily, a matter of serving the national interest: "Even where Canada's interests are not directly engaged, the values of Canadian society lead Canadians to expect their government to respond when modern communication technologies make us real-time witnesses to violence, suffering and even genocide in many parts of the world."[12] As is evident here, there is little reference to, or concern for, Canadian national security interests as it involves failed states throughout the 1990s. If the effects on Canada are expressed, it is more as an affront to Canadian values.

The decade closed with NATO's armed attack on Serbia to protect the non-Serb population of Kosovo. This intervention, conducted with extensive military force and without the authority of the UN Security Council, presented a challenge to Canadian policy, which had tended to favour operations under UN auspices. It also marked one of the more overt efforts to construct a new sovereign entity out of an existing state that the international community had determined had failed, though not so much on the grounds of capacity as on legitimacy. The intervention also demonstrated the increased significance of human rights practices and the introduction of considerations other than a state's capacity to maintain order.

Canadian policymakers concerned about the precedents set by the Kosovo intervention were instrumental in establishing the International

Commission on Intervention and State Sovereignty (ICISS), an ad hoc body of UN members under Australian politician Gareth Evans and Algerian diplomat Mohamed Sahnoun. The commission was asked to develop a set of principles to govern how states and the international community would respond to nations that failed to exercise their responsibilities to their own citizens. In advancing the idea of "responsibility to protect," the international commission advocated for intervention in failed states, and began to redefine the requirements of sovereignty. The ICISS report insisted on "a modern understanding of the meaning of sovereignty" that was clearly different from that expressed in UNGA Resolution 1514 and included much closer attention to the treatment of civilian populations. During this phase, Canada's approach was clearly guided by a concern to promote liberal values and practices in both the political and economic spheres. There was also considerable support for intervention of a direct and overt sort, though ideally conducted through multilateral associations—the UN, regional organizations, or NATO. While interventions were obviously not possible in every state that failed to meet democratic standards, protect human rights, and support free market principles, it remained unclear how to determine the appropriateness of intervention.

The fourth and most recent phase in Canadian policy toward failed states occurred after the terrorist attacks against the United States in September 2001. In the wake of the attacks, the United States identified failed states as its principal security threat, a view with which many in Canada agreed. The US National Security Strategy of 2003 boldly stated that "America is now threatened less by conquering states than we are by failing ones,"[13] a refrain echoed less dramatically in the International Policy Statement released by Prime Minister Paul Martin's Liberal government in 2005: "Failed and failing states dot the international landscape, creating despair and regional instability and providing a haven for those who would attack us directly."[14]

These concerns were repeated in the government's defence policy statement, winning favour with some commentators. Alex Wilner, a senior research fellow at the Macdonald Laurier Institute, contended that "Canada's policy toward fragile political environments must evolve in kind, so that intervention is based less on the promotion of good governance, human rights, and social justice and more on the hard realities of Canadian security and national interest. The post–9/11 era demands

Figure 3: Prime Minister Paul Martin's government released its International Policy Statement in April 2005, underlining the threat posed by failed and failing states after the terrorist attacks of 9/11. (Credit: Dave Chan)

that Canadian foreign policy align itself more wholly with emerging international security prospects and their related strategic concerns."[15] At the same time, others, including political scientist Rob Huebert, questioned such an interpretation, writing that "attempting to explain contemporary terrorism only as a result of failed and failing states is incomplete at best and simply wrong at worst."[16] In response, the Martin government insisted that responding to failed states was not a policy option motivated solely or primarily by humanitarian considerations. It remained unclear, however, how one was to distinguish between those failed states that might be a threat and those that were not. Significantly, one begins to see how the perception of a threat arising from a particular state influences the tendency of policymakers to consider and label that state as failed. In other words, failed states are those states that pose a direct or, in most cases, indirect security threat to Canada.

In summary, these different periods of Canadian response to failed states suggest a mix of concerns, which have seemingly come full circle since Ottawa was first alerted to the challenge emanating from failed states in the 1950s. Three sets of concerns have informed policy. First, the government has worried about security, when failed states represent a direct threat to Canadian interests. This is where policy originated from a concern for the spread of Communist regimes and where it returned in the 2000s out of concern for the spread of terrorism or bases from which terrorists might operate. Second, successive Canadian governments have promoted a liberal, humanitarian world order that has focused on bringing these failed states to a "better" position, where human rights and good governance are respected. Such considerations were most prevalent in the later 1980s and 1990s, when they were informed by the human security initiatives of Liberal prime minister Jean Chrétien and his foreign minister, Lloyd Axworthy. Third, Canadian policymakers have been preoccupied with global order, reconciling failed states with prevailing norms of international order, largely by reinforcing and respecting state sovereignty through policies of recognition and non-intervention.

Reflecting on Canadian Policy

The prominent attention given to failed states by analysts and governments is recent, yet the conditions that define failed states have been prevalent in different states for a number of years. What is new is the realization that these states have an impact on the interests of governments and societies like Canada's, and the idea that Western governments can and should intervene with policies that will alleviate or alter the conditions that are causing states to fail, providing them with greater resilience while reducing the threat that they pose to Canada. This review of the changes that have occurred in Ottawa's approach toward failed states raises several issues worth further attention. The four phases reviewed here demonstrate the variability that exists in thinking about and responding to failed states. They also underline the importance of the factors that have influenced both the perceived need for a response and the form of that response.

The historical overview suggests that there has been a shift in Canadian policy over the past two decades. While some of the features of this policy have been around for decades, others are more recent or more pronounced. There is a tendency, for instance, to treat a failed state as an isolated condition independent of the global context in which these states must operate. There has been little effort to address the broader economic and political factors that affect fragile and failed states.

Moreover, there has been increased support for intervening with non-UN operations in a more selective manner. This reflects the traditional influence of alliance and institutional commitments on Canadian thinking. Alliances and institutions have brought attention to the issue of failed states and helped define and coordinate the Canadian response. Canadian policy in response to failed states has generally been articulated in and around these institutional and alliance commitments. This is not to argue that the Canadian government was always reacting to the practices of allies or following the directives of the UN or regional organizations. Rather, these commitments have had an influence on the timing and content of Canadian policy. Ottawa has also demonstrated a consistent effort to develop policy that is in line with its principal allies and institutional commitments. Its recent interest in reinforcing Canada's NATO connections, for instance, would account, at least to some degree, for the greater willingness to use military force as an instrument of intervention.

Finally, Ottawa has tended to look at failed states in relation to specific national interests. Many Canadian policymakers and analysts consider failed states a security threat demanding a more formidable response from government. The net effect has been to frame an interventionist policy that tends to focus primarily on security considerations and devotes less attention to the economic and political realm in which all states exist.

Reflecting on Canadian experiences with failed states, three key questions come to mind. First, why should Canada care or respond to failed states? For what reason should the condition of states on the other side of the planet be of any concern to Canadians? One possible reason might be humanitarian. Another might be economic, or another material interest. A third might be for security reasons. Should any one of these reasons be considered more important than another? How would giving priority to one of these reasons over the other two generate a different response, or a different set of states with which we would be concerned?

Alex Wilner takes issue with the emphasis that has been given to humanitarianism in influencing Canada's decision about where and when to intervene. Wilner challenges the views of Jim Wright, a former assistant deputy minister at DFATD, who argued in 2006 that if "we are not immediately threatened by the collapse or implosion of these states, our values as Canadians and our responsibilities as global citizens must invariably compel us to action in the face of the victimization, human suffering and misery that are the inevitable result."[17] This sort of thinking, contends Wilner, is misplaced. "Canada's policy toward failed states must begin by looking after the security of Canadians, first and foremost," he insists, "followed only then by a responsibility to protect the globe's victimized citizens."[18] It is problematic that the government is still unable to determine which failed state presents a threat requiring a response and to develop a response that addresses security interests first. Humanitarians for their part lament the inconsistencies and lack of response to many crises, arguing that security considerations or relations with principal allies have focused our attention only on some failed states rather than on the real needs of populations at risk. The proliferation of such states and populations at risk makes prioritizing Canadian resources and responses problematic.

A second set of questions relates to what can or should be done. Does Canada have anything to offer to failed states? Regardless of its motive—humanitarian, economic, or security—can Ottawa contribute anything worthwhile? If so, what, and how, and with whom? As Robert Jackson has argued, "there are many ways to responsibly address the problems of 'failed states' without suspending their sovereignty and patronizing their people."[19] There exists a broad range of economic and political sanctions that can be used, including military force. There seems to be a general consensus that this is an area in which Canada should act only in concert with others. Canada's best option, argues Carleton University political scientist David Carment, "remains to work in unison and alongside our allies and other like-minded states in the United Nations, the North Atlantic Treaty Organization, and other regional groupings. Not only does Canada lack the ability to undertake sustained unilateral intervention, but the nature of rehabilitating dangerous failed states is a long-term and costly affair that requires a coordinated and multilateral approach."[20]

This is, no doubt, an accurate appraisal of the way things are, but it creates an additional set of problems that can make such interventions difficult for the failed state and for Canada's foreign relations. What happens when national policies and the practices of Canada's allies do not converge? In the past, for example, the Canadian and American approaches to training police officers in Haiti has differed.[21] In Afghanistan, as well, there were suggestions that the American and Canadian approaches to Provincial Reconstruction Teams were different in important ways. Coordination may become both more important and more difficult as alliance partners operate with a different range of priorities and capabilities and with different sorts of domestic economic and political pressures.

Canadian governments have found it difficult to develop an effective response to failed states with an effective strategy encompassing different policy responses and agencies. This has led to variations on a "whole of government" approach in which different agencies are encouraged to coordinate their policy responses. The idea here is that failed states require not just the restoration of order but a wholesale transformation, including economic and technical assistance and political reform; hence, one needs to call upon experts from many branches of the public sector and the community at large. The premise makes good sense, but the execution is often difficult, as agency protocols and priorities do not always meld.

A third and final set of questions asks where and when should Canada act? Assuming there will always be competing opportunities for responding, how should the government decide to act? Perhaps this question is answered by the response to the first two questions. If one is more concerned about the effectiveness of Canada's response, Canada should respond where the most positive change can be effected. If one is more concerned about the first question—why should Canada care?—the government should respond to the greatest humanitarian need, or where Canada's economic and security interests are greatest. Carment and his colleagues have taken the view that relevance and effectiveness should be the primary considerations: "Canadian engagement will be most effective when the situation is highly relevant to Canadian foreign policy priorities, and when the potential Canadian contribution is likely to have a significant and positive impact."[22]

The persistence of failed states since the 1950s and the intractable nature of their problems have generated another distinct school of observations among Canadian analysts. Writing in the early 1990s, a prominent realist, Denis Stairs, began to voice concerns over the limitless commitments of a policy designed to rescue failing or failed states: "A more accurate conclusion might be that the conflicts themselves are deeply ingrained in cynically exploited combinations of unhappy history and intractable circumstance. Where such is the case, externally imposed solutions will often require massive interventions along a wide variety of the dimensions of modern government—and for periods lasting a generation or more—if they are to have even a modest chance of success."[23] His skeptical view has been confirmed in numerous observations. For example, a parliamentary committee examining conditions in Haiti in 2006 reflected the complexity and multi-dimensional character of any effective response to state failure, as it noted the need to address insecurity, corruption, the justice system, policing, agriculture, education, inequality, poverty, unemployment, civil society, labour organizations, and private investment.[24] Stairs went on to write that "this raises a series of questions about the sources of legitimacy for such operations—operations which, in another time, might have been described as 'imperialism' and defended on precepts that we can no longer accept."[25] In response, many interventionists underlined the need to be attentive to local agency whenever possible. For example, and again drawing from the Haiti discussion, witnesses maintained that initiatives "would have to respect Haiti's sovereignty, fully reflect Haitian society's needs and enhance Haitians' capacity to sustain and embrace reforms."[26] At the same time, they were equally quick to note the lack of local capacity to meet standards of democracy, policing, and justice.

Overlying the Canadian debate regarding intervention, there remained a persistent view that something can be done and that Canadians are capable of doing it. For example, in his report lamenting the lack of attention to the security implications of failed states, Wilner writes that the "wrinkle for Canadian decision makers is that, while they have developed the military, diplomatic, and reconstructive means with which to assist fragile and failed states, they continue to lack the mechanisms to decide, realistically and strategically, when to use them."[27] The assumption here is that more intrusive forms of intervention, including the use of military force to assist failed states, could be an effective policy. Since the 1990s, policy officials in Canada have leaned heavily on intervention as a necessary or desirable response. There seems to be less interest in a broader range of policy responses, including the kind of financial and technical assistance or trade and aid packages that were employed in the past, which stopped short of overt interference in the internal affairs of these states. There also remains little evidence to demonstrate that Canada has developed the means to assist in a manner that is consistently effective, as developments in both Afghanistan and Libya reveal. The issue thus remains not only "when" to intervene in whatever form, but "if" intervention can be conducted in a way that would actually make things better. In the early 1990s, Stairs himself concluded that "in spite of these unresolved dilemmas ... the optimistic view, rooted in the concept of peace through progress, is widely and deeply held, and it contributes mightily to the insistence that the government must take action in almost every case."[28] Subsequent practice may reflect a more selective application of such actions, but there remains a view that intervention of the type Canada has deployed can remedy the problems of failed states.

Conclusion

Canadian policy has demonstrated ongoing support favouring international interventions to rescue failed states; yet, setting aside Afghanistan, in practice this has often meant selectively supporting a minimal degree of international intervention at little real cost over the long term. These interventions have also tended to ignore the broader economic and political contexts, both past and present, that have given rise to failed states. Canadian policy toward failed states over the past decade has marked an effort to reframe Canada's security policy in a manner that challenges the pre-eminence of the principle of state sovereignty, emphasizes individual security, and creates a permissive environment for intervention. At the same time, it has supported the development of a normative order at the level of international society in support of such practices. The government's approaches to interventions in Kosovo, Afghanistan, and Libya provide a significant illustration of its commitment to use force to protect populations at risk in selected circumstances. This suggests a recasting of national security priorities. Specifically, it reflects a view that so-called failed states present a security threat to Canadian values and interests.

It appears to be one position on which both Liberals and Conservatives agree, having been reasserted by Prime Minister Stephen Harper in 2011:

> That's the kind of thing I think we really have to worry about, where you have not just poverty, but poverty and literally lawlessness becomes the nature of the state. And I do think it's in our broader interests and the right thing to do to try and help people and help countries so that they don't get into that situation.... It's why we're so involved in Haiti. Not to have that kind of a state in our own backyard. I think those kinds of situations are very dangerous.[29]

The debate over how to respond to the conflict in Syria in 2012 illustrated the dilemmas and limitations of Canadian policy toward failed states. It is obvious that in many areas Canada lacks the capacity and the political will to act alone in responding to failed states. It can, and has, adopted some unilateral measures, usually in the form of statements, withdrawing or disbursing assistance, or diplomatic and economic sanctions. While most of these are taken in coordination with the actions of other states and institutions, some can and have been taken alone. Overt forms of response, however, including more direct interventions, require the support and assistance of others, principally the United States, but ideally multilateral agencies like the United Nations or, as has become more common, NATO.

It is even tougher to assess Canadian interests. At one level, Syria presented a clear case of government oppression over its domestic population, putting the security of individual citizens at risk. It was doubtless a candidate for intervention on humanitarian grounds alone. Viewed in a different light, however, Syria is enmeshed in a war contested not only by domestic actors but also by outsiders from the region who have a keen interest in the outcome of the conflict and are intervening to shape it. Intervention in such a situation without close attention to the interests and actions of all of the parties involved is deeply problematic at best, as the experience in Afghanistan has clearly demonstrated.[30]

In certain respects, this policy is vastly different from the modest foreign aid programs launched in response to the Communist threat of the 1950s. Ottawa has also adopted a more expansive view of the characteristics of a failed state, embracing a variety of specific political and economic practices—the absence of elections or restrictions on free markets. In the past, such different approaches to government and the economy were accepted by the Canadian government and were not, in and of themselves, cause for concern, let alone an enticement for intervention. That more hands-off approach has changed. It has been replaced by a commitment to redefine the prerequisites for state sovereignty as implied in such notions as "responsibility to protect" and to intervene where possible to bring about necessary change. It would seem that the ultimate objective remains supporting the transformation of failed states so that they look and act just like western liberal democracies.

Notes

1. CBC News, "Canada recognizes Kosovo, Serbia pulls ambassador," 18 March 2008, http://www.cbc.ca/news/world/canada-recognizes-kosovo-serbia-pulls-ambassador-1.745469 (accessed 1 February 2012).

2. The term "failed state" will be used throughout this chapter, but will not be extensively defined or discussed here. It is important to note that this is a highly contested term. For a discussion of the definition of the concept and some of its conceptual and practical problems see David Carment and Y. Samy, "Engaging Fragile States: Closing the Gap between Theory and Policy," *Global Dialogue* 13, no. 1 (2011): 1–11.

3. R. H. Jackson, *Quasi-States: Sovereignty, International Relations and the Third World* (Cambridge: Cambridge University Press, 1990).

4. See, for example, Dorothy Jones, *Code of Peace: Ethics and Security in a World of Warlord States* (Chicago: University of Chicago Press, 1991); and Gerrit W. Gong, *The Standard of Civilization in International Society* (Oxford: Oxford University Press, 1984).

5. United Nations General Assembly, Resolution 1514 (XV), 14 December 1960.

6. Quoted in K. Van Brabant, "What is Peacebuilding? Statebuilding and Peacebuilding," 2010, http://www.interpeace.org/resource/what-is-peacebuilding-statebuilding-and-peacebuilding/ (accessed 14 November 2015).

7. Chris Roberts, "Canadian Foreign Policy & African State Formation: Responsibilities, Silences, Culpabilities," paper presented at the Annual Meeting of the Canadian Political Science Association, Victoria, B.C., 2013.

8. Cited in Keith Spicer, *A Samaritan State? External Aid in Canada's Foreign Policy* (Toronto: University of Toronto Press, 1966), 22.

9. Donald Barry, "Interest Groups and the Foreign Policy Process: the Case of Biafra," in *Pressure Group Behaviour in Canadian Politics*, ed.

A. Paul Pross (Toronto: McGraw-Hill Ryerson, 1975), 117–47.

10. Asa McKercher, "The Centre Cannot Hold: Canada, Colonialism and the 'Afro-Asian Bloc' at the United Nations, 1960–62," *Journal of Imperial and Commonwealth History* 42, no. 2 (2014): 336.

11. R. H. Jackson, "Morality, Democracy and Foreign Policy," in *Canada Among Nations, 1995: Democracy and Foreign Policy*, ed. M. A. Cameron and M. A. Molot (Ottawa: Carleton University Press, 1995), 34–51.

12. Canada, Department of National Defence, "1994 Defence White Paper" (Ottawa: Queen's Printer, 1994).

13. United States, Department of State, "The National Security Strategy of the United States of America," September 2002, accessed 12 January 2012, http://www.state.gov/documents/organization/63562.pdf.

14. Canada, Department of Foreign Affairs and International Trade, "Canada's International Policy Statement: A Role of Pride and Influence in the World" (Ottawa: Queen's Printer, April 2005).

15. Alex Wilner, "Making the World Safe for Canada: Canadian Security Policy in a World of Failed States" (Halifax: Atlantic Institute for Market Studies, 2008), 3.

16. Rob Huebert, "Failed and Failing States: The Core Threat to Canadian Security," in *In the Canadian Interest? Assessing Canada's International Policy Statement*, ed. Derek Burney (Calgary: CDFAI, 2006), 71.

17. Wilner, "Making the World Safe for Canada," 10.

18. Ibid.

19. Robert H. Jackson, "Surrogate Sovereignty? Great Power Responsibility and 'Failed States,'" Institute of International Relations, University of British Columbia, Working Paper No. 25, 1998, 13.

20. David Carment, "Effective Defence Policy for Responding to Failed and Failing States" (Calgary: CDFAI, 2005), 10.

21. See David Beer, "Peacebuilding on the Ground: Reforming the Judicial Sector in Haiti," in *Building Sustainable Peace*, ed. Tom Keating and W. Andy Knight (Edmonton: University of Alberta Press, 2004), 119–41.

22. David Carment, S. Prest, J. Gazo, T. Bell, and S. Houghton, *Assessing the Circumstances and Forms of Canada's Involvement in Fragile States: Towards a Methodology of Relevance and Impact* (Ottawa: NPSIA, 2006), 7.

23. Denis Stairs, "Contemporary security issues," in Canada, Parliament, Special Joint Committee on Reviewing Canadian Foreign Policy, "Report of the Special Joint Committee Reviewing Canadian Foreign Policy," November 1994, 10.

24. Canada, House of Commons, "Canada's International Policy Put to the Test in Haiti," Report of the Standing Committee on Foreign Affairs and International Development, December 2006.

25. Stairs, "Contemporary security issues," 10.

26 Canada, House of Commons, "Canada's International Policy Put to the Test in Haiti."

27 Wilner, "Making the World Safe for Canada," v.

28 Stairs, "Contemporary security issues," 10.

29 CBC News, "Transcript of Peter Mansbridge's interview with PM Stephen Harper," 8 September 2011, http://www.cbc.ca/news/politics/transcript-of-peter-mansbridge-s-interview-with-pm-stephen-harper-1.985393 (accessed 1 February 2012).

30 Kim Richard Nossal, "Don't Talk about the Neighbours: Canada and the Regional Politics of the Afghanistan Mission," *Canadian Foreign Policy Journal* 17, no. 1 (March 2011): 9–22.

CHAPTER 2

PRESENT AT THE CREATION?
Canada, United Nations Intervention, and the Congo as a Failed State, 1960–64

Kevin A. Spooner

American secretary of state Dean Acheson could justifiably give his autobiography the impressive title *Present at the Creation*. His years at the helm of the State Department, in the critical post–Second World War and early Cold War period, were undeniably pivotal and speak to the diplomat's clear and assertive appreciation of this. Borrowing his title, however, is done in a spirit of irony and with none of Acheson's self-assurance. Few states or individuals would take pride in any role, intended or unintended, in the creation of a failed state; yet in the case of the Congo, Canada may well have been witness, and even unwittingly contributed, to a critical moment when the seeds of a failing state were sown.

Within weeks of the Congo's independence from Belgium, serious political turmoil rocked the new state and challenged the nascent government's authority to maintain order. After the United Nations was asked to intervene, the first of many requests for various forms of assistance arrived in Ottawa from New York, and Canadian peacekeepers were then soon present in the Congo. This chapter addresses the implications of Canadian involvement in the Congo crisis of the early 1960s, and particularly explores Canada's role in efforts to develop a program to retrain and reorganize the Armée nationale congolaise (Congolese National Army, or ANC), identified by the international community as a necessary measure to prevent military interference in the Congo's political development. Particularly among Western policymakers, there was a key, if ethnocentric, assumption that the armed forces of newly independent African nations had to be trained to respect the development of democracy and its related governmental institutions. Notably, this was not an exclusively Western point of view. In 1963, when Congolese prime minister Cyrille Adoula visited Washington and met with American president John F. Kennedy, retraining the ANC was the principal focus of their conversation, and both equally recognized that a disciplined and well-organized Congolese military would help to ensure long-term stability in the Congo. Conversely, the two leaders also shared concerns over the potential consequences for the Congo's future of an undisciplined and unrestrained military.

Despite repeated requests, Canada ultimately chose not to contribute to any large-scale plan to reorganize and retrain the ANC. The international community's failure to effectively address the need for ANC retraining and reorganization left the political evolution of a newly independent Congo vulnerable to military interference at a key period in the nation's development—a weakness Joseph Mobutu was then well positioned to exploit.[1] Mobutu, as the ANC's chief of staff in the Congo's first years of independence, very effectively used his station and resources to shape the course of political events at key junctures and, by 1965, had seized power in a coup that established his authoritarian regime, which lasted more than three decades.

As many of the chapters in this book demonstrate, the very discourse of failed and fragile states, and the related debates over how best to understand their origins and address their consequences, are profoundly complicated. Using such loaded terminology certainly has the dangerous potential to shape international responses that ultimately become self-fulfilling prophecy, a real concern highlighted and addressed by David Webster in his contribution to this volume. That said, few would argue with applying the label of "failed," "failing," or "crisis" state to the nation now recognized as the Democratic Republic of Congo (DRC). By the 1990s, the DRC was spiralling into a fragile state that was increasingly unable to provide a stable and secure socio-political framework, leading to a breakdown in order, impossible living conditions, and ultimately the deaths of more than five million people in one decade. Perennially appearing on *Foreign Policy*'s index of failed states, the DRC finds itself still near the top of the 2013 list: in second position, an unenviable increase in rank from previous years.[2] One of the most systematic and well-known studies defining and quantifying state failure suggests the Congo has in fact experienced state failure for more than half its existence as an independent nation (1960–65, 1977–79, 1984, and 1991–present) and identifies political and military challenges to the Mobutu regime, and its eventual collapse, as key factors in the last and most prolonged period of difficulties.[3]

The reality and consequences of state failure in the Congo may be unambiguous, but the origins of this complex situation are less obvious. If it is accepted that there is a continuum of fragility ending in state failure for the Congo, when did the trouble start? In other words, when was this failed state's point of *creation*? In reality, for the Congo, there is no shortage of potential starting points. The near pathological colonial reign of Belgian King Leopold II, documented well by Adam Hochschild, comes immediately to mind.[4] However, as the Congo's most recent and violent tribulations are tied much more directly to the collapse of Mobutu's regime, it is logical to seek out the roots of this failed state in his rise to power. For this, it is important to turn to the days immediately after the Congo achieved independence in June 1960, when the new state erupted in civil and political turmoil. At the request of the newly formed Congolese government, the United Nations dispatched a military and civilian peacekeeping force, the Opération des Nations Unies au Congo (ONUC), to help restore law and order. While the maintenance of law and order was a consistent ONUC objective, evident in the mission's mandate from the outset, the UN Security Council soon also recognized that it was critical to retrain and reorganize the ANC in order to protect the new state's political development from military interference.

It is worth spending a moment to review the relevant UN resolutions. From 1960 to 1961, five Security Council resolutions were passed and an additional supporting resolution was adopted by an emergency session of the General Assembly, meeting from 17 to 20 September 1960. From its earliest response, in the very first two Security Council resolutions, the UN addressed both the role of the Congolese military and the need to restore order. First, Secretary-General Dag Hammarskjöld was authorized

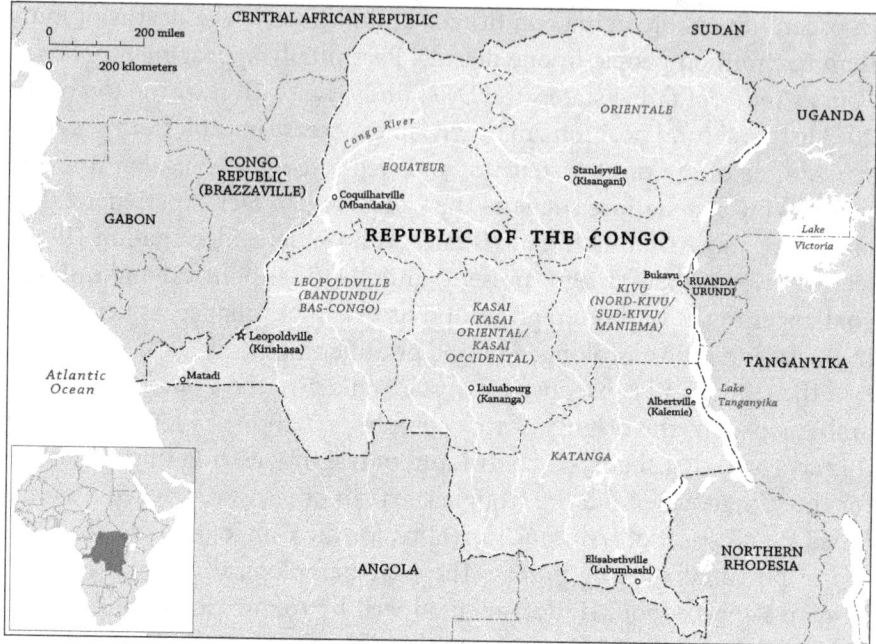

Figure 1: Map. (Credit: Marilyn Croot)

to provide the Congolese government with military support to enable the security forces to carry out their role in maintaining order. Second, the UN recognized that "the complete restoration of law and order" in the Congo would contribute to international stability, so that all countries were urged not to take any action that would undermine or impede the Congolese from restoring "law and order."[5] The provisions of these resolutions were reaffirmed by a subsequent Security Council motion passed at the beginning of August.[6]

By early 1961, the Congo situation had deteriorated further—especially as a result of the assassination of Patrice Lumumba, the first Congolese prime minister. At this point, the Security Council became deeply concerned at the prospect of "widespread civil war and bloodshed" and by the "general absence of the rule of law in the Congo." Once again, provisions in earlier resolutions were reaffirmed, but the Security Council now also urged "that Congolese armed units and personnel should be reorganized and brought under discipline and control, and arrangements made on impartial and equitable bases to that end and with a view to the elimination of any possibility of interference by such units and personnel in the political life of the Congo."[7] A final resolution was passed in November 1961, as fighting erupted between ONUC personnel and the military forces of the breakaway province of Katanga, who were supported by a legion of foreign mercenaries. Once again, the earlier resolutions were invoked and the Security Council unambiguously declared its full support for the central Congolese government, assuring it of UN support for its efforts to maintain law, order, and national integrity.[8]

Taken together, these resolutions demonstrate not only the international community's concern for the breakdown of law and order within the Congo, but also quite specifically the potential role—both good and bad—of the Congolese armed forces in contributing to either the continued turmoil or future stability of the state. In part, this focus on the ANC can be traced to the early days post-independence. The immediate cause of the July 1960 crisis was an uprising within the Force Publique, the Congolese gendarmerie inherited from the colonial period. Along with the Force came a cadré of Belgian officers, including the commander, Lt. Gen. Emile Janssens. The very day the revolt began, Janssens had met with officers and scrawled the phrase "before independence = after independence" on a blackboard.[9] The Congolese rank-and-file quickly and violently demonstrated their unwillingness to cooperate with this arrogant, colonial attempt to carry on "business as usual."

As the mutiny sparked wider political unrest and violence, most notably in the capital but also in other parts of the country, the new Congolese government of Prime Minister Patrice Lumumba and President Joseph Kasavubu immediately moved to Africanize the Force; it was at this point that Mobutu, who had befriended Lumumba while the two were in Brussels in the late 1950s, became its chief of staff. A short two months later, as a brief period of cooperation between Kasavubu and Lumumba came to an abrupt end and the two leaders fought one another for political control, Mobutu took to the airwaves and announced that the army was temporarily taking power. This, Mobutu's first *coup d'état*, was said to be an attempt to neutralize both politicians, but it effectively strengthened Kasavubu and weakened Lumumba. The coup certainly heightened awareness internationally for the need to retrain the ANC to achieve greater distance

Figure 2: Congolese Prime Minister Patrice Lumumba meeting with Prime Minister John Diefenbaker in Ottawa to discuss the prospects of Canadian technical assistance for the fragile new country. 30 July 1960. (Credit: Ted Grant/Library and Archives Canada, e011074241)

between the military and government, and to lessen the likelihood of any future political interference.

The integral role the Canadian Armed Forces played in ONUC—providing vital signals support, serving at force headquarters, and organizing air operations—helps to explain why there were repeated bilateral and multilateral attempts to engage Canada directly in the ANC retraining and reorganization effort. The earliest attempt to involve Canada actually originated with Ghana, just weeks after the Congo Crisis erupted. President Kwame Nkrumah hoped Canada might provide twenty

French-speaking soldiers to cooperate in an initiative to train Congolese cadets at the Ghana Military Academy. Ghanaian motives were immediately questioned. A suspicious member of the Prime Minister's Office observed, "In free Africa, as in free Asia, power politics are regarded as the monopoly of the West—or, at least, of East and West," but added, "can it be, nevertheless, that a game of African power-politics, with strictly African goals and within African regional confines, is also emerging?"[10] The Department of National Defence was also cool to the idea, citing a shortage of French-speaking personnel, and the Department of External Affairs expressed concern at the bilateral rather than multilateral nature of the Ghanaian proposal.

The idea was raised in Cabinet, but by then a competing, and more welcome, training request had arrived from Secretary-General Hammarskjöld. By the end of August 1960, Canada had officially declined Ghana's request and had informed Hammarskjöld that between fifty and one hundred personnel could be provided for the UN scheme. The secretary-general then temporarily shelved the plan, as he dealt with urgent, fast-moving political events taking place in the Congo.[11] This episode was significant, though, because it revealed a key dilemma that ultimately plagued all subsequent efforts to reorganize and retrain the ANC: should this be accomplished through the UN or by direct, bilateral arrangements with the Congolese?

The next approach to Canada for training assistance came directly from the Congolese. It, too, raised the same troubling question of whether military assistance should be provided bilaterally or under a UN umbrella. The Canadian consul general in Léopoldville, William Wood, received inquiries about military studies in Canada, and he was aware that Mobutu had approached a number of Western embassies to discuss officer training. By September 1960, though, the UN General Assembly has passed a resolution that explicitly called upon "all States to refrain from the direct and indirect provision of arms or other materials of war and military personnel and other assistance for military purposes in the Congo during the temporary period of military assistance through the United Nations, except upon the request of the United Nations through the Secretary-General."[12] Once again, Ottawa decided to steer clear of bilateral requests for assistance but remained open to the idea of helping the UN with plans it was developing for an officers' training school located in the Congo, even though this was not an agreeable solution to Mobutu, who preferred the idea of sending candidates abroad for training.[13]

Reform and training of the ANC became an issue again in early February 1961, when Hammarskjöld visited the Congo and concluded that a more active approach was needed. He was supported in this conviction by the new US administration of President John F. Kennedy. In a statement to the Security Council when it reconvened that month, Hammarskjöld called for a number of far-reaching measures, including "the reorganization of the national army, preventing it, or units thereof, from intervening in the present political conflicts in the Congo."[14] He was effectively calling for the disarmament of the ANC, even though the Congolese opposed this. In any case, news soon broke that Patrice Lumumba had been assassinated, and the political upheaval surrounding the deposed prime minister's demise quickly overshadowed any controversy about ANC retraining.

At first, the Congolese authorities greeted Security Council Resolution 161 (1961), passed in the wake of Lumumba's murder, as tantamount to a declaration of war—particularly given its provisions related to the ANC. However, in the months following the resolution, Hammarskjöld dispatched emissaries who managed to smooth over relations. It was in this new spirit of cooperation that Mobutu and the secretary-general's acting special representative, Mekki Abbas, finally reached an agreement that would see ONUC organize the training of ANC officers. Mobutu stipulated that instructors would have to speak French and be either French or Canadian.

Michel Gauvin, by this time Canada's consul general in Léopoldville, having learned of the agreement from a reliable ONUC source, immediately contacted Ottawa. Canada, he presumed, would seriously consider the request if it was raised in the Secretary-General's Advisory Committee on the Congo and if the "more extreme Afro-Asian members" agreed to the plan. He was right. In Ottawa, Secretary of State for External Affairs Howard Green indicated that he was "prepared to give full backing" to the use of Canadian officers as instructors for the ANC. National Defence was already engaged in preliminary planning for a retraining scheme. With both External Affairs and National Defence backing Canadian participation, the UN then failed again to follow through with a retraining plan. Months later, Gauvin met with a frustrated Mobutu, who was still waiting for a response to his request for Canadian or French instructors. Canada,

Mobutu said, was welcome in the Congo. He wondered why Ottawa was so careful not to offend the Afro-Asians. Gauvin reassured him there could be any number of reasons why Canada had not provided officers; the reality was that Canada was still waiting for an official UN request because, to comply with existing UN resolutions, all military assistance had to be channelled through the organization. The matter was dropped and not raised again until September.[15]

That fall, the UN finally approached Canada with a request to provide French-speaking personnel to assist with plans to reorganize the ANC, a request endorsed by the Americans who instructed their Ottawa embassy to ask External Affairs for its "most sympathetic consideration."[16] However, National Defence now proved less optimistic and enthusiastic about the provision of bilingual personnel, concerned about the impact on its other commitments. Before this new attitude could be communicated to External Affairs, open hostilities broke out in Katanga, and Secretary-General Hammarskjöld, en route to the Congo to help end the fighting, died when his airplane crashed.

Overtaken again by events, plans for reorganizing the ANC were suspended until General Iyassu Mengesha, the senior military adviser to the Congolese government, raised them directly with Gauvin in November. He asked Canada to provide eleven officers, and even threatened to resign if the UN did not take action to establish the training school. "If Canada replied affirmatively and quickly," General Iyassu thought, "the U.N. would be willing to fill the most important positions by Canadian officers, leaving other appointments to other nationalities."[17] Given National Defence's reluctance, External Affairs decided not to raise the issue in New York. If the UN broached it, the diplomats would advise the Secretariat that Canada was unlikely to provide the necessary personnel.

The issue did arise again in December, when acting Secretary-General U Thant directly asked Prime Minister John Diefenbaker for fifteen French-speaking officers to assist in the training of the Congolese army. In advising Diefenbaker, Air Chief Marshal Frank R. Miller, chair of the Chiefs of Staff Committee, expressed his reluctance to stretch the French-speaking officer corps any further than it already was; National Defence expected that training the ANC would be a lengthy commitment, so while the request was not rejected outright, it was abundantly clear that the military was not keen. External Affairs drew attention to the request's advantages: retraining the Congolese army would eventually permit the withdrawal of ONUC; providing assistance would be consistent with Canada's support of ONUC and its policy of helping the Congolese help themselves; aiding the Congo would demonstrate that Canadian assistance in Africa was not exclusively for English-speaking countries; and Canada was one of the very few acceptable sources of French-speaking instructors who could exert a Western influence on the Congolese. An uncertain Cabinet reviewed these arguments on 28 December but postponed a final decision because Defence Minister Douglas Harkness was absent.[18]

Under increasing pressure from the Congolese government to address the training issue, the UN pressed Ottawa for a decision. In the Congo Advisory Committee, UN Under-Secretary for Special Political Affairs Ralph Bunche revealed that both Canada and Switzerland had been approached for officers, but the Swiss had turned down the request. "Everything now depended on Canada," according to Bunche.[19] On 26 January, Cabinet debated the merits of providing assistance. Howard Green argued in favour of providing officer instructors; Harkness opposed the plan. The position of the minister of national defence prevailed, primarily because fighting in Katanga highlighted the Congo's political instability and raised doubts as to the wisdom of sending more Canadians. UN Secretary-General U Thant was told no French-speaking officers with the required qualifications were available.[20]

It did not end there, however. U Thant persisted. In a telegram to Diefenbaker, he pleaded, "We are so desperately in need of French-speaking officers for this purpose that I feel that I must renew my appeal to you in a modified form as sole means of avoiding necessity of abandoning training project altogether and informing Congolese of our inability to assist them in this training."[21] The UN launched a lobbying offensive. Bunche approached General E. L. M. Burns, then serving as Canada's principal advisor on disarmament. The two were very well acquainted, having worked closely together while Burns led the United Nations Emergency Force in the late 1950s. Bunche asked Burns to speak directly with the Canadian army on the UN's behalf. Bunche also lobbied William Barton, a diplomat at Canada's Permanent Mission in New York. Sounding utterly desperate, Bunche stressed his hope that Canada would come through with the required officers. The UN, he added, would be happy to use retired or reserve officers, and was no longer expecting Canada to assume sole responsibility for the training mission. Diefenbaker was not unsympathetic, but the prime minister was also unwilling to press this issue with Harkness if the minister felt unable to make any officers available. During a further discussion in Cabinet, the original decision not to provide any officers from the active list was confirmed, but ministers agreed to tell the secretary-general that the government was looking into the possibility of making available six or seven officers from the retired list.[22]

By this time, both Mobutu and Congolese prime minister Cyrille Adoula were growing impatient with the UN. Mobutu, in particular, was opposed to the idea of a school operated by a mixed group of officers from various nations. Adoula wrote to ONUC HQ, "It appears to me that [Canada] which has never been a colonial power which has no political or economic interests in Africa and which possesses good military schools could furnish these few instructors who are needed."[23] Mobutu again spoke directly to Gauvin, asking the consul general to make one last appeal to Ottawa. Though some in the Department of External Affairs began to question the wisdom of Canadian involvement in a school operated by a number of nations, especially if Mobutu was opposed to this UN approach, Ottawa still asked the Permanent Mission in New York to find out the specific appointments, ranks, and qualifications for the six or seven officers Canada could provide. Whether the Congolese government and Mobutu would agree to UN plans for a school operated by officers of various nationalities remained to be seen.[24]

The final round of conflict between ONUC and the separatist elements in Katanga again interrupted the efforts to reorganize the ANC. The project was revisited in early 1963, once the secession was at an end, and attention was focused more directly on what needed to be accomplished to facilitate the withdrawal of ONUC. This time, the United States took the initiative. A plan was developed based on information provided by Colonel Michael Greene of the US Army, who had been dispatched to the Congo the previous year to assess ANC requirements. The Greene plan, as it came to be known, called for a series of bilateral aid programs to train the various services within the Congolese military, all coordinated by the United Nations. Canada, Belgium, Italy, Norway, and Israel were asked to participate. In the ensuing months, Canada was asked to provide training for both officers and communications units, and the senior officer to oversee the entire training mission. Washington, Brussels, and

Léopoldville pressed Ottawa to agree to a Canadian contribution. From Léopoldville, Gauvin reported that Mobutu appeared unwilling to take no for an answer: "Where there is a will there is a way," the Congolese general insisted.[25]

Both National Defence and External Affairs immediately raised the multilateral red flag, arguing that Canada should contribute only if military assistance was directed by and through the UN. Moreover, they argued, the Greene plan appeared problematic because it relied heavily on NATO countries. Canada's permanent representative at the UN, Ambassador Paul Tremblay, was instructed to speak to U Thant and to suggest that African nations, such as Nigeria and Tunisia, be included. The ambassador told the secretary-general that any request for Canadian assistance would only be considered by Ottawa if it came from him and was supported by the Congolese government. Notably, when U Thant subsequently raised the plan in the Congo Advisory Committee, he framed the effort as a program of bilateral assistance, with the UN serving as an umbrella, and guided by a coordinating group of African states, including Nigeria, Ethiopia, and Tunisia.

As anticipated, the plan now ran into political difficulties. Tremblay reported on the Advisory Committee meeting, noting the African and Middle Eastern members "found it psychologically and politically difficult" to approve the plan.[26] The African states were clear: either they should be included in the actual training mission or the plan should be developed entirely on a bilateral basis without any UN involvement. Not including the UN, however, directly contradicted Canada's precondition for participation.

Very quickly, the secretary-general found himself under considerable pressure, from both the Communist Soviet Union and a group of African and Asian states, to keep the UN out of this ANC retraining plan. Indeed, after a further meeting with U Thant, Ambassador Tremblay came to believe that the secretary-general would have to "wash his hands" of it.[27] This left the UN with a significant dilemma. Ideally, the ANC needed to be retrained and reorganized before UN forces withdrew, but political realities now seemed to rule out both direct bilateral military aid and aid provided through the UN. Before the Advisory Committee met again to consider the matter, Prime Minister Adoula wrote to U Thant, insisting that any attempt to prevent the Congolese government from securing bilateral assistance would "constitute an unjustifiable and intolerable restriction on its freedom of action."[28] African members of the committee were divided: some argued that the Congolese government could not solicit bilateral assistance so long as ONUC was present in the Congo, while others came to share the Canadian view that the Congolese should be allowed to make their own arrangements if the UN was unable or unwilling to meet their needs. In the end, noting the lack of unanimity in the committee, Canadian officials correctly anticipated that U Thant would not object to bilateral military training assistance for the Congo. In effect, the secretary-general turned a blind eye to training programs later established with Belgium's assistance. In a report to the Security Council, U Thant simply said, "I have no official knowledge of subsequent developments."[29] Although this diplomatic maneuver enabled the Congo to enlist the help it needed to retrain its army, it also closed the door to any possibility that Canada would provide assistance to the Congo on a multilateral basis through the United Nations.

Though Canada had consistently demonstrated a preference for multilateral over bilateral military assistance, the Congolese persisted in their pursuit of Canadian help. Prime Minister Adoula favoured Canadian support on the grounds that Canada was considered "a non-colonial country politically acceptable to most African opinion."[30] Moreover, he did not want Belgium to dominate completely the training program. The United States also pressed Canada to participate. In Washington, the assistant secretary of state for African affairs, G. Mennen Williams, approached Canadian Ambassador Charles Ritchie and intimated that both Italy and Norway were awaiting a Canadian decision before determining their own participation. Gary Harman, the Canadian diplomat at the embassy in Washington responsible for consultation with the US State Department on African issues, later recalled that the United States was pushing the retraining proposal and counting on Canada to be more supportive.[31] A meeting in Washington between Kennedy and Mobutu in May 1963, when the issue of ANC training was raised and the president asked what steps the United States was taking to secure the participation of other countries, undoubtedly prompted the American overtures.[32] After returning to the Congo, Mobutu grew increasingly impatient. In an interview with the Congolese press, he stated, "Italy, Canada and Norway

Figure 3: Ottawa justified its refusal to join an ANC training mission by citing the substantial burdens already shouldered by Canadian Signalmen in the Congo. (Credit: Department of National Defence/Library and Archives Canada, e010786584)

seem to be hesitating. And I have [the] impression that these countries will not do anything as long as [the] UN does not confer its patronage on this organisation."[33]

A definite decision not to participate in the training of the ANC was finally taken in the fall of 1963 by Prime Minister Lester Pearson's new Liberal government. By then, the UN had decided to extend ONUC's stay in the Congo through to mid-1964. Canadian peacekeepers, because of the key communications and administrative tasks they performed within the peacekeeping mission, were expected to stay until the end. This extended commitment, in addition to an affirmative response to an ONUC request to provide an officer to serve as chief of staff, were cited as the reasons why Canada could not commit further military resources for service in the Congo. In October, Prime Minister Adoula met with President Kennedy, who promised personally to impress upon Canada the importance of assisting with ANC retraining. However, regardless of the pressures applied by Washington, the following month Gauvin in Léopoldville received instructions from Ottawa, advising the consul general to express Canada's regret at being unable to meet the Congolese request, but in doing so to make reference to the "considerable amount of time, manpower and money which [Canada] has expended in Congo to date as evidence of our continuing concern for [the] future stability of [the] country."[34]

From the outset of the Congo crisis, the association between the Congolese military and state stability was a concern for the international community. Mobutu's first *coup d'état* in 1960 illustrated how easily the military could be used to influence the political direction of the country. Was this the point of creation of a failed state? It has been argued that this coup condemned the Congo to political instability and dependence, a situation that even now requires "the Congolese leadership to reorient the military toward external defense by keeping it out of domestic law enforcement" as a means to "constrain the military to stay out of politics by making it uncomfortable in power."[35] While Mobutu did relinquish control for a brief time after the first coup, the precedent was certainly set. Canada's first ambassador to the Congo, J. C. Gordon Brown, was present in the capital for Mobutu's second coup in 1965. He recalls being summoned, along with other members of the diplomatic corps, to meet with Mobutu. According to Brown, Mobutu denied his takeover was a military *coup d'état*, even as he "wryly" acknowledged that the martial music on Radio Leo might have "convinced listeners otherwise."[36]

As an historical case study, this episode is important because it illustrates some of the fundamental issues still associated with international intervention in fragile, failing, and failed states. While ONUC accomplished almost all the objectives established by its mandate, its failure to deal effectively with retraining and reorganizing the ANC from the earliest days of the Congo crisis helped to create a situation whereby Mobutu could readily use his position within the military to seize power and to establish his kleptocratic regime. In this respect, the UN, and Canada as a member nation actively engaged in the failed and protracted diplomacy related to ANC retraining, must shoulder some responsibility for the outcome of events in the Congo. But in this failure, there are also lessons.

Canada's appeal as a potential contributor to so many of the plans for ANC retraining can be attributed partly to the Canadian Forces' bilingual capabilities, but also, critically, to the perception that Canada, though of the West, was not a colonial power. Canada's disinterestedness was key. Without an obvious or hidden agenda in the Congo, Canada was a nation capable of acting without pursuing self-interested motivations; this explains both its attractiveness to the Congolese as a non-threatening contributor/partner, and the persistent and pressing requests for Canadian participation. This does, however, raise an interesting dilemma for current foreign policy. Today much emphasis is placed on self-interest in assessing policy options. Yet intervention in fragile or failing states might best be accomplished through cooperation with nations that have no vested interests—beyond broadly shared humanitarian objectives—in the state concerned. This paradox should be resolved by reconsidering the degree to which self-interest must consistently and universally be applied as the most important determinant in foreign policy.

This episode also demonstrates Canada's clear preference in this period for addressing international crises in newly independent states through multilateral institutions, the UN in particular. This, too, resulted in a particular policy paradox for Canada—this time with respect to sovereignty. Intervention by the international community, even when done at the request of a nation, can be taken as an indication that the state is incapable of governing itself. This was a highly sensitive issue for countries that had only just achieved independence, but remains a point of concern for nations today. It is not unreasonable to expect that states would attempt to protect sovereignty and freedom of action when confronting—indeed, even when welcoming—international intervention. This was most in evidence in discussions over whether military retraining assistance should be provided on a bilateral or multilateral basis. The Congolese government vociferously argued for its right to obtain bilateral assistance to retrain the ANC, but faced stiff opposition in the UN Secretary-General's Congo Advisory Committee, where some members insisted on a multilateral program. Canada was caught in the middle: there was little enthusiasm in Ottawa for a bilateral aid program, and a clear preference in many quarters for schemes organized through the United Nations; but the Canadian government was also supportive of the principle of the Congo's right to secure bilateral assistance, if the UN did not deliver—even if Ottawa had no intention of contributing. This is but one specific example of how intervention in fragile states can be complicated by sovereignty, and in the case of Canada, how a clear preference for multilateralism can sometimes have unintended consequences.

By the summer of 1964, Howard Green had been out of office for months, having been defeated in the 1963 election. He stayed current with world events, though, and was a regular contributor to the *Victoria Colonist*. As ONUC prepared to leave the Congo, Green wrote in his column: "If it turns out that the Congolese authorities cannot cope with the situation which arises upon the withdrawal of the United Nations force the result will be severe criticism of the United Nations and a verdict around the world that it has failed in the Congo. This despite some excellent achievements during the years the force was in the country."[37] Green could not have been more correct. For the most part, ONUC had managed to carry out its complex mandate. But it failed in one important respect: the retraining and reorganization of the ANC. Just as Green predicted, all of ONUC's successes were soon overshadowed and forgotten when, less than two years after its last peacekeepers left, Mobutu's second coup established a ruthless and corrupt dictatorship that endured for more than three decades.

Notes

1. Joseph-Desiré Mobutu is better known as Mobutu Sese Seko; his regime ruled the Congo from 1965 to 1997. In the early 1970s, Mobutu "Africanized" names—both his personal name and many place names. The country became Zaire, and many cities' names were changed (e.g., Léopoldville became Kinshasa). To avoid confusion, and because this chapter addresses the period 1960–64, I will employ names commonly in use at that time.

2. "The Failed States Index," http://http://fsi.fundforpeace.org/rankings-2013-sortable (accessed 14 November 2015).

3. Jack A. Goldstone et al., *State Failure Task Force Report: Phase III Findings* (McLean, VA: Science Applications International Corporation, 2000), 112, http://globalpolicy.gmu.edu/pitf/ (accessed 20 April 2012). Though the methodology of this study's approach has been challenged because of its broad and inclusive definition of state failure, its Congo

findings are consistent with widely supported views of that country. For a critique, see Jonathan Di John, "The Concept, Causes and Consequences of Failed States: A Critical Review of the Literature and Agenda for Research with Specific Reference to Sub-Saharan Africa," *European Journal of Development Research* 22, no. 1 (2010): 15–16.

4   Adam Hochschild, *King Leopold's Ghost: A Story of Greed, Terror, and Heroism in Colonial Africa* (New York: Houghton Mifflin, 1998).

5   United Nations Security Council (UNSC), Resolution 143 (1960) [S/4387]; UNSC Res 145 (1960) [S/4405].

6   UNSC Res 146 (1960) [S/4426].

7   UNSC Res 161 (1961) [S/4741].

8   UNSC Res 169 (1961) [S/5002].

9   Catherine Hoskyns, *The Congo since Independence* (London: Oxford University Press, 1965), 88.

10 Diefenbaker Canada Centre, John G. Diefenbaker Papers, File MG1/XII/C/114: "Memo for Prime Minister: Crisis in Congo and the Role of Ghana, August 1960."

11 Kevin A. Spooner, *Canada, the Congo Crisis, and UN Peacekeeping, 1960–64* (Vancouver: UBC Press, 2009), 88.

12 United Nations General Assembly (UNGA), Resolution 1474 (ES-IV).

13 Spooner, *Canada, the Congo Crisis, and UN Peacekeeping*, 102.

14 Andrew W. Cordier and Wilder Foote, eds., *Public Papers of the Secretaries-General of the United Nations*, vol. 5, *Dag Hammarskjöld 1960–61* (New York: Columbia University Press, 1975), 332–36.

15 Library and Archives Canada [hereafter LAC], RG25, vol. 5222, file 6386-C-40 part 13: "Telegram Leopoldville to External: Training of Congolese Army," 5 April 1961; LAC, RG25, vol. 5222, file 6386-C-40 part 13: "Memo Campbell to Defence Liaison 1: Training of Congolese Army," 7 April 1961; LAC, RG24, vol. 5086, file 3445-34/73: "Memo: Telephone Conversation—Colonel Parker—Lt. Col. Speedie 1130 hours 3 May 1961: Training of the ANC," 3 May 1961; LAC, RG25, vol. 5223, file 6386-C-40 part 15: "Letter Under Secretary to Chairman Chiefs of Staff and Attached Telegram: Training of Congolese Army," 27 June 1961; LAC, RG25, vol. 5223, file 6386-C-40 part 15: "Telegram Leopoldville to External: Follow Up on Visit to General Mobutu," 19 June 1961.

16 LAC, RG25, vol. 5223, file 6386-C-40 part 16: "Memo to Minister: Congo: UN Request for Assistance," 22 September 1961.

17 LAC, RG25, vol. 5214, file 6386-40 part 27: "Telegram Leopoldville to External: UN Request for Military Advisers and Instructors for Congo," 7 November 1961.

18 Spooner, *Canada, the Congo Crisis, and UN Peacekeeping*, 181–82.

19 LAC, RG25, vol. 5214, file 6386-40 part 29: "Memo African and Middle Eastern Division to Mr. Ignatieff: UN Request for French-speaking officers," 10 January 1962.

20 Spooner, *Canada, the Congo Crisis, and UN Peacekeeping*, 181–82.

21 LAC, RG24, vol. 7169, file 2-5081-6 part 15: "Telegram Perm Mission in New York to External: Provision of Instructors for Congolese Army," 2 February 1962.

22 Spooner, *Canada, the Congo Crisis, and UN Peacekeeping*, 186–87.

23 LAC, RG24, vol. 7169, file 2-5081-6 part 15: "Telegram Leopoldville to External: Training of Congolese Army," 24 February 1962.

24 Spooner, *Canada, the Congo Crisis, and UN Peacekeeping*, 187.

25 LAC, RG24, vol. 21487, file 2137.3 part 9: "Telegram Leopoldville to External: Mobutu's Visit and Request," 23 November 1962.

26 LAC, RG24, vol. 7169, file 2-5081-6 part 18: "Telegram Perm Mission in New York to External: Congo Advisory Cttee 73rd Meeting," 20, 21 March 1963.

27 LAC, RG24, vol. 21487, file 2137.3 part 10: "Telegram Perm Mission in New York to External: Congo: ANC Retraining Plan," 28 March 1963.

28 United Nations, *Yearbook of the United Nations 1963* (New York: Office of Public Information, United Nations, 1963), 4–5.

29 Rosalyn Higgins, *United Nations Peacekeeping, 1946–1967: Documents and Commentary*, vol. 3 (Oxford: Oxford University Press, 1980), 361.

30 LAC, RG25, vol. 5217, file 6386-40 part 38: "Memo for Minister: Request for Canadian Assistance in Training the Congolese Army," 8 May 1963.

31 Gary Harman, interview by Kevin Spooner, Ottawa, 31 July 2003.

32 "Memorandum of Conversation," 31 May 1963, in United States, Department of State, *Foreign Relations of the United States (FRUS), 1961–1963*, vol. 20: Congo Crisis (Washington: 1995), 858–62.

33 LAC, RG24, vol. 21487, file 2137.3 part 11: "Telegram Leopoldville to External: ANC Training," 2 July 1963.

34 LAC, RG24, vol. 21487, file 2137.3 part 12: "Telegram External to Leopoldville: Request for Canadian Participation in ANC Training," 25 November 1963.

35 Kisangani N. F. Emizet, "Explaining the Rise and Fall of Military Regimes: Civil-Military Relations in the Congo," *Armed Forces and Society* 26, no. 2 (2000): 224.

36 J. C. Gordon Brown, *Blazes Along a Diplomatic Trail: A Memoir of Four Posts in the Canadian Foreign Service* (Victoria: Trafford Publishing, 2000), 167.

37 Howard Green, "Perilous Times in the Congo," *Victoria Colonist*, 26 June 1964, 44.

CHAPTER 3

THE POLITICS OF AFRICAN INTERVENTION:
Canada and Biafra, 1967–70[1]

Stephanie Bangarth

"Where's Biafra?" enquired Prime Minister Pierre Elliott Trudeau in August 1968 when asked about his position on the civil war raging in Nigeria. Biafra—a small, breakaway state in the West African nation of Nigeria—declared its independence on 30 May 1967. The ensuing Nigerian civil war, which pitted north against south, the oil rich versus the rest of the country, Western interests versus African interests, and Nigerian ethno-religious groups against each other, occupied international attention until its end in January 1970. Biafra was a nightmare for the international community, especially for Britain, France, and—given the initiatives of Presbyterian leader Reverend Ted Johnson—Canada. Trudeau's flippant response and the inaction of foreign affairs minister Mitchell Sharp was "shameful," according to the *Toronto Daily Star*, usually sympathetic to the Liberal Party.[2]

Johnson was unrelenting in his efforts to address the implications of state failure in Nigeria. In February 1969 he led a delegation of church leaders to Ottawa asking for help for starving Biafrans, but was refused. With that rebuff came the creation of Canairelief, supported—without government money of any kind—by Jewish leaders, the Roman Catholic Church, and the major Protestant denominations. In addition, Johnson

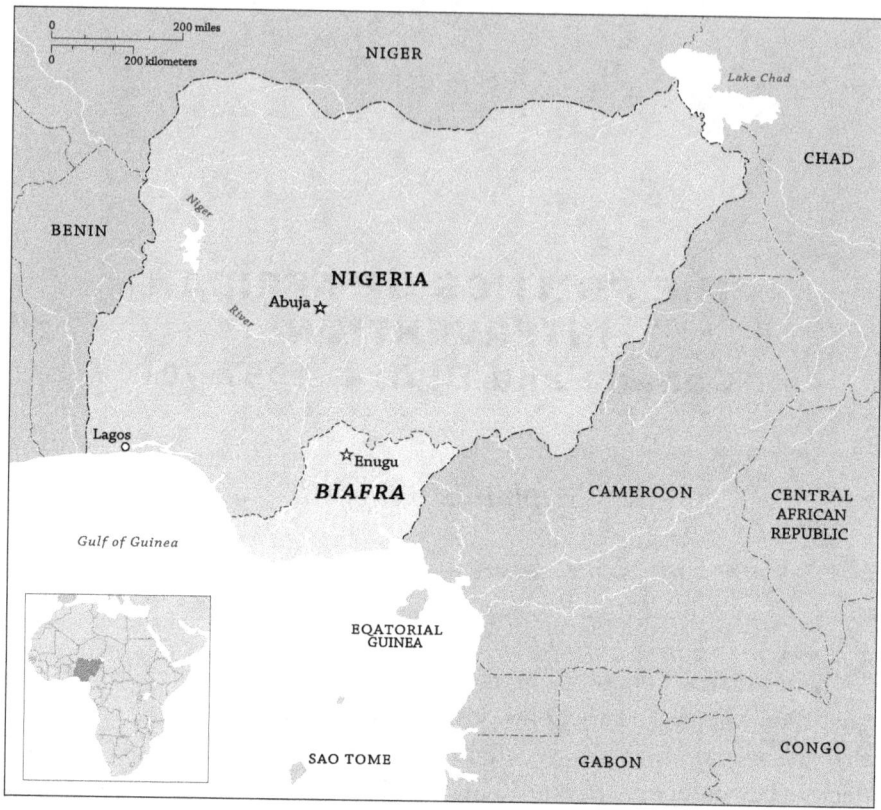

Figure 1: Map. (Credit: Marilyn Croot)

and his team, including Reverend Walter McLean, went the political route and arranged for two members of Parliament—Tory David MacDonald, a United Church minister, and Andrew Brewin, an NDP Anglican—to fly into Biafra on Canairelief on a fact-finding mission. Their report recommended that Canada use its moral suasion to prompt the United Nations into negotiating a ceasefire, participate in relief operations, give money for humanitarian relief, and encourage the United Nations to prosecute Nigerian civil rights abuses. Following their visit, both Brewin and MacDonald attempted to counter the legalistic and ambiguous approach of the Trudeau government to the Biafran conflict. Their advocacy, in conjunction with that of other concerned Canadians, NGOs, and advocacy and religious organizations, will be placed in context in this paper, alongside other issues that were raised by the experience of Biafra, including the legitimacy of a "war on famine," the meaning of genocide, and the limits placed by international law on a nation's sovereignty when it violates basic human rights. Biafra was a lesson unlearned, despite the laudable efforts of churches, NGOs, and some politicians of principle. This was Canada's first encounter with an African relief effort, and Canada, the touted peacekeeping nation, decided not to play a role.

The Biafran situation and its aftermath continues to speak to the phenomenon of "weak," "fragile," or "failed" states, the conflict between ethnic identities and national institutions in many nations, including Canada, and the concerned but sometimes troublesome humanitarian intrusions into the sovereignty of African nations. As scholars Ike Okonta and Kate Meagher point out, Biafra did not begin as a "bid for identity politics, but as a call for a more just and inclusive nationalism." In their view, Biafra emerged from an obligation to federalism, not simply from a desire for separation.[3] Former UN Secretary General Kofi Annan has warned that "ignoring failed states creates problems that sometimes come back to bite us."[4] Indeed, as Biafra symbolized in many ways the legitimacy of a more inclusive nationalism, the legacies of Biafra demonstrate the failure of the Nigerian state to address popular demands for equitable citizenship. Thus, the conflict was about the very legitimacy of post-colonial questioning of federalism and federations, and less about separatism. Trudeau misread the situation as a warning on the issue of Quebec separatism, which dominated domestic policy at the same time. Trudeau viewed all forms of nationalism with suspicion if not outright disdain. Determined to defeat the separatist movement in his own country, he refused to sanction what he perceived as one in another state, and ended up alienating humanitarian opinion in Canada. As a result, while Biafra faded away from popular concern in the aftermath of the Nigerian civil war in 1970, the lessons learned, the tactics employed by mainstream churches, NGOs, and individuals, and the pressure brought to bear on the federal government would serve both as a foundation on which to build future humanitarian relief operations in Africa and as an example of the importance of public mobilization.

Canada Encounters the Nigerian Civil War

The Nigerian civil war of the late 1960s was one of the first occasions when Western consciences were confronted and deeply affronted by the degree of suffering and the extent of violence on the African continent. Accusations of genocide, arms-running by former colonial powers such as Britain, and political machinations carried out by both federal Nigerian and Biafran stakeholders belied the supposed unity of a harmonious state that proponents of Nigerian war policy claimed existed throughout the country's sixty years of colonial rule and the five years of its post-colonial existence as the First Republic. Its fracture represented the fallout from the post-colonial period and placed an extraordinary strain on the Commonwealth. And in that context, Canada was placed squarely in a position of conflict between Britain and Nigeria.

The Nigerian conflict is not generally well known to Canadians, and for good reason. Despite the fact that the Canadian public was, for some time, roused to ire over its government's indifferent response, the historical record is nearly silent on the whole affair. Apart from in-depth reportage from various principals involved in the campaign to send aid to the Biafrans, such as that by Charles Taylor and Clyde Sanger in the *Globe and Mail*, and the reports from MPs Brewin and MacDonald, and Ontario provincial representative Stephen Lewis, there exists little sustained scholarly examination of the subject to provide context for the aforementioned reports.[5] The Nigerian conflict is largely forgotten in the midst of a more widely known conflict—the Vietnam War.

It should be noted that although Nigeria was part of the Commonwealth, its relations with Canada were not particularly close, and the conflict generated little interest in Canada at the outset. The issue of Biafra was first raised in the House of Commons in 1967, but the Liberal government under Lester B. Pearson faced only eight questions.[6] By early 1968, however, Brewin and others began to speak frequently on Biafra. The indexes show numerous instances of Brewin and MacDonald discussing the Nigeria-Biafra civil war in the 1968–69 debates. Broader issues discussed in Parliament regarding Biafra included propaganda, relief, arms sales to combatants, the involvement of other countries (France, the Soviet Union, Portugal), the possibility of bringing orphans to Canada to be adopted, the televising of the conflict, causes of the struggle (ethnic/tribal), Biafran fears of genocide, the Canadian position on the conflict, and Canada's potential to act as a mediator. By 1969, the issue of Biafra turned to debates on post-war relief and rehabilitation. A review of *Hansard* reveals that this conflict and its after-effects were no longer discussed after 1970.

Biafra and the Politicians

As political scientist Donald Barry notes, interest groups began their attempts to influence the government's policy by June 1967. In particular, officials of the Presbyterian Church in Canada were knowledgeable about the situation in both Nigeria and Biafra as a result of their ongoing missionary efforts there. Returned Canadian University Service Overseas (CUSO) volunteers and Biafran students studying in Canada were also among the early campaigners raising public awareness. The Canadian public began to pay attention by July 1968, when pictures of starving Biafran children began appearing on television and in newspapers. Criticism of the government's inaction grew, especially after Trudeau feigned amusement. When asked by a reporter about the possibility of sending Canadian aid to the war's casualties he replied, "You have the funniest questions. We haven't considered this as a government ... I think we should send aid to all needy people but we can't send it to everyone and I'd have to see what our priorities are prior to the Biafra people."[7] At a time when African decolonization and liberation were being viewed with enthusiasm by progressives in the West, Trudeau's statements certainly struck a discordant note. The Biafran crisis dominated the Canadian foreign policy landscape throughout 1968.

Trudeau's flippant remarks are perhaps curious in light of some of the contents of *The Canadian Way*, the foreign policy memoir penned (in the 1990s, it should be noted) by Trudeau and his former advisor, Ivan Head. In it, they describe a meeting with several senior Canadian diplomats in Europe in January 1969, at a time when the Nigerian conflict was being hotly debated in Canada. The diplomats, "to the ill-concealed astonishment of Trudeau and Head," advised the pair "that this major African drama was of little more than passing importance to Canada and of inconsequential

Figure 2: Members of Parliament Andrew Brewin (left) and David MacDonald, who were among the first to champion Biafra in the House of Commons, are shown en route to attend parliamentary hearings on the Nigerian Civil War in October 1968. (Credit: Duncan Cameron/Library and Archives Canada, e011160350)

influence in the web of Canada's external relations. East-West should be the focal point … the driving force of foreign policy, the primary contender for financial and human resources." Trudeau and Head go on to note that they were "concerned about the demonstrable needs of the developing countries and the inexorable influence that they would bring to bear upon future generations of Canadians."[8] It should be noted that Head and Trudeau were the architects of the Canadian International Development Agency (CIDA), an organization created in 1968 to disperse funds for development assistance. About the same time, Trudeau also expanded

Canadian aid to francophone developing countries to match the aid given to Commonwealth nations, as John English notes, via the Colombo Plan.[9]

Pressed to action by various interest groups, chief among them the newly formed Nigeria/Biafra Relief Fund of Canada, the federal government agreed in early July 1968 to make a $500,000 contribution to food aid for Nigeria and promised to assist in the airlifting of supplies, provided that the Nigerian and Biafran authorities granted their approval. However, when it was discovered that the food and medical supplies would be sent to Lagos, Nigeria, and not to Biafra, where it was estimated that six thousand people were dying of starvation each day, criticism of the government increased. The Liberal government then agreed to accept an invitation from the Nigerian Federal Military Government (FMG) to send a Canadian observer to be part of the International Military Observer Team (IMOT) along with Britain, Sweden, the United Nations, and the Organisation of African Unity (OAU), to visit Nigeria to scrutinize the behaviour of federal troops. Still, when Parliament resumed its duties in September 1968, the opposition parties pushed even further with their critiques of the government's Biafra policy. The Progressive Conservative and New Democratic parties persisted in keeping the issue of Biafra on the national agenda over the course of the fall months. Backed by the media and helped by various interest groups, they urged the Trudeau government to secure a ceasefire or a negotiated settlement through the UN; to appeal to nations such as Britain, France and the USSR to stop supplying arms to the combatants; to secure permission from the Nigerian government for relief flights into Biafra; and to boost the flow of aid to Biafra through monetary assistance and aircraft.[10]

Among those voices opposing the government was the Reverend Ted Johnson, moderator of the Presbyterian Church of Canada. On 14 March 1968 he led a delegation of church leaders to Ottawa to request aid for starving Biafrans, but was flatly refused. As a consequence of that rejection, Canairelief was created through the financial support of Jewish leaders, the Roman Catholic Church, and the major Protestant Church denominations (mainly the Anglican, Presbyterian, and United churches), along with a partnership with Oxfam. Canairelief made its first flight on 23 January 1969, and its final trip less than a year later on 11 January 1970. In that short time it completed 670 flights and delivered eleven thousand

Figure 3: Key figures in the global relief effort, shown here in New York in 1968, are, L. to R.: Rev. Viggo Mollerup, Fr. Anthony Byrne, Gen. Ingvar Berg, Bishop. Ed Swanstrom, Mgr. Peter Kuhn, Rev. Ed Johnson, Mr. Jan van Hoogstraten. (Credit: Canairelief.)

tons of desperately needed food and medical supplies into the blockaded state of Biafra.[11]

Two further entreaties to the Liberal government to send aid were also unsuccessful. As historian Robert Bothwell notes, "up to this point, Trudeau had enjoyed a favourable rating from the press: Biafra proved to be the first occasion on which his reason did not appeal to their passion."[12] The opposition parties continued their campaign to call into question Trudeau's reputation as a progressive, and peppered both Trudeau and Mitchell Sharp, the secretary of state for external affairs, with questions on Biafra in the House of Commons. A frustrated Trudeau responded to one such question on 27 September 1968 with the declaration that "we cannot intervene, short of committing an act of war against Nigeria and intervening in the affairs of that country."[13]

But other countries, including France, Portugal, and Israel, were already sending aid directly to Biafra. Johnson and his team responded to Trudeau's stonewalling tactics by stepping up the political pressure, recruiting two MPs—MacDonald, a Progressive Conservative United Church minister, and Brewin, an NDP Anglican layman—to fly into Biafra on a Canairelief flight to embark on a fact-finding mission. Reverend Walter McLean, who was appointed the first CUSO co-ordinator in Nigeria in 1962, indicated recently that he and Johnson were keen to get multi-party representation for their sponsored trip in an effort to show both politicians and Canadians that concern for Biafra cut across party lines. Initially James E. Walker, Liberal MP for York Centre, had expressed a strong interest in participating in the trip with Brewin and MacDonald, but he pulled out. According to McLean, it was not a coincidence that shortly after Trudeau had learned of Walker's intentions, he was appointed as parliamentary secretary to the prime minister.[14]

According to his biographer, the trip "infuriated" Trudeau, who was convinced that support for separatist Biafra was risky. Trudeau's handwritten notes from 1971 hint at the outrage he felt over Conservative and NDP willingness to consort with imperial Portugal in their search for allies on Biafra. "This govt," he sneered, "never supported Portugal in Africa … But NDP & Conservatives were on the side of Portugal in Africa, in its attempt to break up territorial integrity of Nigeria."[15] After French President Charles de Gaulle echoed the separatist slogan "Vive le Québec libre!" during a speech in Montreal on 24 July 1967, and later compared Canada to Nigeria, at the height of separatist tensions in Quebec, Trudeau continued to cast a jaundiced eye on the Nigerian conflict. De Gaulle's not-so-subtle support of Biafra's independence only strengthened Trudeau's opposition to it. By way of example, Trudeau told journalist Peter C. Newman: "To ask, 'Where's Biafra?' is tantamount to asking, 'Where is Laurentia?' the name Quebec nationalists give to the independent state of their dreams."[16]

Trudeau's comments on Biafra following a meeting with Nova Scotia Liberals in October of 1968 were even more revealing. In a lengthy encounter with journalists and protesters, the prime minister expressed his concern with dividing the world along ethnic lines, endorsing the United Nations position in favour of the self-determination of people of heterogeneous origins, "and not of nations, national groups or tribes."[17] Referring to Canada's political climate, Trudeau noted that the proper way to deal with issues of self-determination was to seek remedies, as Canada was doing with Quebec, as opposed to "division," as Biafra was attempting.

36 Hours in Biafra and Beyond

While Brewin and MacDonald's fact-finding mission angered Trudeau, it did generate considerable public interest and even more considerable activity in the House of Commons. Their official report of their fact-finding mission, *Canada and the Biafran Tragedy*, became a book in 1970 that recommended Canada use its influence in the United Nations to negotiate a ceasefire, participate in relief operations, push to uphold Nigerian civil rights and give money for humanitarian relief. They also wrote evocatively about the starvation they had witnessed. Direct news reports also came from Charles Taylor of the *Globe and Mail*, who accompanied Brewin and MacDonald on their trip, and from Stephen Lewis, whose reports were published in the *Toronto Daily Star* and later issued in a single booklet.[18]

As they wrote in *Canada and the Biafran Tragedy*, Brewin and MacDonald hoped their recommendations and observations would be helpful in constructing an international system to prevent the repetition of the Biafran tragedy, one characterized by profound human suffering. They also wanted to arouse the Canadian Parliament and people to act on a double front: pressing for a ceasefire and mounting a massive relief campaign to combat the threat of starvation. They arrived in Biafra in October 1968 when the fortunes of secessionist Biafra were at their nadir, on a relief flight in the dead of night.

There they proceeded with interviews of Biafran officials in the city of Umahia, interspersed with tours of recently bombed areas and hospitals filled with both civilian and military victims. The account of their visit is, not surprisingly, sympathetic to the Biafran cause. Nonetheless, Brewin and MacDonald's account is revealing in terms of how Biafran officials viewed their situation, specifically that they found it difficult to understand Britain's overwhelming commitment to the Federation and the FMG, which, many noted, contrasted sharply with British policy toward such discarded federations as the Central African Federation of Rhodesia, French Africa, the Federation of the West Indies, Malaysia, India, and Pakistan. The visit also revealed that some Biafran officials, including Christopher Chukwuemeka Mojekwu, Commissioner for Home Affairs and Local Government, saw an opportunity for Canada to provide the leadership, either through the Commonwealth or the UN, that the Organisation for African Unity could not, with its divided loyalties to various Western powers.[19]

Upon their return to Canada, Brewin and MacDonald were met with a great deal of public attention; the CBC labelled the visit as "clandestine." The next day, on 7 October, the House of Commons unanimously approved Conservative opposition leader Robert Stanfield's motion, put forward at Johnson's request, to have the Standing Committee on External Affairs and National Defence immediately consider the Nigeria-Biafra question.[20] In the meantime and over the course of October, the Liberal government began to harden its stance toward Biafra, despite joint efforts in the House of Commons by the Progressive Conservatives and the NDP. The government was no doubt encouraged in its stance, as Barry notes, by a recent public opinion poll indicating that notwithstanding the Biafra issue, the popularity of the government was increasing. Moreover, by 27 November, when the House of Commons held a special debate on the Nigeria-Biafra question, public interest had started to wane. Though Sharp announced that the government would provide a further $1.5 million for relief in Nigeria and Biafra, to be delivered by Canairelief, the Liberal government would go no further, easily defeating a joint PC-NDP motion calling on it to press certain countries to cease the shipment of arms to Nigeria.[21]

One of the main issues addressed by Brewin and MacDonald in their report was the question of federalism, and how the Federal Military Government's desire to preserve "One Nigeria" and the Biafran claim to self-determination effectively shaped the attitudes of other nations toward the conflict, including Canada. Brewin and MacDonald carefully argued the speciousness of the comparison drawn between the secession of Biafra and the threat of secession in Quebec. Although government officials denied that the spectre of Quebec separatism influenced Canada's policy, it seems clearly apparent from, among others things, Mitchell Sharp's own statements when he drew attention to the Gabon-Quebec parallel in defending the government's position.²² But as Brewin and MacDonald note, the effect of the Quebec situation was likely to strengthen and rigidify a policy that would have been adopted regardless of separatist tensions.²³ They also maintained that the Nigerian conflict held several important lessons about federalism, specifically whether the preservation of federal structures is an absolute value to be bought at the high price of civil wars and human suffering.

Their report also served to contrast the largely successful efforts of the churches and the International Red Cross in airlifting food and medical supplies into Biafra with the inadequate efforts of governments, including Canada's. They also provided a critical reassessment of the International Military Observer Team. The IMOT reports were, according to Brewin and MacDonald, incomplete, misleading, and served as useful propaganda for the federal side. They concluded, moreover, that the reports lulled the world into a false complacency about the war. They added, however, that if properly constituted with adequate terms of reference, observer teams could play a useful role in the containment and mitigation of similar conflicts. Brewin and MacDonald's report concluded with a recommendation that an international order be built that could effectively intervene to prevent massive loss of human life and the continuation of wars that threatened large numbers of people through genocide or otherwise. Ultimately, Brewin and MacDonald charged that Canada's reluctance to act was largely due to the unwillingness of the Department of External Affairs to change its traditional outlook. They suggested that "the basic reason for Ottawa's refusal to take the Biafran affair to the United Nations has been much more the adherence to a style and attitude in international affairs that has become characteristic of Canada. There is an attitude of caution, an attitude of weighing the views of our allies rather than the merits of the issue."²⁴

On the question of the use of starvation as a weapon of war and whether this constituted genocide, many Canadians who visited Biafra tended to take the view that semantics were pointless. In the words of Stephen Lewis, "Genocide is an ugly, impossible word. I don't know precisely how one defines it. But if it means, even in part, the deliberate, indiscriminate killing of a people or tribe, then there is concrete evidence to be found in the terrible Nigerian-Biafran civil war." He goes on to describe the federal Nigerian troops' mass killing of two to three thousand people in the refugee camp in Urua Inyang, a village at the southernmost tip of Biafra. To Lewis, and to many observers of Biafra who were aware of the 1966 pogroms against people of the Ibo tribe, largely reviled in Nigeria for their near-complete control of elite positions within Nigerian society, genocide was incontestable, and it was nothing but "semantic haggling to talk about what constitutes the nature and quality of genocide." Brewin and MacDonald also took a version of this view, noting that while the Biafran government may have overstated the issue of genocide for the purposes of propaganda, the discussion of genocide "obscures the reality of the tragedy." In their report they asserted that:

> Even if the legal concept of genocide cannot be substantiated, even if the military observers are right in saying that they at least saw no evidence of the necessary intent, the result for the victims ... was much the same: wholesale death by starvation, by indiscriminate bombing, by the slaughter of civilians; wholesale deprivation of the most basic of human rights—the right to live. Fortunately, the international community does not have to depend upon proof of genocide to have the right and indeed the obligation to act.[25]

In addition to pressuring the government in the House of Commons, Brewin also attempted to exert his influence via his international contacts. As he did throughout his career as a politician, Brewin corresponded and consulted with his counterparts in the British Labour Party on the Biafra issue. Recognizing that stopping the war in Biafra required a multilateral effort and coordination on the part of concerned parties, Brewin sent detailed memoranda to MP Philip Noel-Baker, chairman of the Foreign Affairs Group of the Parliamentary Labour Party, who in turn used them to develop their strategy. In return, Brewin often received "insider" advice from Labour Party officials such as MP Michael Barnes, who advised him to press the UN for an arms embargo as a prelude to a ceasefire.[26] Brewin's international contacts on the Nigerian conflict also included US Senator Edward Kennedy, who kept Brewin and MacDonald informed on developments south of the forty-ninth parallel.[27]

Brewin and MacDonald's visit was not without its public critics, however. They were criticized mainly for the "one-sided" nature of their mission, and they readily admitted that they saw and wrote about only one side. They did so in the belief that Biafra was more isolated from the outside world, "with little means of presenting its case to international opinion."[28] In a 5 October 1968 editorial, the *Regina Leader-Post* termed the visit "a breach of protocol." While "the sympathy of most Canadians is with the victims of this prolonged war in Biafra," it argued, "this does not excuse elected officials from the obligations of international good manners."[29] The newspaper also likened their visit to that of a French official, Phillippe Rossillon, who had recently visited Manitoba without the permission of the Canadian government, provoking a storm of outrage among government and opposition members in the House of Commons. As the editorial asked, "By what logic do Mr. MacDonald and Mr. Brewin interpret their decision to visit Biafra without permission from Nigerian authorities as more excusable than a similar action which their parties were swift to condemn recently? The incident has an unsavoury political air to it."[30] Indeed, Rossillon was only one of a number of French officials, with their subterranean links to the French government, whom Trudeau and his advisors suspected of being sent to Canada to stir up trouble and sympathies for the separatist cause. As historians J. L. Granatstein and Robert Bothwell have observed, Rossillon and other "Gaullist travellers" contributed to the already troubled relations between Canada and France.[31]

It would be remiss not to mention oil in relation to the Nigerian civil war. Would the Liberal government have acted differently if it had access to the rich oil reserves in the eastern region of Nigeria, which became Biafra for a time? Subsequent to the division of Nigeria into twelve states, which served to deprive the eastern region of the control of oil resources necessary to its development, the British and Soviet governments favouring the federal side, and the French government on the side of the Biafrans, were not unaware of the potential of access to the oil in Biafra. As Brewin and MacDonald noted in their report, the issue of oil and external influences made "a mockery of complaints of internal interference against those who operated mercy flights. It [made] nonsense of the statement that this was a purely African affair and the world community should not intervene, even for humanitarian reasons."[32] They weren't the only ones making such an observation. A former missionary, long-time Anglican Church layman, and editor of the *Canadian Churchman*, Hugh McCallum, noted as much in a letter to Brewin in December 1969: "It is no longer a black man's war, but with arms being supplied to both sides by white men and with oil playing such a major part in the conflict, the Canadian Government should, in my opinion, move immediately to try and bring about a cease fire so that both sides may get to the conference table."[33] Brewin and MacDonald insisted that Canada could play a central role in such a step principally because "Canada was not inhibited by any important material interests in Nigeria."[34]

The Nigerian conflict continued to reverberate in House of Commons debates and in the press throughout 1969. As noted earlier, in January 1969 Canadian churches and Oxfam organized relief flights to Biafra—Canairelief—and continued to press the government for both financial and diplomatic assistance in obtaining permission from both belligerents for direct relief flights into Biafra. Although Ivan Head went to Nigeria himself to seek such permission, both General Yakubu Gowon, head of the Federal Military Government, and his Biafran counterpart, General Odumegwu Ojukwu, provided obfuscated replies. But then a major breakthrough occurred, which Brewin described as a direct "result of successful pressure on the government by these interested groups and by the public."[35] Finally, on 9 January 1970, the Trudeau government allocated funds for relief, including $1 million for Canairelief. Three days later, however, the Biafran resistance collapsed, rendering useless the monies set aside for Canairelief. Brewin, MacDonald, and their colleagues among the NDP and Progressive Conservative parties nonetheless continued their campaign in the House of Commons. In the aftermath of the cessation of hostilities in Nigeria, Canairelief was unfortunately left holding the proverbial bag, in debt for the planes it had purchased and the salaries of its pilots.

Conclusions

As political scientist David P. Forsythe notes, as a general historical trend, more attention is now paid toward humanitarianism in world affairs.[36] But until the early 1970s, the UN system was not utilized to assist in the management of humanitarian disasters. The major relief players—the International Committee of the Red Cross and Joint Church Aid—were left to solve the problems, with the effect that the attempts to operate in a coordinated fashion stymied the efficient distribution of aid. After Biafra, the UN General Assembly created the UN Disaster Relief Office in 1971. While some have argued that the Biafran relief effort served only to prolong the war, contributing to the deaths of far more civilians than otherwise—"an act of unfortunate and profound folly," according to Ian Smillie, CUSO director, 1979–83[37]—Biafra continues to symbolize the legitimacy of the humanitarian impulse to protect persecuted people from starvation and genocide. Certainly Trudeau's brand of identity politics and federalism prevented a fairer and more sober examination of the Biafran crisis. Just as Biafrans were eager to see their place in a more inclusive federal framework, Quebeckers were asserting their own minority rights throughout the 1960s, but the issues of separation in the late 1960s were not comparable.

Biafra can also be seen as a turning point for many Canadian NGOs, whose focus increasingly shifted from service-oriented practices to ones that were more politicized. Humanitarian groups stopped emphasizing the conditions of the poor and disenfranchised in the Global South, examining instead the systemic global conditions that produced such widespread poverty. As a result of the apparent indifference of the Canadian state, many NGOs became more outspoken in their critiques of the policies of Western nations, which kept the nations of the Global South in unending states of dependency. Following the creation of CIDA in 1968, with its NGO program, Biafra provoked new and more activist Canadian responses to failed and fragile states.

Brewin and MacDonald's recommendations in *Canada and the Biafran Tragedy* were clearly forward-thinking, and certainly foreshadowed a trend of increasing popular internationalism in Canada. Indeed, the historical record indicates that what many Canadians argued for, including Brewin, MacDonald, and Johnson, was a preliminary form of R2P (responsibility to protect), a United Nations initiative established in 1995. While the ineffectiveness of the world community's response to the Rwandan genocide is frequently cited as the genesis of this principle, a close reading of the appeals to Trudeau and Sharp, and to other western governments, reveals remarkably similar ideologies. Successive governments could no longer avoid the shifting international circumstances brought about in a globalizing world. The Conservative government under Brian Mulroney would appreciate this, and throughout the 1980s forged closer relationships with Latin America and served as a world leader in the struggle against apartheid in South Africa. The Canadians who bore witness to the suffering in Biafra and Nigeria recognized this already in the late 1960s, yet Africa remains a challenge today. As the fundamentalist Islamic movement Boko Haram gnaws at the foundations of the Nigerian state, currently listed seventeenth of 178 nations on the Failed States Index, it appears that the tenacious demands for citizenship and self-determination posed more than forty years ago via the Nigerian Civil War will continue to shape the trajectory of Nigeria, and indeed, of Africa, more broadly.

Notes

1   Research assistance for this paper was provided by Emma Swiatek (Cereghini), Matthew Brown, Aileen Gnov, and Caitlin McCuaig, all exceptional History undergraduate students from King's University College. I am grateful for their help. I would also like to acknowledge the anonymous reviewers of this chapter whose comments were invaluable.

2   *Toronto Daily Star*, 21 February 1969.

3   Ike Okonta and Kate Meagher, "Introduction—Legacies of Biafra: Violence, Identity and Citizenship in Nigeria," *Africa Development* 34, no. 1 (2009): 4.

4   Transcript of Press Conference by Secretary-General Kofi Annan at United Nations Headquarters, 21 March 2005, United Nations Information Service—Vienna, http://www.unis.unvienna.org/unis/pressrels/2005/sgsm9772.html (accessed 15 October 2009).

5   Ivan Head and Trudeau (although mainly the former) provide their own self-important interpretations of their foreign policy decisions in *The Canadian Way: Shaping Canada's Foreign Policy, 1968–1984* (Toronto: McClelland and Stewart, 1995). In a broad work about Canadian foreign policy, Dale Thompson and Roger Swanson place the Nigerian civil war within the context of the Trudeau administration's position on the crisis. They stress the desire of the Canadian government to be recognized as a military observer rather than as a liberating force. They note within this context that the federal government did not wish Canada to be labelled as a country that interferes in the internal affairs of another country. In a 1975 book chapter Donald Barry places the Biafran crisis within the context of interest group politics in Canada; Barry's chapter is quite useful for its assessment of

the many interest groups formed in the wake of the crisis and for its judgment of the evolving rationale for in/action on the part of the federal Liberal government. As part of a larger study on Canada's foreign policy in Africa, John Schlegel's positive assessment of the Trudeau government is dismissive of the work of interest groups and the interest of opposition politicians in promoting a contrary discourse on the crisis. More general information may be found, variously, in the scholarly treatments of the life and career of Pierre Elliott Trudeau. Most recently in *Just Watch Me*, the second part of John English's biographical treatment of the life of Pierre Trudeau, the Nigerian conflict is given scant attention; to be fair, Trudeau gave it scant attention, so English's focus is understandable. See Andrew Brewin and David MacDonald, *Canada and the Biafran Tragedy* (Toronto: James Lorimer, 1970); Stephen Lewis, *Journey to Biafra* (Don Mills, ON: Thistle Printing, 1968); Ivan Head and Pierre Trudeau, *The Canadian Way: Shaping Canada's Foreign Policy, 1968–1984* (Toronto: McClelland and Stewart, 1995); Dale C. Thompson and Roger F. Swanson, *Canadian Foreign Policy: Options and Perspectives* (Toronto: McGraw-Hill Ryerson, 1971); Donald Barry, "Interest Groups and the Foreign Policy Process: The Case of Biafra," in *Pressure Group Behaviour in Canadian Politics*, ed. A. Paul Pross (Toronto: McGraw-Hill Ryerson, 1975); John P. Schlegel, *The Deceptive Ash: Bilingualism and Canadian Policy in Africa, 1957–1971* (Washington, D.C.: University Press of America, 1978), chs. 3–4 (I am grateful to Jean Daudelin for this reference).

6   Canada, House of Commons, *Debates*, 27th Parliament, 18 January 1966–23 April 1968.

7   James Eayrs, *Montreal Star*, 16 September 1968. By 1967 the Miles for Millions walks engaged thousands of schoolchildren across Canada, walking to aid Third World children. Walter McLean notes that it brought in money for Biafra. Interview, Rev. Walter McLean in discussion with the author, Waterloo, ON, January 5, 2012. Recent work by Tamara Myers covers the Miles for Millions walkathons but does not specifically mention Biafran relief: "Blistered and Bleeding, Tired and Determined: Visual Representations of Children and Youth in the Miles for Millions Walkathon," *Journal of the CHA* 22, no. 1 (2011): 245–75.

8   Trudeau and Head, *The Canadian Way*, 68–69.

9   English, *Just Watch Me*, 65.

10 Barry, "Interest Groups," 119.

11 Hugh McCallum, "Remembering the Nightmare of Biafra," *Presbyterian Record* (September 2004): 2; Brewin and MacDonald, *Canada and the Biafran Tragedy*, 12.

12 Robert Bothwell, *Alliance and Illusion: Canada and the World, 1945–1984* (Vancouver: UBC Press, 2007), 307.

13 House of Commons, *Debates*, 27 September 1968, 535.

14 Interview, Rev. Walter McLean in discussion with the author,

15 Waterloo, ON, 5 January 2012. When he was first elected to parliament as MP for Waterloo in 1979, McLean was the only member who had lived anywhere in the developing world.

15 English, *Just Watch Me*, 66 [emphasis in original].

16 Peter C. Newman, *Here Be Dragons: Telling Tales of People, Passion, and Power* (Toronto: McClelland and Stewart, 2004): 341–42. At a 9 September 1967 press conference, de Gaulle revealed "happily" that the world had experienced the dissolution of a number of federations, including all former British colonies: Canada, Rhodesia, Malaysia (Singapore's secession), Cyprus, and civil war–ravaged Nigeria. J. L. Granatstein and Robert Bothwell, *Pirouette: Pierre Trudeau and Canadian Foreign Policy* (Toronto: University of Toronto Press, 1991), 133–34.

17 "Trudeau defends stand against outside interference in Nigerian civil war," *Globe and Mail*, 23 October 1968.

18 Charles Taylor's reports appeared in the *Globe and Mail* on the following days: 5, 7, 9–12, 14 October 1968. Stephen Lewis's reports appeared in the *Toronto Daily Star* on 9–12, 14 October 1968. Following Brewin and MacDonald's visit, NDP MP Lorne Nystrom and Liberal MP Ralph Stewart traveled to Nigeria for two weeks to observe the situation on both the Biafran and the federal sides of the conflict. Interview, Lorne Nystrom in discussion with the author, 25 June 2012.

19 Brewin and MacDonald, *Canada and the Biafran Tragedy*, ch. 1; Lewis, *Journey to Biafra*, 14.

20 House of Commons, *Debates*, 7 October 1968, 842.

21 Barry, "Interest Groups," 138.

22 House of Commons, *Minutes of Proceedings and Evidence*, Standing Committee on External Affairs and National Defence, 10 October 1968, 144.

23 This line was indicated independently to me by both Rev. McLean and Rev. David MacDonald. Interview, Rev. Walter McLean in discussion with the author, 5 January 2012; Interview, Rev. David MacDonald in discussion with the author, 4 August 2011.

24 Brewin and MacDonald, *Canada and the Biafran Tragedy*, 135.

25 Lewis, *Journey to Biafra*, 35–36; Brewin and MacDonald, *Canada and the Biafran Tragedy*, 118–20.

26 Library and Archives Canada [hereafter LAC], Brewin Papers, MG 32 C 26, vol. 74, file 15: "Letter, Rt. Hon. Michael Barnes to Brewin, 18 Nov. 1968."

27 LAC, Brewin Papers, vol. 75, file 4 "Biafra—Correspondence with Senator Edward M. Kennedy, 1968–71"; Interview, Rev. David MacDonald in discussion with the author.

28 Brewin and MacDonald, *Canada and the Biafran Tragedy*, 7.

29 "A breach of protocol," *Regina Leader-Post*, 5 October 1968.

30 Ibid.

31 Granatstein and Bothwell, *Pirouette*, 132–34.

32 Brewin and MacDonald, *Canada and the Biafran Tragedy*, 6. For more on contemporary accusations of oil influence, see Robert Fitch and Mary Oppenheimer, "Biafra: Let Them Eat Oil," *Ramparts* (7 September 1967): 34ff., as quoted in Appendix A of *Canada and the Biafran Tragedy*.

33 LAC, Brewin Papers, MG 32 C 26, vol. 75 file 3: "Letter, Hugh McCallum to Brewin, 22 December 1969."

34 Brewin and MacDonald, *Canada and the Biafran Tragedy*, 138–39.

35 LAC, Brewin Papers, MG 32 C 26, vol. 75, file 3: "Letter, Brewin to Donald Barry, 9 June 1971."

36 David Forsythe, "International Humanitarianism in the Contemporary World: Forms and Issues," in *Multilateralism Under Challenge: Power, International Order and Structural Change*, ed. Edward Neuman, Ramesh Thakur, and John Tirman (Washington: Brookings Institution Press, 2006), 237–38.

37 Ian Smillie, quoted in Alex de Waal, *Famine Crimes: Politics and the Disaster Relief Industry in Africa* (Bloomington: Indiana University Press, 1997): 77.

CHAPTER 4

FAILING FRAGILE STATES:
Canada and East Timor

David Webster[1]

Canada's approach to failed and fragile states has been linked to the wave of decolonization that swept Asia and Africa in the second half of the twentieth century, and its often chaotic aftermath. One decolonization that made small but still noticeable ripples in Ottawa was the Democratic Republic of Timor-Leste, normally referred to as East Timor. This small half-island state joined its fellow Portuguese colonies Angola, Mozambique, and Guinea-Bissau in starting on the path to independence in 1974. After an internal conflict, it declared independence on 28 November 1975. Yet, just over a week later, on 7 December, Indonesian troops launched a full-scale invasion. The subsequent twenty-four years of military occupation cost some 200,000 lives out of a population of 680,000 people, a bloody toll that, along with the Khmer Rouge genocide in Cambodia, knows few parallels in modern Southeast Asian history. In 1999, finally, a United Nations (UN) referendum saw the Timorese vote overwhelmingly for independence. Under an interim UN administration, the Democratic Republic of Timor-Leste regained its independence in 2002, using the same name and flying the same flag as the short-lived state of 1975. Amidst some post-independence troubles, it celebrated the tenth anniversary of regaining independence in 2012, a year also marked by its third free election and a peaceful transition of power. The government changed again peacefully in 2015, when the prime minister stepped down in favour of a leading member of the major opposition party.

In 1975, East Timor was called an impossible state, too small and poor to do anything but fail. Similar rhetoric preceded East Timor's passage to independence in 1999, and continues into the twenty-first century. Constructivist political scientists have pointed out that rhetoric matters: the languages used to describe overseas conflicts often shape how Western publics view faraway lands and underpin government policy decisions about them. The argument of this chapter is that this rhetoric of state failure is derived from outside, not based on any reality on the ground. More importantly, the rhetoric of "failure" has helped to construct the very thing it warns against. If a state like East Timor is a "failed" state, the "failure" comes from outside.

It is worth taking into account some of what has been written to challenge the prevailing notion of "failed states." With regard to Haiti, *Globe and Mail* columnist Rick Salutin has suggested "that 'failed' could also be used the way 'disappeared' is now used in Latin America: as an *active* verb. Countries can 'fail' other countries, the way the police or army 'disappear' protesters." This does not suggest a simple failure to act; it means that at times the "international community"—meaning, usually, Western governments—works actively to *ensure* failure through intervention, economic pressure, or other means.[2] The constructed image of a state as "failed" can then be used to justify intervention, as it has been in Afghanistan.[3]

It matters what rhetoric is used to frame debates on East Timor, and on the idea of "failed states" more generally, because the rhetoric itself is one of the most powerful factors in deciding which states are "failed," "fragile," "in danger," and so on. There is little reason to throw good money after bad in aid to a state that has been damned by the designation "failed." If a state is dubbed "fragile," then donors might prefer to send their aid through non-governmental organizations, even if this risks undermining the legitimacy and capacity of the local state as provider of social security. Although "paved with good intentions,"[4] this road may lead to unintended consequences that actually harm the prospects of states struggling to develop their capacity. Canada's problematic role in Haiti serves as example here. How a government is labelled matters, and helps shape the policies of Canada and other governments. This is especially problematic when labels

Figure 1: José Ramos-Horta at a solidarity movement gathering in New York City in the 1980s, prior to a meeting of the UN Decolonization Committee. Ramos-Horta was the leading Timorese diplomat and eventually won the Nobel Peace Prize in 1996 for his work with activist groups around the world to advance the cause of Timorese self-determination. (Credit: Elaine Brière)

like "failed" and "fragile" mislead, as they have done and continue to do in the case of East Timor.

In 1996, the Nobel Peace Prize went to two Timorese leaders: Bishop Carlos Ximenes Belo and José Ramos-Horta. The Nobel Prize was understood, both by the award committee and the Timorese activists, as a step against silencing and forgetting. But the prize came up against two long-standing narratives. One, which this paper will return to, was "civil war" rhetoric, the claim that without Indonesian military rule, the Timorese would immediately start fighting one another. The second was "lost cause" rhetoric, which claimed that Timorese independence was completely hopeless, and that therefore the cause should be given up. Taken to its logical, albeit misguided, conclusion, "lost cause" rhetoric argued that it was, in fact, *immoral* for outsiders to support Timorese independence, because it only preserved false hopes.

One example of "lost cause" rhetoric came from journalist Marcus Gee of the *Globe and Mail*, Canada's national newspaper. The point is not to single out and criticize Gee; indeed, it should be noted that he was in fact a supporter of human rights, rather than an apologist for the Indonesian military regime. Nonetheless, in an article entitled "Nobel prize is no help to East Timor," Gee wrote that Bishop Belo and Ramos-Horta were "by all accounts brave and honourable men. But they are linked to a lost cause: the independence of East Timor." Independence was impossible for this "small place in a little-known part of the world, with no allies and an implacable opponent."[5] When the Indonesian dictator Suharto fell from power in 1998, a window seemed to open for change on East Timor—Suharto had been among the major obstacles to an Indonesian policy shift on its troublesome colony. "But experts say the separatists are fooling themselves if they expect the new government in Jakarta to set the former Portuguese colony free in the near future," Gee wrote.[6]

"Experts" in this context referred to one Australian scholar, but there were many observers in academia, the commentariat, and government who agreed. This expertise was wrong—as some voices, especially from Australian non-governmental circles, pointed out at the time regarding the academic "Jakarta lobby."[7] "Expertise" was far from objective. Throughout the period of Indonesian rule over East Timor, researchers seeking to develop expertise on or portray Indonesia worked under constraints. They required research visas to visit Indonesia and do their work. Such visas lay in the gift of the Indonesian Academy of Sciences, which worked at arm's length from the government but was hardly independent. In conflict areas, including East Timor, researchers required special travel permits (*surat jalan*) granted by Indonesian state or military agents. Academics who became too critical of Indonesia risked being blacklisted (*dicekal*) along with human rights activists. The same people cited as "experts," in other words, were also dependent for their continued expertise claims partly on the Indonesian government. It is little wonder that they pulled their punches or offered compliant quotations to journalists seeking expert quotes to bolster their stories. The expert quoted by Marcus Gee, for instance, was part of an "Indonesia lobby" of Australian academics.

More directly, the received wisdom of experts became a factor justifying Western policies of inaction, or even complicity, in Indonesian military rule over East Timor, which these same experts generally agreed was poorly treated, with little respect for human rights. It continued to exert a firm hold over much commentary even in the days leading up to the 1999 referendum, when hope for independence seemed real at last. Marcus Gee repeatedly preached the hopelessness of Timorese aspirations. Independence, he wrote two years later, would be "a leap in the dark. The independent nation of East Timor would be a flyspeck on the world map." Unable to stand on its own, "East Timor would have to throw itself on the mercy of the international community."[8]

This "lost cause" rhetoric was more than just a way of writing and talking about East Timor. It was also a factor in shaping policy. Indonesian rule over East Timor was never inevitable. Knowing this is not a matter of mere hindsight. East Timorese independence from Portugal was not only plausible in 1975 but in fact became a reality, albeit briefly. Indonesian rule quickly became well entrenched, but only as a result of the active diplomatic, economic, and military support lent to the Suharto regime by its patrons in the West. Policymakers from Ottawa to Tokyo to Canberra chose to portray Timorese independence as "hopeless," and therefore proclaimed that it was folly to support it. Maybe. But *if* the cause was hopeless, that was largely because Indonesian rule was so deeply entrenched, thanks to overseas support for its government. The logic was circular. Once policymakers and press pundits adopted the "lost cause" thesis, they shaped their actions accordingly. Policy did not begin to shift until the Timorese demonstrated convincingly that their cause was far from lost. An assumption that the case for independence was hopeless encouraged rhetorical assertions that defined the limits of the possible—limits that were then reified and used to excuse lacklustre policy decisions. All too often, many Western policymakers said, in essence: "It won't work, so we shouldn't try." The documents make it fairly clear that the concept of failure reinforced existing inclinations to side with pro-Western Indonesia against a Third World nationalist struggle. There was in this process little space for Timorese voices, which tended to be ignored even when heard.

Even before East Timor declared independence in 1975, Canadian diplomats were working in quiet opposition. Their main concern was Indonesia, a pro-Western outpost in a region where communism was on the rise, strategically located, and a potentially lucrative trade partner, made all the more important because it was home to the world's largest Muslim population. The Trudeau government highlighted Suharto's Indonesia as "a nascent power among the non-Communist nations because of its position and population, and the development potential of its natural resources."[9] When Ottawa contemplated specific bilateral partners in Asia, it identified Japan, South Korea, Australia, and the five countries of the Association of Southeast Asian Nations (ASEAN)—a neutral but implicitly pro-Western group in Southeast Asia. As Prime Minister Pierre Trudeau acknowledged, the decision meant devoting special attention to Indonesia, ASEAN's largest member by far. Canadian aid to Indonesia from 1950 to 1965 had accounted for less than one percent of total Canadian bilateral aid to Asia, but in 1970 the first Canadian International Development Agency (CIDA) review of priorities picked Indonesia as the only "country of concentration" outside the Commonwealth and former French empire.[10] Aid was designed to help transform Indonesia from "aid recipient to trading partner."[11] Canada and Indonesia, meanwhile, worked well together on the International Commission of Control and Supervision in Vietnam in 1973, and enjoyed harmonious relations on North-South issues in general.

Along with development aid, Canadian investment in Indonesia began to rise. Toronto-based Inco's nickel mine in Sulawesi became the second-largest source of foreign investment in Indonesia, placing Canada fourth among foreign investors. At the Inco mine site, Foreign Investment Board chairman Mohammad Sadli, with his eyes "round as saucers," told Canada's ambassador W. T. Delworth that "Indonesia has never seen so much money."[12] Between entering Indonesia in 1968 and the end of the century, Inco invested US $2,074 million in the mine and associated operations.[13] When Suharto made his first official visit to Ottawa in 1975, the Canadian government teamed up with the major chartered banks to offer an innovative $200 million line of credit as "the centrepiece of the visit." Trade quickly soared from $30 million to $300 million a year.[14]

Yet Indonesia's economy was soon teetering over a debt crisis brought about by over-borrowing by the state oil company, Pertamina. Consequently, the Toronto Dominion Bank cancelled its line of credit to Indonesia soon after agreeing to be part of the $200 million Canadian loan package. The Canadian government, however, maintained its faith in Suharto and also the government-backed credit that his government could draw upon.[15] The TD Bank's analysts had decided that Indonesia was not a good credit risk. Despite that, Ottawa decided for political reasons to maintain support. There could be few examples that fit today's definition of "fragile state" better than the Suharto regime, challenged by soaring dissent, without democratic avenues to channel protests, dependent on an oil boom, and at risk of defaulting on its foreign debt. The Indonesian debt crisis, brought on by Pertamina's reckless moves, placed the regime in real danger, just a decade after massacres in Indonesia saw the army topple the country's first president, an event that had entailed casualties of up to one million people. Was this a stable state? The case was at least debatable. Yet state fragility was in the eye of the beholder. Indonesia, as an important Cold War ally and potential trade partner, could not be considered as fragile—whatever the rational calculations of economists said. Policymakers in Ottawa maintained their idealistic faith in Jakarta, and helped provide the tools that allowed the Suharto regime to survive.

By the time the decolonization of Portuguese Timor appeared on the Western political agenda in 1975, Western policymakers were inclined to accept Indonesian strategic concerns. Canadian observers hoped that the Timorese could be persuaded to accept the Indonesian declaration of Timorese "integration" into Indonesia. Covert Indonesian efforts to annex East Timor were acceptable, so long as the *appearance* of self-determination was respected. If that meant an invasion, Canada would maintain "some sympathy for Indonesia's dilemma."[16] Canadian diplomats accepted at face value Indonesian arguments that an independent East Timor would not be a viable state—in other words, that it could only "fail" if allowed to be independent. The inevitability of failure was especially prominent in Australian government documents. One worried about "a poor, uneducated, probably unstable, independent East Timor on our doorstep."[17] Canadian officials often looked to Australia for the lead on how to act with regard to East Timor, so Australian views mattered. So, too, did those of neighbouring New Zealand, from which Canadian diplomats obtained much of their information about developments in East Timor in the early years. New Zealand ambassador to Indonesia Roger Peren visited in 1978 and reported that the Indonesian annexation was "plainly irreversible." The "irreversible" doctrine became official New Zealand policy from 1978 to 1995, influencing Canada's embrace of the same belief.[18]

Even while putting forward this case of inevitable failure due to East Timor's too-small size and low level of economic development, Indonesian diplomats argued that East Timor might be not only viable, but viable enough to pose a threat to regional peace and security. It could become, in the words of one Indonesian source, "another Cuba," threatening Indonesia from close by in the same way that the US government argued that Communist Cuba under Fidel Castro's leadership threatened the United States.[19] East Timor was allegedly especially threatening in 1975, when South Vietnam's pro-American regime was toppled by Communist-led Vietnamese nationalists and Communist governments came to power in Cambodia and Laos, Vietnam's Southeast Asian neighbours. Australian Prime Minister Gough Whitlam was among those who accepted Indonesian arguments, saying an independent East Timor would be "an unviable state and a potential threat to the area."[20]

Added to both those arguments—lack of viability leading to failure, and alleged viability as a threat—was the argument that Timorese peoples were so divided that only outside rule would prevent a civil war among them. It was an argument much like the one offered by Dutch colonial rulers in the early twentieth century against Indonesian independence, now echoed by the rulers of independent Indonesia.[21] East Timor was too small to be viable, Suharto told his hosts on a mid-1975 visit to Ottawa. Canadian officials looked to Australian counterparts for guidance and learned that they would acquiesce in an Indonesian takeover.[22] This coincided with Canada's own active interest in the region; as one briefing paper noted, "stability in the Southeast Asian region is of significance for Canada."[23] In other words, the invasion was not a "surprise," as recalled by Derek Burney, who directed the Pacific Affairs Bureau in External Affairs.[24] Canadian officials, like their Australian and American counterparts, knew it was coming and chose not to deter it when speaking to Indonesian counterparts.

Shortly after Indonesian troops launched a full-scale invasion of East Timor on 7 December 1975, the United Nations General Assembly issued the first of several resolutions calling for Timorese self-determination. Canada's delegation, ordered by Ottawa not to support any criticism of Indonesia, abstained in company with most of its Western allies. The following year, External Affairs Minister Allan MacEachen promised to be guided by ASEAN views.[25] Accordingly, Canada continued to abstain until 1980, and then began voting with Indonesia against Timorese self-determination. Canadian aid to Indonesia the year after the invasion reached a record level of $37 million, third among Canadian aid recipients.

Canada's UN vote was guided by the "lost cause" claim. Officials at the Department of External Affairs argued against "taking up every lost cause in the world" and against UN resolutions that preserved "false hopes and a false issue."[26] A major part of the reason why no progress on East Timor appeared possible was that the Western alliance was collectively lending support to the Indonesian occupation; in other words, it was a self-fulfilling prophecy. From 1980 onward, Canada's UN mission sided with Indonesia, voting against resolutions affirming East Timor's right to self-determination. Human rights advocacy was not absent, but it was deflected toward less controversial causes. Canadian officials, like those in the Carter administration in the United States, concentrated their human rights talk on the release of political prisoners, an issue that did not directly challenge the legitimacy of the regime.[27] Advocating prisoner releases allowed a focus on the "abuses" of an authoritarian regime; support for human rights in East Timor would have required a more fundamental critique of the basis of Indonesia's military-dominated government and wrecked Canadian hopes for increased trade in an emerging Asian market. Visiting Jakarta in 1983, Prime Minister Trudeau admitted that the East Timor issue "raised the problem of self-determination of peoples," but insisted that his government had "decided that stability of the region should be the foremost concern and thus had supported Indon[esia]."[28] There was no question, for the Trudeau government, that the need for "stability" outweighed any temptation to advocate for human rights.

In 1983, the Australian newspaper *The Age* reported that Indonesian forces had used incendiary devices in bombing runs over East Timor. Australian officials denied the story. Yet Timorese leaders and human rights groups continued to insist that the Indonesian armed forces had used bombs in this way, and had even used napalm—specifically, a version known as "opalm" purchased from the Soviet Union. In a rare display of unwitting superpower cooperation, they dropped the Soviet opalm from American-supplied aircraft. To this day, the Indonesian government denies the use of napalm. Recently declassified Australian documents, however, confirm the use of napalm and the Australian government's knowledge.[29] Canadian documents add to the evidence, confirming the use of opalm and demonstrating that the Department of External Affairs was aware of this atrocity. Canada's embassy in Jakarta confirmed "that bombing runs with napalm and cluster bombs began on September 23."[30] The high commission in Canberra confirmed with Australian counterparts that the chemical dropped was opalm, "a more virulent form of napalm."[31] Canadian diplomats chose not to act on the information and withheld it from members of the Canadian Parliament in a subsequent briefing note on East Timor. Instead, the note blamed internal Timorese divisions for provoking an Indonesian intervention and argued against any Canadian support for Timorese self-determination at the UN on the grounds that Indonesian rule was "unchangeable."[32]

Timorese independence activists raised insistent cries that the cause was not, after all, completely hopeless. They could change the dynamic, they insisted, if the international community ceased backing Indonesia. The key and vital achievement of Timorese diplomats and the international solidarity networks formed to support them was to disrupt the "lost cause" thesis. It is useful to consider this process using the model of transnational advocacy networks, which emerge and gel through the use of "common languages." As Margaret Keck and Kathryn Sikkink argue, when campaigners in one country are blocked by their own government, they can often succeed by making common cause with civil society allies overseas. A "boomerang" effect sees these overseas groups place pressure on their own governments and on international organizations, which in turn can pressure the home government.[33]

The "boomerang" effect certainly operated in East Timor. Over time, Timorese and foreign supporters evolved common languages centred on human rights. They were able to disrupt Indonesia's overseas support, leading to increasing international pressure. During the 1990s, East Timor emerged as a world issue, tied up with global debates over the meaning and extent of human rights. Indonesia's government, in common with Malaysia, China, Singapore, and other authoritarian regimes, asserted an "Asian values" thesis that saw human rights as Western-derived, arguing for less emphasis on individual rights and more acceptance of undemocratic governments. Asian human rights groups rejected the thesis, joining battle on rhetorical terrain about the meaning and applicability of human rights. Timorese diplomats were prominent among these non-state networks, advancing a language of universal human rights to bolster their claim to the right to self-determination.[34]

In Canada, East Timor initially received little attention—there were none of the missionary links, diasporas, or hopes for trade that shaped

Canadian relations with other Asian countries. This began to change, however, with the launch of Amnesty International's 1985 global campaign for human rights in East Timor. Timorese non-state diplomats increasingly stressed the language of human rights, partly under the influence of the Timorese Catholic Church. In the 1980s, Canadian churches funded the creation of two organizations centred on raising public awareness of East Timor: the Indonesia East Timor Programme in Ontario, and the East Timor Alert Network (ETAN) in British Columbia. There was also an active Nova Scotia East Timor Group, which in the late 1980s merged into a single national ETAN group. ETAN would in time become a national network, supported by core funding from the Catholic, Anglican, United, and Presbyterian churches. The Canadian Catholic Organization for Development and Peace (CCODP) joined with others in the church-sponsored Asia Partnership for Human Development to call for international pressure for human rights in East Timor. Canadian Catholic bishops' calls for a more human-centred development in northern Canada aligned well with critiques of Indonesian state-led "development" (*pembangunan*) from Bishop Carlos Ximenes Belo and others in East Timor.

ETAN was increasingly effective in raising awareness, especially with the arrival in Canada of Timorese students-turned-refugees. Abé Barreto Soares and Bella Galhos subsequently became important representatives for the Timorese diplomatic network. After lobbying from Canadian activists and exiled Timorese bishop Martinho da Costa Lopes, Canadian Catholic bishops became more willing to speak out in support of East Timor, asking the Canadian government to promote peace talks and ban arms sales to Indonesia. ETAN was also able to gain the backing of the Canadian labour movement, especially for its arms embargo campaign. All of this made it increasingly difficult for Canadian government representatives to carry on business as usual with their Indonesian counterparts. "We continue to seem to be prepared to have our NGO community dictate our actions," Canada's ambassador Lawrence Dickinson complained in the mid-1990s, adding that there were no concessions made to lobbyists on Vietnam and other countries.[35] Indonesian foreign minister Ali Alatas similarly claimed that "Canadian NGOs are the most ferociously anti-Indonesian in the world."[36] Transnational activist networks became a powerful weapon for the Timorese resistance forces.

But Indonesia still had much to offer those other, less romantic non-state actors: transnational corporations. The 1990s saw the peak of admiration for Asian "miracle economies" grouped in a menagerie of tigers, dragons, and flying geese. Indonesia was more valuable than ever. Canadian and American governments enthusiastically backed the Suharto regime in Indonesia as a "little tiger" in economics, a reliable voice in international politics, and a stabilizing factor in chaotic Southeast Asia. True, it was no respecter of human rights, but the fashionable thinking of the day was that "soft authoritarian" governments were delivering an "economic miracle" in eastern Asia and that growth would eventually bring about democratization.[37] External Affairs acknowledged that severe human rights abuses had occurred between 1975 and 1980 but argued that the situation was improving rapidly. "Like most other nations," wrote Conservative Foreign Minister Joe Clark, "Canada believes that the situation has become irreversible." Given that belief, the goal was to build "an environment conducive to the awareness and promotion of human rights."[38] Once more, the rhetoric of hopelessness was deployed to justify a policy of complicity on East Timor.

The end of the Cold War removed the strategic reasons to back Indonesia, right or wrong. Hoping to position Canada as a leading voice for global human rights, Conservative Prime Minister Brian Mulroney made passionate declarations at the 1991 summit meetings of the Commonwealth and La Francophonie that Canada would "no longer subsidize repression and the stifling of democracy."[39] Less than a month after Mulroney uttered those words in Zimbabwe, East Timor provided the first test case. Indonesian soldiers opened fire on a pro-independence march in Dili, East Timor's capital, on 12 November 1991, with film footage of the killings broadcast around the world. The massacre received extensive coverage on the Canadian Broadcasting Corporation's nightly television newsmagazine *The Journal*. Reaction to the killing produced a global upsurge in activism and reinforced the solidarity movement, with a host of new ETAN groups forming in Canada. The Canadian ambassador in Jakarta, Ingrid Hall, was ordered to inform her hosts of the rising public concern.[40]

The Mulroney government also froze three major aid projects worth a collective $30 million. Foreign minister Barbara McDougall added an unofficial ban on any arms export permits.[41] Nevertheless, existing aid and export promotion efforts continued unhampered. The Mulroney government's response was intended to express disapproval through a careful targeting of sanctions in such a way that core trade and investment ties would not be harmed. Indonesia remained a Canadian trade priority, with two-way trade up reaching $563 million in 1992, a 47 percent increase on the previous year.[42] Indonesian officials exempted Ottawa from the angry reprisals that it directed at the Netherlands when the Dutch government linked aid to human rights. In Canada, though, rumours that frozen aid would be restored were never fulfilled, apparently for fear of public reaction.[43] The aid freeze remained in place until the fall of the Conservative government in 1993.

Concerned with high unemployment at home and a big government deficit, Jean Chrétien's Liberal government redoubled the emphasis on trade with Indonesia, hailing it as one of the Asian "miracle" economies. It permitted the resumption of new aid to Indonesia and began to authorize arms sales once again, part of a larger strategy to kick-start the Canadian economy by boosting exports. By 1994, Canadian investment in Indonesia stood at $3 billion and rising; more than fifty companies reported exports to Indonesia in excess of $50 million. "Indonesia offers the best fit for Canadian economic interests I have seen," Canada's ambassador Lawrence Dickinson declared.[44]

Ottawa's aid arm, CIDA, meanwhile funded two CCODP projects strengthening the Dili diocese's ability to reach and involve more lay people: a radio station and a peace and justice commission. Ottawa was looking for ways to involve Canada in East Timor without raising thorny human rights issues that could affect trade prospects. Visiting Jakarta that year for the Asia Pacific Economic Cooperation (APEC) summit, Chrétien argued that increased trade would give Canada more leverage to promote human rights. As in the 1970s, rights advocacy tended to be diverted into safe channels. Chrétien's foreign ministers, André Ouellet and Lloyd Axworthy, refused to ban arms sales to Indonesia or to take a lead on the East Timor file. Axworthy, an exponent of "human security" and niche diplomacy, diverted rights advocacy into a closed-door "bilateral human rights dialogue," and pointed to that as evidence of Canadian quiet diplomacy for human rights. This gave him an answer to critics who argued that human security doctrine required stronger action on East Timor: Canada

Figure 2: A protester is arrested at the 1997 Asia Pacific Economic Cooperation (APEC) summit at the University of British Columbia in Vancouver. Protesters were attempting to perform a "citizen's arrest" of Indonesian President Suharto, a campaign organized by the East Timor Alert Network of Canada. (Credit: Elaine Brière)

was active on that front using the "niche" opportunity of a bilateral dialogue on human rights.[45]

Canadian rights groups hotly contested government assertions that trade advanced rights. The clash of views was best symbolized by the 1997 APEC summit, held at the University of British Columbia in Vancouver. When ETAN posted pictures of Suharto captioned "Wanted: For Crimes Against Humanity," enraged Indonesian officials made the group an issue in bilateral relations. Suharto threatened to boycott the APEC summit, a vital symbol of the Chrétien government's Asia trade strategy. Axworthy pleaded with Indonesian Foreign Minister Alatas, saying "we did not want ETAN to win a victory and they would claim victory if [the] President did not come."[46] Once again the government claim, grounded in the rhetoric of "hopelessness," clashed with NGO demands for a positive policy of support for Timorese self-determination. Under heavy pressure from

Jakarta, Canadian authorities agreed to ensure that Suharto would not be confronted by protesters. Keeping this promise required the use of pepper spray to clear away protestors and to allow the APEC motorcade to pass through campus undisturbed by signs of dissent.[47] No longer was Canada the wealthy donor and Indonesia the supplicant. Instead, Canadian wheat exporters looked to companies controlled by Suharto's business cronies as leading customers, and Canada was prepared to ignore human rights and its own traditions of political protest as a cost of doing business.

That changed when a financial crisis swept through Asia in 1998, toppling Suharto from the Indonesian presidency he had occupied since the mid-1960s. When the new president, B. J. Habibie, agreed to let Timorese voters choose autonomy or independence, Timorese leader Xanana Gusmão wrote to Lloyd Axworthy to argue that Canada, as a new Security Council member, was "in a unique position to play a lead role during the upcoming transition in East Timor, which I believe is _inevitable_ [emphasis added]."[48] Inevitability, it seemed, had changed sides. Even if officials in Ottawa did not necessarily agree with Xanana that Timorese independence was inevitable, neither did they cling any longer to their earlier belief that it was impossible. Once Axworthy and his officials freed themselves of the "lost cause" thesis, they became able to make valuable, creative contributions. But it took the debunking of the rhetoric of hopelessness to open the window to any action.

With the "lost cause" rhetoric disrupted, there was one other challenger: civil war rhetoric—in other words, the rhetoric of a "failed state," or a state certain to fail. Indonesian government publications and officials argued that there had been a civil war in East Timor in 1975, stopped only by Indonesian intervention. True, there had been a civil war, but it lasted for only a few weeks before order was restored and the pattern since then had been of increasing unity among Timorese groups. Suharto's roving ambassador on East Timor, Francisco Lopes da Cruz, travelled the world with one message: if Indonesian troops left, there was certain to be another civil war.

Without denying the existence of internal divisions within East Timor, it should be pointed out that civil war rhetoric was essentially an Indonesian state strategy to prevent East Timor's independence by arguing that an independent East Timor would instantly "fail" in the absence of the stabilizing Indonesian armed forces. This is an argument that has been used by many colonial rulers—not least, the former Dutch colonial rulers of Indonesia, who had once argued that Indonesia's great diversity meant that it would dissolve into chaos without the stabilizing Dutch presence. This civil war rhetoric, like the rhetoric of the "lost cause," was debunked as Timorese parties gradually came together in a series of resistance coalitions and demonstrations of Timorese unity, aimed almost exclusively at swaying the opinions of international observers.

Portuguese-Indonesian negotiations at the UN produced an agreement for a referendum on Timorese autonomy within Indonesia or independence early in 1999. Indonesian officials had predicted an internal conflict among the Timorese. When this failed to materialize, figures in the Indonesian military set about creating one by encouraging, funding, and arming pro-Indonesia militia groups and giving them a licence to terrorize pro-independence Timorese.[49] Despite these efforts, over 98 percent of Timorese voters turned out for the referendum on 30 August 1999, and 78.5 percent chose the independence option. The Indonesian military response was to unleash a wave of violence by the militias, which put East Timor on front pages and top-of-evening newscasts around the world. No longer convinced that self-determination was hopeless, Canadian diplomats worked hard to pressure Indonesia to invite an international peacekeeping force. That pressure, added to similar pressure from other governments and international organizations, forced President Habibie to surrender and invite peacekeepers in; the UN then supervised a transition period leading to Timorese independence in 2002. The cause so long portrayed as hopeless had succeeded after all.

There was nothing uniquely Canadian about supporting Indonesian military rule in East Timor: it was also the policy of the United States, Australia, Japan, Britain, France, Germany, and other allies. But the rhetorical justifications offered by Canadian policymakers may have leaned more on the rhetoric of hopelessness; where American officials could couch their policy in realpolitik, Canadian officials perhaps needed to claim they *wanted* to do the right thing—but it was impossible.

Self-defensive rhetoric could become self-congratulatory, too. Again, Marcus Gee's commentaries in the *Globe and Mail* serve as examples. As Indonesian troops finally departed in 1999, Gee offered a contribution to a new, emerging narrative: that "we" in the West, who "tend to romanticize those who struggle for national liberation," were "the midwives of East

Timorese independence" who had "rushed in to restore order, the sword of righteousness in our hands." The disconnect from the *very* recent past was startling. "We intervened in defence of human rights," he wrote.[50] Perhaps. But if so, it was only after more than two decades of quieter intervention on the other side. The new narrative construct tells of a twenty-four-year-long "fit of absence of mind," followed by a righteous rescue mission, and it plays a part in denying calls for an international tribunal on mass atrocities in East Timor, for any duty to make amends or reparations, for any acknowledgement of past actions. Instead, Western governments are shrouded in the glory of a brief moment in 1999, and all previous complicity is consigned to the realm of forgetting.

This is very bad history, and it teaches some unfortunate lessons. We now have a new false assumption, that East Timor is one of the fragile states that threaten global stability. The language of the "failed state" is bandied about, creating once again a sense of hopelessness. To read the occasional media mention of East Timor, it would be easy to get a picture of a nation in crisis, an Asian Somalia with few prospects. This is often tied to a political crisis, including a mutiny by demobilized soldiers in 2006, but the language of "failed state" began earlier: it is not simply the result of the 2006 crisis. It started even before the restoration of independence. Richard Woolcott, who as Australian ambassador to Indonesia in 1975 played an important role in shaping Australian acquiescence in the invasion of East Timor, greeted the arrival of Australian peacekeepers in 1999 with dismay, saying he feared "an obligation to support with substantial aid a broken back, mini-state within the Indonesian archipelago."[51] More on the same lines followed in the first years of independence.[52] The 2013 Failed States Index ranks independent Timor-Leste as "in danger," at number thirty-two. Using new categories, it gets an "alert" status and ranks thirty-first in the rebranded 2014 Fragile States Index.[53] This grouping is part of a zone of instability that includes almost the entire—and undifferentiated—developing world. Even in rebranding away from the term "failed states" to "fragile states," the index makers maintain the implication that some states—all in the Global South—are "fragile," while others are not, an implication easily avoided by using the more neutral term, State Stability Index.[54] The country has risen as high as eighteenth on the Failed States Index (in 2010, a year of improvements in the eyes of most observers).[55]

Yet Timor-Leste is a country with a vibrant and non-violent party system, with higher voting rates than Canada. It has ratified more human rights covenants than either the United States or Canada, and its lively, engaged civil society is better able to influence public debates than its Canadian counterpart. It has seen two peaceful handovers of power from one prime minister to another, with no violent changes of power at all. Without romanticizing prospects or minimizing setbacks, this is a country that can point to substantial accomplishments in a decade of independence, and whose non-governmental organizations are effectively holding the government to account. It is no simple "failed state" today.

In spite of this, Canadian governments, for more than twenty years, were captives of the "lost cause" argument. Since Timorese self-determination was impossible, they did not advocate it until 1998, by which time Timorese advocacy had shown that self-determination was in fact entirely possible. Canada was not silent because no one in Ottawa *cared* about human rights. Rather, the "lost cause" thesis made strong rights advocacy appear pointless, even counter-productive. It had the power to convince officials that the most humane approach was to convince the Timorese to abandon their independence campaigns and acquiesce to Indonesian rule in exchange for a lighter ruling hand. Timorese activists never accepted this defeatist rhetoric and, together with their supporters in transnational advocacy networks, proved able to debunk the argument. By forming themselves into a single independence coalition, they were also able to undermine the "civil war" narrative. Once freed from these false constructs, the Canadian government was able to frame constructive policies for goal-oriented rights promotion for a short time around 1999. False constructs, however, once again dominate the Canadian government's outlook on East Timor. The insidious idea of East Timor as a state on the road to "failure" feeds a sense of hopelessness and becomes another self-fulfilling prophecy. It absolves governments like Canada's—which has ended bilateral aid to East Timor despite promises to remain for the long term—from any role in reinforcing the new nation. It permits Australia, for example, to reject Timorese calls to negotiate a sea border in the oil-rich Timor Sea, with the claim being advanced that Timorese are less able to manage oil resources than Australians since their government lacks capacity.[56]

The Timorese are trying to regain some control over the rhetorical terrain. Many observers blur the two concepts of "failed" and "fragile" states.

If some states have "failed," others may be *fragile*, yet far from the point of failure. A fragile state, after all, can recover. The notion of "fragility" has the potential to restore some agency to the countries often consigned to the conceptual grab bag of "failed states." This is part of the reason East Timor has taken the lead in forming the g7+, a group of nineteen self-declared fragile and conflict-affected states who seek to regain a collective voice and help set the aid and peacebuilding agenda, while rejecting any suggestion that they have "failed."[57] In the words of South Sudan's finance minister at the 2011 g7+ meeting: "the only way you can drive is from the driver's seat, not from the back seat, and this is what we want to tell our friends."[58]

In spite of the evidence of substantial progress and the lack of violent conflict within Timor-Leste, the "failed state" accusation continues to be levelled. Timorese non-state diplomats struggled against the claim that they were fighting for a "lost cause" throughout the final quarter of the twentieth century. In the first years of the twenty-first century, they were confronted with a similar "failed state" claim and forced to battle it on the same rhetorical terrain. An article in *Foreign Affairs* in 2014 lamented that Timor-Leste "has struggled in almost every facet of economic and political management."[59] Former UN mission chief Ian Martin and Timorese cabinet minister Agio Pereira are among those who have pointed out the flaws in the "failure" claim, with Martin saying Timor-Leste was not "failed" but young, and Pereira mustering statistics and references to Timor-Leste's rise to "medium human development" on the UN Development Programme's Human Development Index.[60] On the HDI, Timor-Leste ranks alongside Honduras and is fourth in the world in its index improvement in the 2000–13 period.[61]

In acknowledging his country's challenges, Timorese researcher Guteriano Neves offers a thoughtful deconstruction of the "failed state" claim in an article published on the Timorese presidency's semi-official blog. (The publication of critical analysis of government policy by that same government is, incidentally, another sign of vibrant political debate.) "Viewing these challenges as the product of social and political dynamic and using these challenges as the basis to claim that Timor-Leste is a failed state is ahistorical, missing the context, and it is an oversimplification of the issue," he writes.[62] Canadians analyzing Timor-Leste might benefit from listening to local voices, rather than labelling Timor-Leste as "failed" in the same way they once labelled it a "lost cause."

Notes

1. An earlier, shorter version of this article was published as "Self-fulfilling prophecies and human rights in Canada's foreign policy: the case of East Timor," *International Journal* 65, no. 3 (2010): 739–50.

2. Rick Salutin, "Failed States All Over," *Globe and Mail*, 5 March 2004. This version from Salutin's column was reposted on rabble.ca: http://rabble.ca/columnists/failed-states-all-over (accessed 30 January 2012).

3. John Warnock, *Creating a Failed State: The US and Canada in Afghanistan* (Halifax: Fernwood, 2008), 21–24.

4. Nikolas Berry-Shaw and Dru Oja Jay, *Paved with Good Intentions: Canada's Development NGOs from Idealism to Imperialism* (Halifax: Fernwood, 2012).

5. Marcus Gee, "Nobel Prize Is No Help to East Timor," *Globe and Mail*, 16 October 1996.

6. Marcus Gee, "East Timor Hopes for Freedom Premature, Experts Say," *Globe and Mail*, 3 June 1998. Like many Indonesians, Suharto has no first name.

7. David Scott, *Last Flight out of Dili: Memoirs of an Accidental Activist in the Triumph of East Timor* (North Melbourne: Pluto Press Australia, 2005), 59–62.

8. Marcus Gee, "East Timor Would Be Wise to Stay," *Globe and Mail*, 25 August 1999, A11.

9. Department of External Affairs, *Foreign Policy for Canadians*, Pacific Booklet (Ottawa: Queen's Printer, 1970), 7.

10. *A Report on Canada's External Aid Programs 1965–66* (Ottawa: External Aid Office, 1966); Canadian International Development Agency, *Canada and the Developing World* (Ottawa: Queen's Printer, 1970).

11. "Canadian policy towards Southeast Asia," undated note prepared for Commonwealth prime ministers' meeting, Singapore, 14–21 January 1971, in Library and Archives Canada [hereafter LAC], RG25, G-25, vol. 9801, 19-1-DA-IND-1971/1: "Visit of PM Trudeau to India, January 1971," briefing book.

12. LAC, RG25, vol. 10861, file 20-INDON-2-2: "Canadian Embassy in Jakarta confidential memorandum on Inco operations," 22 June 1971.

13. Arianto Sangadji, "Inco in Indonesia: A Report for Canadian People," 7 January 2000, http://www.miningwatch.ca/inco-indonesia-report-canadian-people (accessed 14 June 2015).

14. Peter Johnston, *Cooper's Snoopers and Other Follies: Fragments of a Life* (Victoria: Trafford 2002), 122, 129. Inco's role in Indonesia is discussed in Robin Gendron, "PT Inco and the Culture of Business in Indonesia: The case of Tjendra v. Jessup," paper presented to the Canadian Association of Asian Studies Conference, Waterloo, November 2008, and will be included in Gendron's upcoming book, *Mother Inco in Paradise: The International Nickel Company of Canada in New Caledonia, 1960–1988*.

15 LAC, RG19, vol. 5456, file 7875/I43: Canadian Embassy Jakarta to DEA, 19 December 1975.

16 LAC, RG25, vol. 8586, file 20-TIMOR [2]: R. L. Rogers memorandum, 3 December 1975.

17 Australian Ambassador to Jakarta Bob Furlonger to Feakes, 30 July 1974, in *Documents on Australian Foreign Policy: Australia and the Indonesian Incorporation of East Timor, 1974–1976* (Melbourne: Melbourne University Press, 2000).

18 "East Timor: Ambassador's Visit," 13 January 1978, New Zealand government document cited in Maire Leadbeater, *Negligent Neighbour: New Zealand's Complicity in the Invasion and Occupation of Timor-Leste* (Nelson, New Zealand: Craig Potton Publishing, 2006), 80. The abandonment of the "irreversible" doctrine is discussed in Leadbeater, 170–75.

19 LAC, RG25, vol. 8586, file 20-TIMOR [1]: Canadian High Commission Canberra to DEA, 20 September 1974.

20 Scott, *Last Flight out of Dili*, 149.

21 Peter Carey, "To struggle for freedom: Indonesia yesterday, East Timor today," *Inside Indonesia* 49 (January–March 1997), http://www.insideindonesia.org/to-struggle-for-freedom-indonesia-yesterday-east-timor-today (accessed 14 June 2015).

22 Clinton Fernandes, *Reluctant Saviour: Australia, Indonesia and the Independence of East Timor* (Melbourne: Scribe Publications, 2004).

23 LAC, RG25, vol. 8586, file 20-TIMOR [2]: "Portuguese Timor," Pacific Division background paper, 3 October 1975.

24 Derek Burney, *Getting it Done: A Memoir* (Montreal: McGill-Queen's University Press, 2005), 37.

25 LAC, RG25, G-25, vol. 9801: "Record of meeting between Allan MacEachen and Indonesian foreign minister Adam Malik," 26 August 1976; "Visit of the Secretary of State for External Affairs to Indonesia," 23–26 August 1976.

26 LAC, RG25, vol. 8664, file 20-TIMOR [6]: Asia Pacific division memorandum, 9 October 1979; McMaster University Archives, East Timor Alert Network papers: Department of External Affairs, memorandum for the minister, 27 October 1980.

27 Bradley Simpson, "'Illegally and Beautifully': The United States, the Indonesian Invasion of East Timor and the International Community," *Cold War History* 5, no. 3 (August 2005): 281–315.

28 "Twenty Years in East Timor: A Chronological Overview," unattributed 1994 memorandum, DFAIT file 20-TIMOR.

29 Philip Dorling, "Australia knew about Indonesia's napalm plans in Timor Leste," *Sydney Morning Herald*, 9 May 2015, http://www.smh.com.au/national/australia-knew-about-indonesias-napalm-plans-in-timor-leste-20150508-ggwxod.html (accessed 11 May 2015); Clinton Fernandes, *Companion to East Timor*, http://hass.unsw.adfa.edu.au/timor_companion/invasion_and_

conventional_war/napalm.php (accessed 11 May 2015).

30 LAC, file 20-TIMOR: J. Scott, counsellor Jakarta, a personal and confidential letter to DEA, 10 October 1983. This and other documents on the use of napalm are posted at https://davidwebster.wordpress.com/2015/05/11/a-crime-against-humanity-confirmed-indonesian-use-of-napalm-against-east-timorese-civilians-1983/.

31 LAC, file 20-TIMOR: Canadian Embassy in Canberra, telegram to DEA, 3 November 1983.

32 LAC, file 20-TIMOR: "Situation in East Timor," House of Commons briefing note, 16 January 1984.

33 Margaret E. Keck and Kathryn Sikkink, *Activists Beyond Borders: Advocacy Networks in International Politics* (Ithaca: Cornell University Press, 1998).

34 I have explored these themes in "Languages of Human Rights in Timor-Leste," *Asia Pacific Perspectives* 11, no. 1 (August 2013): 5–21, and "Human Rights: Across the Pacific Both Ways," in Akira Iriye and Robert David Johnson, eds., *Asia Pacific in an Age of Globalization* (Basingstoke, UK: Palgrave Macmillan, 2015).

35 LAC, file 20-TIMOR: Jakarta telegram 3040, 7 March 1995.

36 LAC, file 20-TIMOR: Canadian embassy in Jakarta to Foreign Affairs, 7 March 1995; Embassy in Jakarta to DFAIT, 3 November 1998.

37 J. W. Morley, ed., *Driven by Growth: Political Change in the Asia-Pacific Region* (Armonk NY: M. E. Sharpe, 1999).

38 East Timor Alert Network Papers: "Joe Clark to Christine Stewart MP."

39 Mulroney speech at Commonwealth heads of government meeting in Harare, Zimbabwe, 16 October 1991.

40 LAC, file 20-TIMOR: Jakarta telegram, 20 November 1991.

41 McDougall interview, cited in David Webster, "Canada expands export of military goods to Indonesia," *Catholic New Times*, 25 June 1995.

42 Malia Southard, Southard, *Looking the Other Way: The Indonesian Bond, Partnership or Plunder?* (Victoria: South Pacific Peoples Foundation of Canada, 1997), 117–18, 159.

43 Chris Dagg, "Linking Aid to Human Rights in Indonesia: A Canadian Perspective," *Issues* 7, no. 1 (Winter 1993).

44 Canada, Department of Foreign Affairs and International Trade, *Indonesia: A Guide for Canadian Business, 1995–96* (Ottawa, Queen's Printer, 1995).

45 David Webster, "Canada and Bilateral Human Rights Dialogues," *Canadian Foreign Policy* 16, no. 3 (2010): 43–63.

46 University of British Columbia Archives, British Columbia Civil Liberties Association papers, APEC inquiry exhibits, box 1: Memoranda on Axworthy meetings in Jakarta, July 1997.

47 University of British Columbia Archives, British Columbia Civil Liberties Association fonds (hereafter BCCLA), box 1: Jakarta e-mail, 12 Sept. 1997; "Liaison

visit by Indonesia, Sept. 8–9, 1997," RCMP memorandum; Jakarta e-mail, 10 Sept. 1997; BCCLA, box 2: "Bilateral meeting with President Soeharto [sic] of Indonesia," memorandum for the PM, November 1997.

48 LAC, file 20-TIMOR: Xanana Gusmão to Lloyd Axworthy, 20 February 1999.

49 Geoffrey Robinson, "East Timor 1999 Crimes against Humanity," report commissioned by the Office of the UN High Commissioner for Human Rights, July 2003, http://www.cavr-timorleste.org/chegaFiles/finalReportEng/12-Annexe1-East-Timor-1999-GeoffreyRobinson.pdf (accessed 14 June 2015).

50 Marcus Gee, "Where Does East Timor Head Now?", *Globe and Mail*, 6 October 1999.

51 Leadbeater, *Negligent Neighbour*, 209.

52 For a media example, see "East Timor Could Become a 'Failed State'—Aid Agency," Reuters wire report, 19 May 2004, http://www.etan.org/et2004/may/15-21/19etrisk.htm (accessed 15 January 2012); for an academic article that saw Timor-Leste "sliding towards becoming a 'failed state' only three years after finally achieving independence," see Clive Schofield, "A 'Fair Go' for East Timor? Sharing the Resources of the Timor Sea," *Contemporary Southeast Asia* 27, no. 2 (August 2005): 255–80.

53 The Fund for Peace, "Fragile States Index 2014," http://fsi.fundforpeace.org/rankings-2014 (accessed 14 June 2015).

54 The Fund for Peace, "Failed States Index 2013,"fsi.fundforpeace.org/rankings-2013-sortable. For an argument that highlights the continued patronizing nature of the FSI, see Heath Pickering, "Terminology twist: from failed states to fragile states," *The Strategist*, 1 July 2014, http://www.aspistrategist.org.au/terminology-twist-from-failed-states-to-fragile-states/ (accessed 28 September 2014).

55 "Failed States Index 2010," http://fsi.fundforpeace.org/rankings-2010-sortable (accessed 14 June 2015).

56 See, for instance, Frank Brennan, "Time to draw the line between Australia and Timor Leste," *Eureka Street*, 13 May 2013, http://www.eurekastreet.com.au/article.aspx?aeid=36275#.VX3uL_lViko (accessed 14 June 2015).

57 g7+ founding statement, Dili, Timor-Leste, 10 April 2010, See Annex, http://www.g7plus.org/sites/default/files/basic-page-downloads/Dili-Declaration.pdf (accessed 14 November 2015); Kai Thaler, "Timor-Leste and The g7+: A New Approach to the Security and Development Aid Nexus," *IPRIS Lusophone Countries Bulletin* 18 (2011): 4–7.

58 Kosti Manibe, Minister of Finance, South Sudan, cited in "The g7+: A Paradigm Shift for Fragile States," World Bank Institute, 28 November 2011, http://wbi.worldbank.org/wbi/stories/g7-paradigm-shift (accessed 30 January 2012).

59 Madhu Narasimhan, "The World's Youngest Failed State: Letter From East Timor," *Foreign Affairs*, 12 August 2014, https://www.foreignaffairs.com/articles/east-asia/2014-08-12/worlds-youngest-failed-state (accessed 28 September 2014). Academic analyses along similar lines include Jarat Chopra, "Building State Failure in East Timor," *Development and Change* 33 (2002): 979–1000, and James Cotton, "Timor-Leste and the discourse of state failure," *Australian Journal of International Affairs* 61, no. 4 (2007): 455–70.

60 Ian Martin, "Timor-Leste was not a failed state, it was a young state!", 10 Anos da Independência, http://10anosindependencia.blogs.sapo.tl/12695.html (accessed 28 September 2014); Agio Pereira, "Timor-Leste Success: Why It Won't be the Next Failed State," *Foreign Affairs*, 26 August 2014, https://www.foreignaffairs.com/articles/east-timor/2014-08-26/timor-leste-success (accessed 28 September 2014).

61 UNDP, "Human Development Index Trends, 1980–2014," http://hdr.undp.org/en/content/table-2-human-development-index-trends-1980-2013 (accessed 14 June 2015).

62 Guteriano Neves, "Is Timor-Leste a failed state? Life at Aitarak Laran," 15 September 2014, https://aitaraklaranlive.wordpress.com/2014/09/15/is-timor-leste-a-failed-state/ (accessed 28 September 2014).

CHAPTER 5

ENTANGLED:
Canadian Engagement in Haiti, 1968-2010

Andrew S. Thompson

Introduction

Since the late 1960s, Haiti has occupied a disproportionately large place in Canadian foreign policy decision making. Despite its small size, Haiti—perhaps the quintessential fragile state—has been, and continues to be, a strategic priority for Canada.[1] For more than four decades, Canada has been engaged in an ongoing international reconstruction effort in Haiti, an engagement that has only increased since the earthquake of 12 January 2010 that levelled the capital, Port-au-Prince.

This chapter offers a brief survey of Canada's involvement in Haiti from the Duvalierist period to the earthquake of 2010. The record is mixed. At times Canada used its diplomatic, economic, and military resources to advance and protect democracy and human rights. Yet there were other moments when its motives and actions were less benevolent, even counter-productive. Given the long history of relations between the two countries, this variation is hardly surprising. For nearly half a century, Canada has been entangled in Haiti's affairs, unable to divorce itself from the tiny Caribbean island nation's troubles. Although it is a rich source of talented, francophone professionals, who maintain their homeland's political profile in Canada, Haiti's strategic and economic value to Canada is minimal. However, its geographic proximity to the United States, which has a strong stake in regional stability, and the centrality of the Canada-US relationship, means that Ottawa does not have the luxury of being able to ignore this island country.

Although it is by no means a passive actor, much of Canada's involvement in Haiti has been reactive, responding to both internal conflicts and exogenous threats. Indeed, the history of Canada's involvement in Haiti is as much the story of Haitian agency as it is about Canada's attempts to bring stability to a fragile state, and the relationship between the two countries has been far from asymmetrical, even though the former is a member of the G7 and the latter the poorest country in the western hemisphere. Broadly, Haiti is representative of the central dilemma that fragile states pose to developed countries in an age of globalization and interconnectedness: they are too complex to "fix," yet too volatile to be left alone.

Duvalierism

Dr. François "Papa Doc" Duvalier preyed on Haitians with a ruthlessness that made the regime an international pariah during his fourteen-year reign as Haiti's president, from 1957 to 1971. Black, rather than a member of the mulatto population (who comprised the island's traditional economic and political elites), charismatic, nationalistic, educated, and fluent in French and Creole, Duvalier seemed the ideal candidate to lead Haiti, at least in the eyes of the Haitian military, which hoped he could win the support of the people without diminishing the authority of the army. But as Michel S. Laguerre argues in his pioneering book *The Military and Society in Haiti*, those who backed him underestimated him. Elected in 1957, Duvalier understood power—not only how to acquire it but also how to consolidate and hold onto it. He did so through a combination of tactics: practising divide-and-conquer politics, neutralizing and even eliminating real and potential opponents, engaging in strong-man rule, and employing state terror through his infamous henchmen, the Tontons Macoutes.² Declaring himself "President for Life" in 1964, he finally relinquished control of the country on 21 April 1971, dying peacefully in his sleep, but not before naming his son, Jean-Claude "Baby Doc" Duvalier, as his successor.

The "Baby Doc" era began with cautious hope in Haiti and abroad that things would be different. Duvalier advocated what he called "Jean-Claudism." According to political scientist Robert Fatton, Jr., this was a "relatively 'open' technocratic project" in which the president liberalized the economy, "stopped the worst excesses of the macoutes, tolerated some dissent, and rehabilitated the army as an institution."³ Encouraged by the prospect of reform, international donors—including Canada—responded by funding millions of dollars' worth of development assistance. In 1973, the Canadian International Development Agency (CIDA) gave Haiti a modest grant of US$150,000 to subsidize existing agricultural projects being administered by France; the amount of the subsidy was later increased to US$7.24 million.⁴ The following year, CIDA sponsored two additional projects worth almost US$5 million.⁵ CIDA subsequently added another US$2 million over a five-year period, and sent US$1.17 million in food assistance.⁶ In 1977–78, CIDA committed an additional US$39 million to Haiti over the next four years, US$21 million of which was allocated to a soil rejuvenation project in Nippes.⁷ By the end of the decade, Canadian bilateral assistance to Haiti was second only to that of the United States. Much of the money was channelled through development organizations and faith-based groups, many of whom had been operating in the country since the 1940s.⁸ Nonetheless, by the early 1980s, as Duvalierism began to flounder, officials at CIDA began to doubt the merits of its programs and to pull back funds on the grounds that the Haitian government had not contributed its share of funds for joint projects.⁹

The timing of Canada's development assistance to Haiti coincided with Washington's re-engagement with the Caribbean country through the 1970s. From 1976 to 1978, the United States Agency for International Development (USAID) issued nearly US$43 million in government-to-government grants, and worked closely with the Inter-American Development Bank (IDB) and the Pan American Health Organization (PAHO) on a Disaster Preparedness Project. It also pledged an additional US$86 million over five years for a food-for-work program to bolster agricultural production.¹⁰

USAID assistance to Haiti was, in part, a response to Washington's concerns about illegal immigration. During the 1970s, large numbers of unskilled Haitians had fled the country in tiny wooden ships headed for other Caribbean countries and the US mainland.[11] By the early 1980s, "Haitian boat people" had become a contentious political issue in a number of southern states, most notably Florida and Missouri. The issue was made worse in 1981, when Haiti's precarious economy was hit hard by a series of external and internal shocks. Hurricane Allen and an outbreak of African swine fever virus devastated much of Haiti's agricultural production.[12] To further Haiti's economic woes, the country's bauxite reserves were almost depleted and tourism was on the decline. USAID responded to the swine fever crisis by launching the controversial, and largely ineffective, Interim Swine Repopulation Project, which imported pigs from the United States to Haiti, while Republican President Ronald Reagan provided US$5 million in emergency economic aid in return for an agreement with the Duvalier government that permitted the US Coast Guard to repatriate any Haitian intercepted at sea.[13]

But "Baby Doc" Duvalier proved as repressive as his father, and by the early 1980s, confidence in the new regime had collapsed, so much so that Washington cut off aid on the grounds that Haitian authorities had violated its citizens' freedoms.[14] Within the country, Haiti's faltering economy and massive trade deficit, combined with widespread tax evasion and embezzlement of foreign aid by government officials, fuelled the flames of anti-Duvalier sentiment. By 1986, the nation had had enough. Anti-Duvalier riots broke out across the country. To escape, "Baby Doc" boarded a US plane for France, while Tontons Macoutes were dragged into the streets and killed by angry mobs, thus bringing a violent end to twenty-nine years of Duvalierism.

Transition

Jean-Claude Duvalier's departure put immediate pressure on international donors to assist Haiti with its transition from dictatorship to democratic rule. USAID asked Congress to fund programs aimed at promoting both the welfare of the population and private sector development in light assembly manufacturing.[15] Similarly, in March 1987, CIDA granted US$10.51 million in bilateral assistance—roughly three times the amount given the year before—to help prepare Haitians for the upcoming elections.[16] Minister for External Relations Monique Landry even travelled to Haiti to discuss Canada's role in supporting the country's new Interim Development Program, and invite the country's new leadership to attend the summit of La Francophonie, which was to take place in Quebec City in September.[17] Little did anyone know at the time that the transition from dictatorship to democracy would prove so difficult, violent, and costly.

To fill the void left behind by Duvalierism, a provisional military government, the Conseil National de Gouvernement (CNG), was established under the direction of General Henri Namphy. The initial activities of the CNG were encouraging. Upon assuming office, Namphy scheduled the first and second rounds of the presidential elections for November 1987 and February 1988. He also created a constitutional assembly with an assortment of Haitian stakeholders charged with rewriting the constitution to check the power of the president and the military.[18] On the human rights front, he freed political prisoners, welcomed back exiles, and announced that the Macoutes would be disbanded.[19] Moreover, a team of UN observers led by Canadian Michel Gauvin—an experienced and outspoken diplomat who had previously served in Vietnam, the Congo, and the Dominican Republic—reported that it was satisfied that the CNG was relying less on terror and intimidation to govern and more on due process of law. Of the six human rights cases it presented to the United Nations Human Rights Commission, only one involved a violation that had occurred after Duvalier's departure.[20]

But Haitians were no more empowered after the revolution than they had been under Duvalier. They had displaced the president and the Tontons Macoutes, but the military quickly filled the vacuum. The months leading up to the November 1987 presidential election were particularly violent. In July, wide-scale, state-sponsored violence broke out as reports emerged that the CNG was using force to bar church groups and unions from fielding candidates. Four weeks later, the human rights group Washington Office on Haiti reported that the Tontons Macoutes, in league with wealthy landowners, had massacred between three hundred and seven hundred farmers in the rural town of Jean-Rabel who were suspected of belonging to the popular peasant group Tet Ansanm (Heads Together).[21]

The violence mounted as Duvalierists launched an aggressive campaign to reclaim power. On 2 November, supporters of the former president, who were barred from holding office under the new constitution, burned down the Provisional Electoral Council headquarters, attacked human rights activist and leader of the Christian Democratic Party Sylvio Claude, and fired machine guns at a voter registration office.[22] On election day, 29 November, roughly thirty voters in Port-au-Prince were gunned down while waiting to cast their ballots. Namphy responded by suspending the election. The Haitian military then arrested and executed forty-six Haitians from the area for having involved themselves in pro-democracy demonstrations.[23]

The brutal act was met with widespread international condemnation. After the massacre, USAID slashed its bilateral assistance from US$96.5 million to $36.9 million.[24] In Canada, the opposition Liberal Party called on the Mulroney government to reduce aid or cut it off altogether. The Conservatives replied that any action taken would be in concert with UN Security Council resolutions.[25] Meanwhile, Ottawa recalled its ambassador to Haiti in protest nine days after the incident. On 8 January 1988, CIDA announced that until there was a legitimate election all funds for Haiti would be channelled through NGOs, private Canadian businesses, and multilateral organizations.[26] At first, the decision to use aid as leverage for democratic reforms seemed to be working. Shortly after the aid transfers stopped, Namphy announced that a new round of presidential elections was scheduled for 17 January 1988.

Historian Leslie Manigat won the election, but many in the international community contested the legitimacy of the results, in part because of reports of widespread human rights violations.[27] Washington considered the election to be undemocratic. In the Canadian House of Commons, the Liberals denounced the events in Haiti, calling it a "Macoute election," and asked the government whether it would recognize the newly elected Haitian government. The parliamentary secretary to the minister for external relations admitted that all the government could do was denounce the election, conceding that the CNG was the effective governing authority.[28] In March, a Canadian parliamentary delegation travelled to Haiti to meet with President Manigat, hoping that diplomatic pressure would convince Haiti's new leader that new elections were urgent.

Meanwhile, the situation in Haiti continued to disintegrate. Six months after the election, the UN reported that conditions in Haiti had become as oppressive as those under Duvalierism, estimating that more than five hundred Haitians had lost their lives to political violence.[29] According to Professor Michel S. Laguerre, the loss of funds from the international community angered the country's economic elite, whose livelihood depended, in part, on the revenue from aid projects. Namphy's answer to the instability was to re-take power, deposing Manigat on 19 June 1988. Two months later, soldiers killed eleven people, injured another seventy, and burned down St. Jean Bosco Church in a failed attempt to assassinate the popular Catholic priest (and future president) Jean-Bertrand Aristide.[30] Predictably, mass opposition to the government erupted. Fearing a popular rebellion, the military hierarchy took matters into its own hands. Six days after the St. Jean Bosco burning, the Haitian army under the command of Lieutenant-General Prosper Avril removed Namphy from office.

The Avril regime was little better than the one it succeeded. A UN Human Rights Council (UNHRC) fact-finding mission reported in February 1989 that human rights conditions were only slightly more humane under the new government.[31] Nevertheless, both Washington and Ottawa agreed to assist Avril with the transition to democracy. In the US, Congress pledged US$50 million in economic assistance once a new government was democratically elected.[32] For its part, CIDA granted US$22.1 million ($10.16 million of which was in the form of direct bilateral assistance) and launched a four-year AIDS prevention program with McGill University, the Pan American Health Organization, and the World Health Organization.[33] Under close and sustained international scrutiny for his government's lacklustre human rights record, Avril was eventually forced to concede the presidency to civilian Ertha Pascal-Trouillot in March 1990.[34]

Like her predecessors, Pascal-Trouillot's principal responsibility was to organize a new round of presidential elections. Once again, both Washington and Ottawa offered significant material support for the elections. In addition to a number of development projects, USAID provided technical assistance and elections training programs. Similarly, four days after taking office, CIDA rewarded the new Haitian leader with an initial US$150,000 in humanitarian aid. This was followed up with US$1 million in food aid and "small, labour-intensive community projects," and another US$1 million through Elections Canada in support for the election.[35] To her credit, Pascal-Trouillot was good on her promise to hold new elections, thus bringing to an end five years of turbulence marked by mass human rights violations.

Aristide

On 16 December 1990, Aristide and his Lavalas Party won 67 percent of the popular vote in what observers considered to be Haiti's first legitimate election since the 1986 revolution. After twenty-nine years of Duvalierism and five years of military rule, it finally seemed as though the difficult transition from dictatorship to democracy was over. A populist, Aristide implemented political and economic reforms that would redistribute wealth within the country, steps that certainly angered the Haitian elite. As a result, on 30 September 1991, eight months into Aristide's term, Lt.-General Raoul Cédras and the Front pour l'Avancement et le Progrès Haitien (FRAPH) staged a *coup d'état* that forced Aristide to flee the country.

Predictably, the coup aroused widespread condemnation and prompted the international community to intervene. On 3 October, the Organization of American States (OAS) called on foreign governments and the UN Security Council to impose diplomatic sanctions and suspend all commercial relations. Six days later, it sent a civilian-led mission to Haiti, the "OAS-DEMOC," to negotiate Aristide's return to office.[36] At the same time, Amnesty International reported that in the first few days of the coup, the army had murdered more than fifty civilians living in the Cité Soleil district of Port-au-Prince, another thirty or forty in the district of Lamentin 54, and six more in Gonaïves.[37]

Canadian prime minister Brian Mulroney was particularly vocal in his opposition to the coup. In the House of Commons, he denounced Cédras and his followers as a "gang of hoodlums," and promised that Canada would do everything in its power to restore Aristide to his rightful position as president.[38] Parliament unanimously supported Mulroney's decision to place a moratorium on the return of any Haitian refugee claimants in Canada and to cut off all development aid to the Haitian government. Two weeks later, Barbara McDougall, who had been Canada's representative on the OAS mission investigating the coup, told the UN General Assembly that neither the international community nor the people of Haiti would accept Cédras's military regime. She encouraged the UN to use its "moral force and political will" to return Aristide to power so that the crisis did not threaten democracy in the western hemisphere.[39]

President Bush, however, had reservations about intervening in Haiti. At a press conference on 4 October—at which Aristide was present—he acknowledged the crisis in Haiti but refused to send US troops unless American lives were in danger.[40] Left-wing critics attributed Washington's reluctance to intervene to US commercial interests in the Caribbean country. According to the National Labor Committee (NLC), companies such as Walmart, J. C. Penny, and Sears had been taking advantage of Haiti's inexpensive labour by paying textile workers the equivalent of US$0.14 per hour without benefits or pensions. One of Aristide's first measures had been to convince the Haitian parliament to raise the minimum wage to US$0.37, a policy opposed by many US-based multinationals.[41] Nonetheless, by the end of October, as the situation continued to deteriorate, Bush was forced to act, issuing Executive Order 12779, which required US companies to freeze their Haitian assets, halt payments to the regime, and suspend trade with Haiti with the exception of food products.[42]

Canadian, American, and international pressure notwithstanding, the human rights situation in Haiti continued to worsen. In January 1992, Amnesty International reported that Cédras and his supporters had, in the three months since taking control, eliminated all grassroots organizations, re-established the authority of regional governors known as the "Chefs de Section," issued "hit lists" on the radio, burned houses, attacked domestic and foreign clergy, and permitted soldiers to use rape as a "weapon of terror."[43] Moreover, by February 1992, the United Nations estimated that roughly twenty thousand Haitians had fled the country.[44] Within months, that number had grown to an estimated thirty-four thousand, the majority of whom were destined for the United States. Anxious to avoid a mass influx of refugees, Bush issued Executive Order 12807, the *Interdiction of Illegal Aliens*, on 24 May, which instructed the Coast Guard to repatriate Haitians without first trying to determine their refugee status.[45]

Meanwhile, negotiations were underway to secure Aristide's return to Haiti, but progress was slow as Cédras played for time, even staging parliamentary elections in January 1993. Slowly the economic sanctions, ineffective at first, began to bite. By the spring of 1993, pressured to find

Figure 1: In the early 1990s, Canada and other countries in the ad hoc group "Friends of Haiti" set about rebuilding the country's battered justice system. In this 1994 photo, RCMP Inspector Joe Healy lectures Haitian police recruits on criminal law in Port au Prince. (Credit: Joe Healy)

a solution by the "Friends of Haiti," an ad hoc group that included the United States, Canada, France, and Venezuela, government and opposition representatives met at Governors Island, New York, on 27 June. Following six days of negotiations, the two sides agreed to give Aristide the authority to choose a prime minister in exchange for an end to the sanctions and amnesty for Cédras. The Governors Island Agreement also promised international help to reform Haiti's justice system, the resumption of development assistance, the establishment of a new police force, the naming of a new commander-in-chief of the armed forces, and Aristide's reinstatement on 30 October. Furthermore, the agreement was to be monitored by the newly created peacekeeping mission, the UN Mission in Haiti (UNMIH) and the UN Civilian Mission in Haiti (MICIVIH). An addendum, the New York Pact, called for an end to arbitrary arrests and torture, the release of political prisoners, respect for fundamental freedoms, and compensation for coup victims.[46] To ensure compliance, the

UN Security Council passed a resolution on 16 July imposing a total oil and arms embargo until 27 August.

Once again, Cédras proved unwilling to comply and played for time. His *de facto* government refused to cooperate with international forces, and even barred the USS *Harlan County*, a US naval vessel carrying 25 Canadian and 193 US peacekeepers, from docking.[47] On 11 October 1993, three days after presenting Parliament with a proposal to create a new civilian police force, Aristide's minister of justice, François-Guy Malary, was assassinated. The UN Security Council responded with resolution 873, re-imposing the oil and arms embargos, and resolution 875, which promised "further necessary measures," thus opening the door to a military intervention.[48]

Throughout the negotiations, the refugee exodus had continued, despite a plea from Aristide to his fellow Haitians not to circumvent the "floating Berlin Wall" that now surrounded the country.[49] In the US, domestic criticism of American policy began to mount. In early 1994, the Congressional Black Caucus submitted two bills calling on US authorities to ensure that their policies toward Haitians intercepted at sea were consistent with standards codified in international human rights law. US civil society actors also levelled sharp criticism at Washington. On 12 April, Randall Robinson, the executive director of TransAfrica, began a high-profile twenty-seven-day hunger strike on behalf of Haitian refugees that drew international attention to US repatriation practices. Weeks later, Amnesty International issued a report documenting seventeen cases of persecution of Haitians who had been returned to Haiti by US immigration officials, further underscoring the need for an urgent resolution to the situation.[50]

The situation remained at an impasse as both sides upped the ante in an attempt to force the other to back down. On 26 May, the border between Haiti and the Dominican Republic was closed, a move designed to cut off the military's access to illegal goods. Cédras countered by expelling MICIVIH on 11 July, which effectively forced the UN's hand. At the end of July, the Security Council adopted resolution 940, creating a Multinational Force (MNF) whose mandate was to

> use all necessary means to facilitate the departure from Haiti of the military leadership, consistent with the Governors

Island Agreement, the prompt return of the legitimately elected President and the restoration of the legitimate authorities of the Government of Haiti, and to establish and maintain a secure and stable environment that will permit implementation of the Governors Island Agreement.[51]

Backed by the MNF and the threat of invasion, President Bill Clinton sent former President Jimmy Carter, former Joint Chiefs of Staff chairman Colin Powell, and Senator Sam Nunn, chairman of the Senate Armed Services Committee, to Haiti on 17 September to persuade Cédras to comply with the Governors Island Agreement. Sensing defeat, Judge Emile Jonaissant, whom Cédras had named provisional president, agreed to allow Aristide to return and to let Haitian and US forces provide security jointly. In return, Cédras was granted asylum in Panama.

Sadly, but perhaps not unsurprisingly, governing in the post-coup period proved difficult despite the UN/OAS presence in the country, as deep divisions fostered a climate of political paralysis. During the mid-1990s to early 2000s, during the first René Préval administration and the early days of the second Aristide administration, the UN had several security missions in Haiti, the final one coming to an end in February 2001. As the UN mission wound down, the political situation in Haiti became increasingly unstable. Aristide had been re-elected in 2000 under disputed circumstances. During his second term he came to rely increasingly on his armed militias (Les Chimères) in order to maintain his authority. By 2004, anti-Aristide sentiment within the country had grown considerably while his international support, especially in Washington, dwindled.

The Insurrection

On 5 February 2004, a group of former military and paramilitary officials known as the "Cannibal Army," led by Guy Philippe, a former army officer and police commissioner, and Louis-Jodel Chamblain, the former second-in-command of the FRAPH, launched an anti-Aristide insurgency that began in the north and quickly made its way south to Port-au-Prince. By the end of the month, the situation had deteriorated to the point of crisis. Unlike the situation in the early 1990s, when the international community had been willing to intervene in Haiti, there was little appetite for putting down the rebels. Instead, the UN allowed Aristide to be forcibly boarded onto a US plane destined for the Central African Republic before the Security Council passed resolution 1529, creating a Multinational Interim Force (MIF) to re-establish order in the country,[52] and Supreme Court President Boniface Alexander was sworn in as interim president, thus bringing an end to the insurgency. The following week Gérard Latortue, a former economist with the UN, was appointed prime minister of an interim government whose principal mandate was to organize a new round of elections, which eventually resulted in René Préval becoming president for a second time in February 2006.

Canada's engagement in Haiti has been controversial since 2004. In the wake of the insurrection, Canada responded by contributing five hundred soldiers to the MIF, which also consisted of troops from the United States, France, and Chile. Once the UN Stabilization Mission in Haiti (MINUSTAH) was established and the situation on the ground steadied, Canada withdrew the bulk of its forces. Nonetheless the decision to send Canadian security forces to Haiti was heavily criticized by civil society and Haitian solidarity groups in Canada, even though the UN Security Council had authorized the intervention. At issue was President Jean-Bertrand Aristide's departure from office. US Secretary of State Colin Powell defended the decision to remove Aristide from Haiti, telling the media that the UN had "averted a bloodbath."[53] Others, most notably critics on the left, such as the Canada Haiti Action Network, found this argument to be disingenuous, accusing the Canadian government of supporting of a US-led coup against a democratically elected government.[54]

Following the insurrection, Ottawa made—and continues to make—a sizeable financial commitment to the international reconstruction effort. From 2004 to 2006, Canada pledged US$97 million to Haiti through the international Interim Cooperation Framework, a commitment surpassed only by the United States and the European Union. In May 2006, Conservative Prime Minister Stephen Harper's recently elected government pledged an additional $48 million for good governance, human rights, and debt forgiveness programs, primarily aiming to strengthen the Haitian parliamentary system. A month later, Canada committed $15 million in additional aid, and, on 25 July 2006 at the International Donors'

Conference for the Economic and Social Development of Haiti, the federal government pledged another $520 million in aid over the next five years. And more seemed likely. A December 2006 report from the Standing Committee on Foreign Affairs and International Development, entitled "Canada's International Policy Put to the Test in Haiti," recommended that Canada "continue to affirm its commitment to a long-term human security, development and democratization strategy for Haiti," and that it do so for a period of at least ten years.[55] Harper's trip to Haiti in July 2007, when he ventured into the slums of Cité Soleil, and Minister of Foreign Affairs Maxime Bernier's subsequent visit to Port-au-Prince in February 2008, were touted as further evidence of the Canadian government's public commitment to bringing stability to the Caribbean nation.

Since 2004, CIDA has funded numerous projects and initiatives designed to foster economic growth, strengthen the delivery of basic services, advance democratic reforms and human rights (especially human rights for women), and provide election support. According to political scientist Stephen Baranyi, the effects of these projects will not be known for many years; however, there are elements in these initiatives, such as support for programs to deal with gender-based violence, that have the potential to have a positive impact on the lives of Haitians.[56] These initiatives, particularly those relating to state building, occurred in the context of a larger policy shift by the Canadian government, first initiated by Prime Minister Paul Martin and subsequently adopted and expanded by Prime Minister Harper, to make good governance programming a central component of Canada's development assistance policies, particularly with respect to investments in fragile and failed states.[57] Perhaps the most striking example of this priority shift was the creation within CIDA of the Office for Democratic Governance in October 2006 to promote "freedom and democracy, human rights, the rule of law and open and accountable public institutions in developing countries."[58] Parliament was also supportive of the good governance agenda. In July 2007, the House of Commons Standing Committee on Foreign Affairs and International Development released a major report on Canada's democracy promotion programs, in which it recommended that Canada become a "world leader" in the promotion and advancement of democratic governance to the developing world.[59]

By its own admission, CIDA (which was merged with the Department of Foreign Affairs and International Trade in 2013) does not have a great track record when it comes to successful development in Haiti, particularly with respect to good governance programming. In December 2004, the agency submitted a report to the Organisation for Economic Co-operation and Development (OECD) titled "Canadian Cooperation with Haiti: Reflecting on a Decade of 'Difficult Partnership.'" As the title suggests, CIDA has found operating in Haiti to be a challenge. From 1994 to 2004, Canada spent $300 million on development assistance to Haiti, bring its total aid expenditure since 1968 to $600 million.[60] The money was not necessarily well spent. According to the report, in the mid-1990s Canada ceased funding programs aimed at reforming the security and justice sectors; the reason cited was "disappointing results," which were attributed both to corruption and to "President René Préval's leadership, which stagnated from political deadlock."[61]

While the significance of the internal political feuding within Haiti should not be minimized, several scholars and observers have been equally critical of CIDA's past operations. Robert Muggah, a specialist on post-conflict state-building in fragile states, has argued that between 1998 and 2002, "exogenous factors have played an equally insidious role in shaping the contours" of Haitian politics. Among other things, international donors withheld roughly $340 million in aid because of World Bank concerns relating to "political instability, woefully poor governance and corruption."[62] The impact was tremendous, although surely foreseeable. Funding for the very sectors most in need of assistance, specifically in areas relating to security sector reform, was largely abandoned by 2000 in response to controversies surrounding Aristide's re-election, a decision that undoubtedly contributed to dysfunction within the criminal justice system.[63] On top of this, Canada, like the US and EU, placed strict conditions on aid and channelled money through civil society organizations instead of the national government, both of which undermined Aristide's ability to govern.[64]

The coordination of aid, or "donor harmonization," has also been a problem for CIDA, as well as for the international community in Haiti. In its December 2006 report, the House of Commons Standing Committee on Foreign Affairs and International Development faulted CIDA for engaging in "too many small short-term projects having little cumulative effect."⁶⁵ Finally, Muggah has suggested that the international aid strategy to date has been "overambitious," "erratic," unevenly funded, and, perhaps more fundamentally problematic, it has never been "'owned' in any meaningful sense by Haitians and the process was hardly 'inclusive' beyond consultation in the capital of Port-au-Prince and to a lesser extent in the regions."⁶⁶ Much of the reason for this stems from a lack of trust in Haitian authorities to govern effectively, as well as a lack of systematic understanding of realities on the ground.⁶⁷

Haiti, more than most countries, is susceptible to external shocks that have the effect of exacerbating political paralysis.⁶⁸ In this respect, 2008 was a particularly difficult year for the country. In February, the global food crisis that saw international prices for staples rise sharply had a dramatic effect on Haiti, which is a net food importer. With the price of rice out of reach for the majority of Haitians, riots broke out in Port-au-Prince, which resulted in the impeachment of Préval's prime minister, Jacques Édouard Alexis, in April, a move that compromised the government's ability to function. Only in the fall of 2008, after two hurricanes and two tropical storms hit Haiti in a period of three weeks, did Parliament finally approve a new prime minister, Michèle Pierre Louis, who had been Préval's third choice for the job. Although faint, there were signs that life in Haiti was improving in 2009. Thanks to the worst natural disaster to hit Haiti in two hundred years, however, these gains were fleeting.

The Earthquake

In the early morning of 12 January 2010, an earthquake measuring 7.0 on the Richter scale rocked Port-au-Prince and its surrounding districts. The death toll was estimated at more than 230,000, while another 1.3 to 1.5 million Haitians were driven from their homes and forced to live in "temporary" displacement camps. Damage to property and infrastructure was estimated to be between $8 and $11 billion.⁶⁹ The state infrastructure was also reduced to rubble: fifteen of seventeen government ministry buildings were destroyed, as was the Presidential Palace, the Parliament building and the Supreme Court. Had it not been for the rapid international response and MINUSTAH's existing presence on the ground, the disaster could have been much worse.

For their part, Canadians reacted with overwhelming sympathy to the situation. The day after the earthquake, Canada's Governor General, Haitian-born Michaëlle Jean—who had been in Haiti just days before and who would become UN Special Envoy to Haiti later that year—made an impassioned plea to Canadians and the world to lend a hand to Haiti.[70] According to Baranyi, Canadians responded by donating "a record $220 million to Haiti," which Ottawa matched, and "at the International Donors' Conference on 31 March, Canada pledged an additional $400 million over two years."[71] In addition to this substantial financial commitment, Canada was actively involved with the Interim Haiti Recovery Commission, a temporary body consisting of Haitian and international actors that was responsible for developing and coordinating the reconstruction effort.

Yet in the half-decade since the earthquake, Haiti remains in a perilous state. Although there were elections in 2011, the country is fragmented politically. Despite the infusion of billions of dollars of aid money, the economy remains fragile. Moreover, the displacement camps that were supposed to be temporary remain in place, with few signs that they will be closed any time soon. Just as troubling, there have been reports of forced evictions and widespread sexual violence in the camps, as both domestic and international police have struggled to provide security to those vulnerable to attack.[72] All the while, Haiti has also become a *de facto* UN trusteeship, as donors have been unwilling, at least for the time being, to allow Haitian authorities full control of the affairs of the country.[73]

Conclusion

There is a common view—in Canada and abroad—that Haiti's problems are intractable. It is, sadly, a sentiment that is not completely unwarranted, in part because of internal problems but also because international attempts at nation building have yet to produce anything beyond very limited and short-lived successes. If it thought that it could, Ottawa would undoubtedly disengage from Haiti; at various times since the late 1960s it has been tempted to do so. But there are compelling reasons to remain

Figure 2: Following the massive earthquake of January 2010, Canadians rallied in support of Haiti. In this photo, a Haitian family receives an emergency cooking and water storage kit. (Credit: CIDA/Benoit Aquin)

involved. Many Canadian faith-based and development organizations have deep roots in Haiti, and the country is an important source of talented francophone immigrants. More important, until the day comes when Haiti's problems no longer concern Washington, Canada will have little choice but to play a role in shaping the fate of Haitians, whether it wants to or not. As long as Haiti's instability is deemed to pose a threat to international peace and security, this tiny Caribbean island country that presents no direct danger to Canadian national security will remain a fixture of Ottawa's foreign policy.

Notes

1. Despite billions of dollars in aid money, technical assistance, and military support that the international community has provided to the country, contemporary Haiti has never been able to shed its reputation as the "basket case" of the Western hemisphere. It suffers from a host of political, economic, social, and environmental ailments, many of which are internal and of its own making. But it is also acutely vulnerable to exogenous threats such as volatility in the global economy and natural disasters brought on by extreme weather that hinder development and exacerbate the state's inherent inability to provide for the basic needs of Haitians. See Jared Diamond, *Collapse: How Societies Choose to Fail or Succeed* (New York: Viking, 2005), 341. For an excellent analysis of Haiti's fragility and vulnerability, see Amélie Gauthier and Madalena Moita, "External Shocks to Fragile States: Building Resilience in Haiti," in *Fixing Haiti: MINUSTAH and Beyond*, ed. Jorge Heine and Andrew S. Thompson (Tokyo: United Nations University Press, 2011), 27–40.

2. Upon winning the election, Duvalier institutionalized the Tontons Macoutes—the unofficial, pro-Duvalier militia—in order to create a rival force to the army. For details, see Michel S. Laguerre, *The Military and Society in Haiti* (Knoxville: University of Tennessee Press, 1993).

3. Robert Fatton, Jr., "The Fall of Aristide and Haiti's Current Predicament," in *Haiti: Hope for a Fragile State*, ed. Yasmine Shamsie and Andrew S. Thompson (Waterloo, ON: Wilfrid Laurier Press and Centre for International Governance Innovation, 2006), 18.

4. Of the $150,000, $40,000 was in the form of immediate disbursements, while $110,000 was earmarked for future commitments. CIDA, *Annual Aid Review* (Ottawa: Government of Canada, 1974), 41.

5. CIDA, *Annual Report, 1974–75* (Ottawa: Government of Canada, 1975), 12.

6. CIDA, *Annual Report, 1975–76* (Ottawa: Government of Canada, 1976), 59, 135.

7. CIDA, *Annual Report, 1977–78* (Ottawa: Government of Canada, 1978), 20.

8. See Sean Mills, "Quebec, Haiti, and the Deportation Crisis of 1974," *Canadian Historical Review* 94, no. 3 (September 2013): 424; Ruth Compton Brouwer, "When Missions Became Development: Ironies of 'NGOization' in Mainstream Canadian Churches in the 1960s," *Canadian Historical Review* 91, no. 4 (December 2010): 661–93.

9. CIDA, "News Release," No. 81-58, 28 November 1981, 1–2.

10. USAID, *Congressional Presentation, Fiscal Year 1978, Annex III: Latin America and the Caribbean* (Washington, DC: GPO, 1979), 129, 143.

11. The problem of illegal immigration from Haiti was not unique to the United States. As Mills explains, Canada had its own "deportation crisis" in 1974, when the Trudeau government attempted to deport

1,500 low-skilled Haitians, a move that prompted widespread public outcry from the Haitian diaspora community, as well as sympathetic civil society, faith, and Quebec nationalist groups. See Mills, "Quebec, Haiti, and the Deportation Crisis of 1974," 405–35.

12 United Nations General Assembly, A/40/432, 25 October 1985, 5–6.

13 "Message to the Congress Transmitting Proposed Caribbean Basin Initiative Legislation, 17 March 1982," *Public Papers of the Presidents of the United States: Ronald Reagan* (Washington, DC: GPO, 1983), 315.

14 In 1973, Amnesty International issued its first comprehensive assessment of the human rights situation in Haiti. It found evidence of roughly four hundred cases of political prisoners who had been detained and charged with violating the 1969 Anti-Communist Law, which gave the government the authority to imprison, and even execute, anyone it deemed a threat to national security. Moreover, it found evidence of prisoners being subjected to torture and ill-treatment; those who became ill were denied both medical care and the opportunity to speak with a priest. See Amnesty International, "Report on the Situation of Political Prisoners in Haiti, 1973" (London: Amnesty International Publications, 1973), 3; Amnesty International, "Amnesty Hints at Haiti's 'Cynicism and Deception' Over Political Prisoners" (London: Amnesty International Publications, 1 March 1973), 1; Amnesty International, "News Release," (London: Amnesty International Publications, 9 January 1977); Amnesty International, "Haiti: Human Rights Violations, October 1980 to October 1981" (London: Amnesty International Publications, November 1981), 3; Americas Watch, "Haiti: Report of a Human Rights Mission, 26–29 June 1983" (New York: Americas Watch in conjunction with the Lawyer's Committee for International Human Rights, August 1983), 8.

15 USAID, *Congressional Presentation, Fiscal Year 1988, Annex III: Latin America and the Caribbean* (Washington, DC: GPO, 1988), 234–35.

16 CIDA, "News Release," no. 87-17, 9 March 1987, 1.

17 CIDA, "News Release," 24 November 1986.

18 For two excellent assessments of the significance of the 1987 Constitution on Haiti's political culture see Robert Fatton, Jr., "Haiti's Unending Crisis of Governance: Food, the Constitution and the Struggle for Power," and Mirlande Manigat, "The Legacy of the 1987 Constitution: Reform or Renewal?", both in *Fixing Haiti: MINUSTAH and Beyond*, 41–65, 66–77.

19 United Nations General Assembly (UNGA), A/41/PV.23, 6 October 1986, 60.

20 UNGA, A/41/PV.100, 12 December 1986, 12.

21 Washington Office on Haiti, "Action Alert" (Washington, D.C.: Washington Office on Haiti, 1 July 1987); Washington Office on Haiti,

"Action Alert" (Washington, D.C.: Washington Office on Haiti, 28 July 1987).

22 Washington Office on Haiti, "Democratic Process in Jeopardy in Haiti" (Washington, DC: Washington Office on Haiti, 3 November 1987), 1.

23 For an account of the deterioration of the human rights climate in Haiti during this period, see Andrew S. Thompson, "Haiti's Tenuous Human Rights Climate," in *Haiti: Hope for a Fragile State*, 53–56.

24 USAID, *Congressional Presentation, Fiscal Year 1989, Annex III: Latin America and the Caribbean* (Washington, D.C.: GPO, 1989), 222.

25 *Hansard*, 30 November 1987, 11306-308

26 CIDA, "News Release 88-03," 8 January 1988, 2–3.

27 For international condemnation of the election results at the United Nations, see UN, Economic and Social Council (ECOSOC), E/CN.4/1988/NGO/48, 16 February 1988, 2; UN, ECOSOC, E/CN.4/1988/SR.34, 1 March 1988, 19; and UN, ECOSOC, E/CN.4/1988/SR.35, 1 March 1988, 2.

28 *Hansard*, House of Commons, 21 January 1988, 12177-8.

29 UN, ECOSOC, E/CN.4/1988/NGO/6, 10 June 1988, 2.

30 Amnesty International, "Haiti: Current Concerns" (London: Amnesty International Publications, November 1988), 3.

31 UN doc. E/CN.4/1989/40, 6 February 1989, paragraphs 45–90.

32 USAID, *Congressional Presentation, Fiscal Year 1991, Annex III: Latin America and the Caribbean* (Washington, DC: GPO, 1991), 149.

33 CIDA, "News Release," no. 89-63, 1 December 1989, 1.

34 See Thompson, "Haiti's Tenuous Human Rights Climate."

35 CIDA, "News Release," no. 90-13," 14 March 1990; CIDA, "News Release," no. 90-17, 25 March 1990.

36 United Nations Security Council (UNSC), S/23109, 3 October 1991, 3–4; UNSC, S/23132, 9 October 1991, 2–3.

37 Amnesty International, "Haiti: Human Rights Violations in the Aftermath of the Coup D'état, October 1991" (London: Amnesty International Publications, October 1991), 3.

38 *Hansard*, House of Commons, 1 October 1991, 3052.

39 UNGA, A/46/PV.31, 18 October 1991, 19–21.

40 "Exchange with Reporters Prior to Discussion with President Jean-Bertrand Aristide of Haiti, 4 October 1991," *Public Papers of the Presidents of the United States: George Bush* (Washington, DC: GPO, 1992), 1260.

41 According to the NLC, USAID had also objected to the reform on the ground that it would make Haiti less competitive and stifle economic growth. See NLC, "Sweatshop Development," *The Haiti Files: Decoding the Crisis*, ed. James Ridgeway (Washington, DC: Essential Books, 1994), 135–44.

42 "Executive Order 12779—Prohibiting Certain Transactions With Respect to Haiti," 28 October 1991, http://www.presidency.ucsb.edu/ws/?pid=20157 (accessed 17 May 2014).

43 Amnesty International, "Haiti: The Human Rights Tragedy—Human Rights Violations Since the Coup" (London: Amnesty International Publications, January 1992), 2–8.

44 UN, ECOSOC, E/CN.4/1992/SR.45, 3 March 1992, 5.

45 See "White House Statement on Haitian Migrants," *Public Papers of the Presidents of the United States: George Bush*, 818; and "Remarks and a Question-and-Answer Session with the Mount Paran Christian School Community in Marietta," *Public Papers of the Presidents of the United States: George Bush*, 831–32.

46 UNGA, A/47/1000, 13 August 1993.

47 Roland I. Perusse, *Haitian Democracy Restored, 1991–1995* (New York: University Press of America, Inc., 1995), 55.

48 UNSC Resolution 873, 13 October 1993, 1; and UNSC Res. 875, 16 October 1993, 2.

49 UNGA, A/48/931, 29 April 1994, 4.

50 Amnesty International, "USA/Haiti: The Price of Rejection—Human Rights Consequences for Rejected Haitian Asylum-Seekers" (London: Amnesty International Publications, May 1994), 6.

51 UNSC Res 940, 31 July 1994, 2.

52 UNSC Res 1529, 29 February 2004.

53 Jim Garamone, "Powell Visits Haiti, Says U.N. Action Averted 'Bloodbath,'" American Forces Press Service, 6 April 2004.

54 See, for example, "CIDA's Key Role in Haiti's 2004 Coup d'État: Funding Regime Change, Dictatorship and Human Rights Atrocities, One Haitian NGO at a Time," *Press for Conversion* 61 (September 2007).

55 Canada, Standing Committee on Foreign Affairs and International Development, "Canada's International Policy Put to the Test in Haiti," Ottawa, December 2006, 2, 25.

56 Baranyi, "Canada and the Travail of Partnership," in *Fixing Haiti: MINUSTAH and Beyond*, 205–28.

57 Canada, "Government Response to the Eighth Report of the Standing Committee on Foreign Affairs and International Development *A Focus on Democracy Support*," 2 November 2007, http://cmte.parl.gc.ca/cmte/CommitteePublication.aspx?SourceId=216092 (accessed 21 November 2007).

58 http://www.acdi-cida.gc.ca/cidaweb/acdicida.nsf/En/NIC-54102116-JUN (accessed 8 November 2007).

59 Standing Committee on Foreign Affairs and International Development, "Advancing Canada's Role in International Support for Democratic Development" (Ottawa: Government of Canada, July 2007), 13. For a critique of Canada's good governance programming, see Ian Smillie, "Boy Scouts and Fearful Angels: The Evolution of Canada's International Good Governance Agenda," in *Exporting Good Governance: Temptations*

and *Challenges in Canada's Aid Program*, eds. Jennifer Welsh and Ngaire Woods (Waterloo, ON: The Centre for International Governance Innovation and Wilfrid Laurier University Press, 2007), 41–71.

60   CIDA, "Canadian Cooperation with Haiti: Reflecting on a Decade of 'Difficult Partnership'" (Ottawa: Government of Canada, 2004), 6.

61   Ibid., 8.

62   As quoted in Robert Muggah, "The Perils of Changing Donor Priorities: The Case of Haiti," in *Exporting Good Governance*, 171.

63   For a critique of current Canadian initiatives relating to security sector reform, see Stephen Baranyi, "Le Canada, Haïti et les dilemmes de l'intervention dans les 'États fragiles,'" Ébauche présentée au Congrès de LASA à Montréal, 5–8 septembre 2007, 9–12.

64   Muggah, "The Perils of Changing Donor Priorities," 183.

65   Standing Committee on Foreign Affairs and International Development, "Canada's International Policy Put to the Test in Haiti," Ottawa, December 2006, 10.

66   Muggah, "The Perils of Changing Donor Priorities," 172–73.

67   Baranyi, "Le Canada, Haïti et les dilemmes de l'intervention dans les 'États fragiles,'" 5.

68   See Amélie Gauthier and Madalena Moita, "External Shocks to Fragile States," 27–40; and Robert Fatton, Jr. "Haiti's Unending Crisis of Governance," 41–65.

69   Maguire, "US Policy toward Haiti," 230; Jorge Heine and Andrew S. Thompson, "Introduction: Haiti's Governance Challenges and the International Community," in *Fixing Haiti: MINUSTAH and Beyond*, 2.

70   Tonda MacCharles, "Governor General delivers tearful statement on Haiti," *Toronto Star,* 13 January 2010, http://www.thestar.com/news/world/2010/01/13/governor_general_delivers_tearful_statement_on_haiti.html (accessed 11 April 2015).

71   Baranyi, "Canada and the Travail of Partnership," 222.

72   See Amnesty International, "Haiti: After the Earthquake—Initial Mission Findings, March 2010" (London: Amnesty International, March 2010).

73   Fatton, "Haiti's Unending Crisis of Governance," 56.

CHAPTER 6

DIAGNOSTIC CONFUSION AND MISSED OPPORTUNITIES:
Canada and Pakistan's "Failed State"[1]

Julian Schofield

Since the end of the Cold War, Canada and its Western allies have had a strong global interest in reducing the incidence of failed states. At first glance, Pakistan seems to fit this profile, as it confronts widespread poverty, terrorist groups, possibly insecure nuclear weapons, and substantial tracts of territory beyond the control of its central government.[2] Indeed, in 2008, the *Economist* described Pakistan as the world's most dangerous state. Yet neither Canada, nor its Western allies, are as deeply engaged in Pakistan as this description would warrant. This chapter tackles this paradox, exploring Canada's long and fitful engagement with Pakistan.

Pakistan only partially meets the failed state criteria, and it remains sufficiently strong to deter foreign intervention and resist external efforts to re-engineer its social and political institutions. As a result, neither Canada nor its allies have treated Pakistan as a failed state, despite the rhetoric of failure. Historically, Canada has mobilized aid to support Pakistan, in conjunction with its Anglo-American allies, only when the Asian nation has been under acute threat. At the same time, Canada tried to promote stability in Indo-Pakistani relations, notably through its participation in the United Nations (UN) peacekeeping mission in Kashmir from 1949 until 1978.[3] Although Canadian politicians have tilted slightly to one side or the other—Prime Minister John Diefenbaker favoured Pakistan while Prime Minister Lester B. Pearson supported India—Canada has been consistently impartial.[4] For example, Diefenbaker declined to support Pakistan's goal of a plebiscite for Kashmir,[5] and Prime Minister Pierre Trudeau refused to downgrade relations with Pakistan in the early 1970s, despite an appeal by Indian Prime Minister Indira Gandhi.[6]

Ottawa was heavily involved in offering aid to Pakistan during the early stages of the Cold War, but reduced its effort in the 1970s as the bipolar conflict in Asia eased following the end of the Vietnam War. Similarly, Canada re-engaged with Islamabad after the destabilizing terrorist attacks on the United States of 11 September 2001 and the collapse of the Taliban government in neighbouring Afghanistan. Compared to the stakes of the US, China, India, and Saudi Arabia, Canada's direct political influence is comparatively weak. Nevertheless, a long, cordial relationship has guaranteed a persistent minimum baseline of Canadian help for Pakistan and has ensured Ottawa's persistent engagement, however marginal, in Pakistan's survival.

Qualifying Pakistani State Failure

Pakistan is neither a failed, fragile, or weak state, nor is it under threat of imminent collapse. According to former US ambassador to Pakistan William Milam, "Pakistan is not a failed state.... But it is a country of failed politics with a failed political class."[7] Pakistan is perhaps best characterized as a multi-ethnic, semi-industrialized developing state. The three most commonly identified avenues toward contemporary state failure in Pakistan all include scenarios of state hijacking, the probabilities of which are all remote: a military-Islamist coup, civil war, or an Islamist electoral victory.

The prospects of an Islamist coup seem far-fetched. Pakistan has seen eight coup attempts between February 1951 and October 1999, and in all cases no coup has proceeded beyond the planning phase without the approval of its military, the guardian of the secular elite. Coups that did not receive this endorsement failed abruptly (1951, 1971, and 1973), including an Islamist-inspired attempt in 1994. Consent for a coup must come either from the chief of the general staff, in consultation with his principal subordinates, or from the corps commanders' conference, which has become a routinized aspect of the Pakistani army's process of policy deliberation. The physical barrier to a successful coup is the 111th Brigade, which protects Pakistan's capital, Islamabad, and its military headquarters in Rawalpindi, buttressed by several significant corps-sized formations located nearby.

Nor is a coup likely to originate from an intelligence organization,[8] given their subordinate status within the military hierarchy. In effect, for an Islamist coup in Pakistan to produce a failed state outcome would require the conjunction of a collapse of the cohesion of the Pakistani army, a thorough political Islamist infiltration of that institution, and the emergence of a centrifugal Islamist regime. While the second outcome is plausible, the latter is more likely to be socially centripetal, given the shallow public support for Islamist governance in Pakistan.[9]

Pakistan is also unlikely to collapse as a result of civil war. Concerns in 2009 and 2010, mainly regarding Pashtun Islamist insurgents in the Swat Valley, a mere hundred kilometres from some of Pakistan's nuclear facilities, exaggerated the country's vulnerability. For the last two centuries, there have been no successful, sustained penetrations by Pashtun insurgents into the Punjab, the demographic and industrial core of Pakistan. The reasons are obvious: Pakistan's formidable military consists of 600,000 volunteers, organized in 28 divisions and equipped with 2,400 tanks, 4,200 artillery pieces, and almost 400 combat aircraft. More importantly, Pakistan has shown itself capable of effectively suppressing domestic opposition: the Bengalis of East Pakistan in 1971; the Baloch in five separate campaigns; Sindhi separatists; and the Mohajirs in Karachi in the 1990s. Efforts to interdict the sanctuaries of the Pakistan Taliban (the Tehreek-e-Taliban), the government's principal adversary along the Afghan frontier, were ongoing as of 2014. Only an upheaval in Pakistan's core, the Punjab, would have any hope of displacing the military. Revolts originating in the periphery are rarely strong enough to challenge Pakistan's army, which has little difficulty maintaining domestic control.[10] If Pakistan were to succumb to an Islamist regime at the conclusion of a civil war, the new regime would likely be at least as centralized and developmentally oriented as current secular regimes, making state failure an unlikely outcome.[11]

Outside of the Punjab, however, Pakistan's parochial and unrepresentative methods of governance have generated periodic separatist movements (mentioned above), most notably in East Pakistan in 1970–71. When unrest occurs in conjunction with foreign intervention, as it did when Indian support for East Pakistan produced the breakaway state of Bangladesh, Pakistan's weak consolidation of peripheral populations has brought it very close to failed state status. Its success in surviving Bangladesh's secession attests to its strength and resiliency.

Finally, some analysts have speculated that Islamist political parties might capture segments of the Pakistani state through the electoral process, resulting in a failure in domestic governance.[12] This too seems very unlikely. Religious parties in Pakistan typically win just 5 to 10 percent of the popular vote, rising to as much as 20 percent when boosted through ballot manipulation by domestic intelligence agencies. One leading Islamist party, Jamiat-i-Islami, did not even field candidates in the 2008 elections due to its low prospects. Moreover, Islamic political influence has been strongest when operating in conjunction with powerful military or political partners, whose support for the unity of the *ummah* (community) is likely to enhance the cohesion of the Pakistani state rather than undermine it. Clearly, Pakistan is not a traditional failed state, though it might more appropriately be described as a developmentally feeble state.

Chronic Underdevelopment

The principal source of instability in Pakistan is its chronically underdeveloped and neglected population. With an adjusted Purchasing Power Parity 2010 Gross Domestic Product (GDP) per capita of just $2,400, close to 60 percent of the population lives on less than $2 a day.[13] Pakistan consequently ranks 145th out of 187 states on the United Nations Development Programme's 2011 Human Development Index.[14] It is plagued by high infant and maternal mortality rates, and its gender-discriminating education system, which reaches only 5 percent of the population, is inadequate to the task of helping the 61 percent of Pakistan's population that is under the age of twenty-five to escape unemployment and poverty.[15]

Though Pakistan's bureaucracy is comparatively well organized, it has limited reach into society, as indicated by the fact that only 2 percent of earners pay income tax.[16] This problem is not the result of military government or shadow influence: military regimes in Pakistan usually promote macroeconomic stability and growth, and there is little evidence that reducing the defence budget would produce a peace dividend available for social spending.[17] Moreover, military-owned manufacturing can be a sensible form of industrial policy in some sectors. Similarly, Islam is not a genuine obstacle to development in Pakistan, despite its perceived hostility to Western policy goals. Its role in promoting madrassahs—religious schools—the majority of which are peaceful, mostly helps to fill an educational vacuum on behalf of the marginalized. Islam often fosters and promotes the cultural unity of Pakistan, and sustains a favourable distribution of wealth, facilitating Pakistan's comparatively good Gini co-efficient score of 3.0 (comparable to Canada's rating).[18]

Pakistan's main impediment to development is its landed and industrial elites, whose vested interest in plentiful and low-wage labour and whose desire to preserve the social order maintains a system of widespread poverty.[19] This neglect has not been sufficient to arrest socio-economic development, though. Foreign direct investment starting in the 1950s, socialist and pro-labour policies in the 1970s, and a focus on manufacturing and infrastructure through to the 1990s have contributed substantially, though slowly, to socio-economic transformation. Approximately 50 percent of Pakistanis live in towns or larger cities. Industrialization, and the capitalization and mechanization of agriculture, are proceeding, though predominantly in the Punjab. Pakistan is therefore not a failed state in the conventional sense, but a state with a feeble developmental priority, where there is an unwillingness to provide a social-political framework in which citizens can meet their basic needs. In the obstacles it faces and its development statistics, Pakistan is not much different from India.

Canadian Aid Policy in the Context of Alliance Politics

Canada's primary interest in Pakistan is linked to its involvement in Afghanistan and its response to the North Atlantic Treaty Organization's (NATO) invocation of Article V for Collective Defence after the terror attacks of 9/11.[20] Despite the rhetoric around Pakistan's failed state status, Canadian involvement in South Asia is largely a product of Pakistan's strategic importance and not the result of a focus on the country's domestic weaknesses.[21] Indeed, Ottawa's strategic interests coincide with those of its major allies: supporting a democratic, united India, and reconstructing a secure, stable Afghanistan.[22] Canadian engagement with Pakistan has been inadequate to the task of addressing issues of nuclear security and clandestine support for Islamist militants, even when these have directly affected Canadian operations in Afghanistan.

In Ottawa, Canada's Pakistan policy springs from two locations. In the short run, Afghan policy, which drives Canada's current approach to South Asia, has been centralized within the Prime Minister's Office (PMO) and the Privy Council Office.[23] The two central agencies have drawn upon help from the Canadian International Development Agency (CIDA), the Department of Foreign Affairs and International Trade (DFAIT), and the Treasury Board.[24] Pakistan's nominal failed state status provided these policymakers with a convenient political fiction to explain NATO's failures in Afghanistan and a tool to bolster public support for its military efforts in Afghanistan. Encouraged by the Ottawa bureaucracy, the national media easily cast Pakistan as a prototypical failed state.[25]

Yet, despite social fragility, Pakistan remains a strong state, and is regionally pivotal, with significant strategic impacts on Afghanistan, India, and China, and even on Saudi Arabia and Iran.[26] Pakistan possesses a virtual veto over the success or failure of NATO's mission in Afghanistan, where it carefully pursues a sound and deliberate foreign policy focused on neutralizing Kabul as a source of Pashtun separatism, as opposed to indicating a lack of state capacity.[27] This inaccurate failed state discourse has encouraged Canada to allow its larger allies to manage the complicated relations with Pakistan and to join NATO in making unreasonable requests of Pakistan.[28] These include pressing Islamabad to sign the Non-Proliferation Treaty (NPT) and to shut down insurgent sanctuaries, without a *quid pro quo* from Kabul on its non-recognition of the Pakistan-Afghan frontier.[29] One recent and concrete policy setback, which highlighted Canada's failure to appreciate fully Islamabad's strategic interest in weakening Afghanistan, was Ottawa's proposal for joint Pakistan-Afghanistan border security, raised repeatedly in 2009, 2010, and 2011. The proposal for joint action to control borders, customs, and narcotics smuggling was ignored by the two rival states, which viewed the scheme as an unwelcome intrusion.[30]

The second, long-run influence on Canada's Pakistan policy is the historical isolation of CIDA from DFAIT. This division explains the steady persistence and consistency of Canada's developmental assistance, despite a range of troubling political incidents within Pakistan that have led Canadian allies like the United States to reduce their aid. Historically, CIDA has been reluctant to secure and wield diplomatic influence. However, in the Asian context, where Canada has traditionally put an emphasis on security at the behest of its allies, this view has been challenged, with critics complaining that Canada has not clearly linked its aid program to tangible foreign policy objectives.[31] Canada's initial support for Colombo Plan aid, which aimed to raise the standard of living in South Asia to offset the attractions of Cold War communism, was explicitly political. But this had largely wound down by the 1970s, and along with it, direct Canadian influence. Ottawa continued development aid to Pakistan until its Western allies reduced their support following the 1971 civil war in East Pakistan and India's 1974 nuclear test.[32] Instead, Canada shifted aid to Africa, the Caribbean, and Latin America, and never returned to its earlier level of activity in South Asia, even as the US and Britain backed Pakistan against the Soviet Union in Afghanistan in the 1980s. By the same token, neither did Canada reduce its support much when Soviet forces withdrew in 1989.[33] Canada has thus had a more consistent aid presence than many of its more powerful allies.

Canada's Legacy of Development Assistance

Canada shifted its preference for aid disbursement from the UN to the Commonwealth Colombo Plan with the outbreak of the Korean War in 1950.[34] The threat of the spread of Communist insurrection in the underdeveloped areas of the world prompted Canada to join its liberal allies in providing development assistance to Asia.[35] Pakistan in particular was viewed as suffering from widespread poverty, but it was run by a pro-Western elite, with which Canada has been able to maintain good relations for over six decades.[36] Significantly, Canada never required any political change in Pakistan as the price of its decades of largesse.[37] Between 1950 and 1967, Canada sent a third of its $227 million in Colombo Plan aid money to Pakistan.[38] By the 1990s, Canadian official development assistance (ODA) help for the Asian nation totalled almost $2 billion.[39] Of Canada's five major industrial development projects overseas between 1950 and 1965, three were in Pakistan, highlighting Canada's significant efforts.[40] By 1967, Canada ranked fourth among donors to Pakistan. But the focus on Cold War security rather than governance helped reinforce weak government institutions.[41] In the early 1980s, Canada reduced, but did not end, its economic assistance to Pakistan.[42] Pakistan's civil war in 1971, the emergence of a socialist government in Islamabad focused on corporate expropriations and debt moratoria, and the development of regional nuclear tensions in the mid-1970s created pressures from India to suspend aid, but Canada did not. Instead, it followed the US in maintaining a presence in Pakistan, variously justifying its efforts as measures to prevent regional conflict, to promote market access, and to advance human rights.[43] Through the 1980s, Canada's goals continued to include the provision of emergency assistance.[44] After 1970, Canada's ranking as a Pakistani aid donor was never higher than fourth (at 6.4 percent of aid),[45] and often lower, and absolute amounts were either static or gradually reduced from $47 million in 1970 to $36 million in 1989.[46] Overall, of the US$19.5 billion in foreign aid to Pakistan between 1950 and 1982, Canada provided US$961 million, or 4.92 percent of the total, an economically significant but politically immaterial amount.[47]

In 1965, Canada and Pakistan agreed to establish the Karachi Nuclear Power Plant (KANUPP) reactor to provide electricity to the city's 3.5

Figure 1: For much of the Cold War, Canada used its foreign aid to woo pro-Western Pakistan and promote economic linkages. The 1959 atomic energy agreement, signed by Prime Minister John Diefenbaker and High Commissioner for Pakistan Samuel Martin Burke on 14 May 1959, did both. (Credit: Duncan Cameron/Library and Archives Canada, e010836507)

million inhabitants.[48] Once construction was completed in 1971, Canada contracted to assist Pakistan in building a nuclear fuel production plant, including heavy water and parts.[49] Subsequent to India's 1974 nuclear test, however, Canada terminated the agreement when Pakistan refused to enact full-scope safeguards. This resulted in Pakistan suffering serious slowdowns and technical challenges in the operation of KANUPP, and had a significant, negative short-term impact on Canadian-Pakistan relations.[50] Canada's efforts at segregating the nuclear dispute from Canada's broader aid assistance to Pakistan, together with its generous aid offering of C$700 million in 1979, helped preserve good relations. When Pakistan was suspected of developing a nuclear weapon in 1980, Canada complained to Islamabad, but did not, as the US did, suspend all aid.[51]

Current State of Canada's Assistance

Canada's development assistance to Pakistan changed little in the 1980s.[52] With the end of the Cold War, aid shifted to a focus on social spending, specifically nutrition, education, and women's issues.[53] Canada's ranking as an aid donor shifted between fourth and fifth in the 1990s, with annual aid valued between $39 and $52 million, consistent with amounts disbursed in the 1970s, adjusted for inflation.[54] In 1992, for example, Canada accounted for 2 percent of Pakistan's aid. Canada's reluctance to engage Pakistan was further tempered by human rights issues and concerns among the Western allies regarding Pakistan's nuclear proliferation efforts.[55] Japan, for example, cut off half a billion dollars in aid in response to Pakistan's nuclear test in 1998, and did not resume aid assistance until 2005.[56] Ottawa also believed that Canada's strategic interests would be better served in developing ties with the newly liberated states of Central and Eastern Europe, as opposed to increasing aid to Pakistan.[57]

American engagement in Afghanistan immediately after the terrorist attacks of September 2001 led to an increase in all forms of aid to Pakistan by as much as 200 percent, followed by a general decline in ODA over the next ten years as rifts emerged between Washington and Islamabad.[58] US aid from 2001 to 2011 totalled US$13.3 billion in security assistance and US$7.3 in economic and developmental aid.[59] By 2008 Pakistan was receiving US$1.5 billion in ODA annually, up from $1 billion in the 1990s, of which the top contributor was the European Union (EU).[60] Canada's annual contribution increased from C$62 million in 2002 to C$80 million by 2011. Though a significant proportion of this was in response to specific floods and earthquakes, overall ODA was consistent with levels in the 1980s and 1990s.[61] By 2010–11, Canada's bilateral aid shrank back to C$30 million ($83 million with multilateral aid),[62] placing Canada thirteenth among ODA donors to Pakistan, out of a total pool of US$1 billion.[63]

Canada's involvement in Afghanistan led it to define Pakistan as a fragile state and to resume higher levels of direct aid.[64] Canada's interest in educational programs in Pakistan also reflects its link with Afghanistan and the need to create educational alternatives to the radical madrassah network.[65] These are consistent with Canada's millennium goals, which focus on eradicating poverty, universal primary education, gender equality, reducing child mortality, improving maternal health, disease control, and ensuring environmental sustainability.[66] Efforts in Pakistan fit into Canada's overall plan of targeting the world's fragile states with C$800 million in ODA, supplemented by a further C$1.2 billion in multilateral aid.[67] Canada briefly emerged as a top-five humanitarian aid donor in 2008, following floods in Pakistan that year.[68] In 2009, Canada identified Pakistan as a "country of focus," meaning it was one of twenty states receiving 80 percent of CIDA's funding.[69]

But aid has translated into little real influence upon efforts to bolster the Pakistani state. There have been problems with the effectiveness of Canadian aid to Pakistan arising from nepotism in the aid community, and the dominant position occupied by an elite group of approximately fifty NGOs out of some 95,000 agencies operating in the country.[70] Canada has been slow to implement projects, which get bogged down by Ottawa's preoccupation with financial accountability.[71] Pakistan furthermore claims that what aid has been delivered is miniscule, given the 35,000 Pakistani casualties and the claimed US$68 billion in costs to Pakistan associated with NATO's engagement in Afghanistan since 2002.[72] In 2013, Pakistan ranked just fifteenth among Canada's bilateral aid recipients (with Afghanistan in first place).[73]

What success Canada has had in obtaining diplomatic influence from ODA has largely to do with the Pakistani elite's memory of historical Canadian contributions to Pakistan's development and their trust in Canadian intentions. This has translated into open access for Canadian aid programs and good local working relations, even with Islamist social groups.[74]

The Remaining Instruments of Influence: Commerce, Domestic Values, and Military Ties

Canada's relatively weak influence in Pakistan also stems from the two countries' limited bilateral trade.[75] The historical level of trade has remained low despite numerous attempts to increase it through such missions as Prime Minister Jean Chrétien's 1995 trade initiative in South Asia.[76] The principal reasons for this low level of bilateral trade are perceived unfair contract competitions, institutional impediments to imports, including protectionism and corruption, and a lack of interest in Pakistan by Canadian exporters and investors. Pakistani exporters have also failed to appreciate the Canadian market, while its importers rarely think of Canada as a source for high-tech and other high-value products.[77] Pakistan's focus has instead been on trade with the US and EU.[78]

The possibility that Canada might exert some influence over Pakistan by mobilizing the diaspora community and its Canadian values has been mitigated by the small size of the expatriate communities in Canada and Pakistan. South Asian immigration to Canada grew steadily after 1962 until it numbered in the hundreds of thousands in the 1970s.[79] This has resulted in as many as 300,000 Pakistani-Canadians.[80] Two federal Pakistani-Canadian members of Parliament have represented this community: Rahim Jaffer (Edmonton-Strathcona, Conservative, 1997–2008) and Wajid Khan (Mississauga, Liberal 2004–2007, Conservative 2008).[81] But neither they nor the broader Pakistani community have tried to marshal their forces to impress Pakistan's interests on Canadian legislators.[82] Foreign Affairs officials considered reaching out to the diaspora to leverage their ties but considered it too fragmented and under-mobilized to proceed.[83] Canada's contact with the Ismaili Agha Khan Foundation has facilitated some trade and immigration but affects only a small segment of Pakistan's population.[84] Nor does the small number of Pakistani students and tourists travelling to Canada represent an effective bridge between the countries.[85] In 2005 there were 502 student visas, growing to just 902 by 2009.[86] Pakistani tourists, though the trend is headed upward, totalled a miniscule 18,700 in 2010.[87]

Canada's military influence on Pakistan comes through two avenues: its historic peacekeeping role in the region and direct military-to-military ties. Canada was an early participant in the United Nations Military Observer Group in India and Pakistan (UNMOGIP), set up in 1949 to police a ceasefire in Kashmir.[88] Peacekeeping ties were buttressed by Canada's military links with Pakistan's military academies, especially after 1993, when the High Commission in Islamabad added a military attaché and arranged for a Canadian Forces major-equivalent to be posted to the Pakistani army's staff college at Quetta.[89] These ties were further strengthened when a small number of future Pakistani generals completed courses at the Canadian Army Staff College in Kingston during the 1990s. Canadian

Figure 2: Canada has sustained a long military presence in Pakistan, beginning in 1949, when it joined the UN Military Observer Group in India and Pakistan (UNMOGIP). Brigadier H.H. Angle (right with UN armband), the first Canadian to command a UN mission, is seen checking the positions of opposing troops in Kashmir in January 1949. (Credit: UN Photo 83976)

policymakers hoped that nurturing close links with the army, given its pre-eminent role in Pakistan and its growing exposure to radical Islamist pressures, would facilitate the transmission of Canadian values.[90] However, Canada's influence on the Pakistani military has always been significantly smaller than that of the US, UK, or China, and it was realized that Canada realistically exerted very little influence.[91] The Pakistan army's consistent preference for technocratic political forms, and occasional tolerance of democracy and secularism, had far more to do with the British political legacy than any influence Canada has exerted.[92] All ties between the Canadian and Pakistani militaries were terminated in 2001 following 9/11, though some links have since been re-established.[93]

Net Diplomatic Influence and Policy Implications

Canadian aid to Pakistan has formed part of a broader historical effort by the West to combat the appeal of hostile, illiberal ideologies—communism during the Cold War and radical Islamism since the early 1990s. According Pakistan failed state status helped legitimize these efforts, even as the label became increasingly inaccurate. The relative lack of Canadian foreign aid, low levels of bilateral commerce, and the limited range of Canada's direct domestic and military-to-military contacts have significantly limited Canada's influence on Pakistan, despite generally cordial relations. Moreover, Canada's weak position in Pakistan stands in sharp contrast to the much more dynamic roles occupied by Saudi Arabia, China, the US, the EU, Japan, and even the United Arab Emirates.[94] Ottawa is simply not in a position to push forward policies designed to avert state failure in Pakistan, even if they were required. Pakistan is too large and too complex for Canada and its small local footprint to have a meaningful impact.

Historically, fragile state rhetoric has hidden this simple truth from Canadian policymakers, who have often responded to Pakistani developments with unrealistic interventionist policies.[95] Canadian prime minister Louis St. Laurent, for instance, alienated Pakistan with his reluctant support for a Kashmiri plebiscite in the late 1940s.[96] Two decades later, Canada's neutral stance during the 1965 Indo-Pakistani War led an angry mob to tear down the Canadian flag at the High Commission.[97] Ottawa's efforts to convince Pakistan to abide by the NPT in 1998 similarly failed, because Canadian policymakers ignored Pakistan's strong strategic interest in deterring India and overestimated the value of Ottawa's diminished aid.[98] More recently, Canadian attempts to foster a Pakistan-Afghan dialogue collapsed in the face of Pakistan opposition.[99] Observers with considerable knowledge of both Canada and Pakistan consider the attempted imposition of Canada's Western, liberal values as foolhardy and inappropriate.[100]

A reasonable Pakistan policy for Ottawa would be one that encourages Pakistan to moderate its domestic and foreign policies, encourages a reduction in defence expenditures and non-proliferation, promotes trade and investment, and obtains access for ODA—all policies that Canadian diplomats have in fact been pursuing with reasonable consistency.[101] To that extent, Canada's policies are most similar to those of the EU, with a shared emphasis on human rights and democratization.[102] What Canada should not do, because it lacks the power and the domestic support, is to play a major role in Kashmir, or intercede between Afghanistan and Pakistan, or India and Pakistan.[103] Canada needs to recognize that as a middle power it can follow no third path, but must remain within the policy range of its alliances.

Notes

1. Considerable thanks are due to four former high commissioners to Pakistan who aided me in this project: Marie-Andrée Beauchemin, David Collins, Louis Delvoie, and Doug Small. Further thanks are due to Victor Carvel for his insights from CIDA's standpoint.

2. Kanti Bajpai, "India and Canada: Moving Ahead," in *Canada Among Nations 2009–2010*, ed. Fen Osler Hampson and Paul Heinbecker (Montreal: McGill-Queen's University Press, 2010), 160.

3. W. M. Dobell, "Canadian Relations with South Asia," in Paul Painchaud, ed., *From Mackenzie King to Pierre Trudeau* (Quebec: Les Presses de L'Universite de Laval, 1989), 356.

4. Dobell, "Canadian Relations with South Asia," 355.

5. M. Raziullah Azmi, *Pakistan-Canada Relations 1947–1982* (Islamabad: Quaid-i-Azam University, 1982), 28–29.

6. Dobell, "Canadian Relations with South Asia," 361.

7. William Milam, *Bangladesh and Pakistan: Flirting with Failure in South Asia* (London: Hurst, 2009), 243, cited in Richard Bonney, Tridivesh Singh Maini, and Tahir Malik, eds., *Warriors after War* (Oxford: Peter Lang, 2011), 31.

8. Here I refer specifically to the Inter-Services Intelligence (ISI), Military Intelligence (MI), Investigation Bureau (IB), or the Federal Investigation Service (FIS).

9. Julian Schofield and Michael Zekulin, "Appraising the Threat of an Islamist Military Coup in post-OBL Pakistan," *Defense and Security Analysis* 27, no. 4 (December 2011): 181–92.

10. Julian Schofield, "Pakistan's Counter-Insurgency Doctrine," in *Routledge Handbook of Insurgency*

11. Julian Schofield, "The Prospect of a Populist Islamist Takeover of Pakistan," in *Escaping Quagmire: Strategy, Security and the Future of Pakistan*, ed. Usama Butt and N. Elahi (New York: Continuum, 2010), 215–32.

12. Ajai Sahni. "A New Government Takes Charge," 9 June 2005, http://satp.org/satporgtp/sair/Archives/1_19.htm#assessment1.

13. Global Humanitarian Assistance, *Briefing Paper: Pakistan: Country Aid Factsheet* (Somerset: August 2010), 1.

14. United Nations Development Programme, "Human Development Reports," http://hdr.undp.org/en/statistics/ (accessed 14 January 2012).

15. Foreign Affairs, Trade and Development Canada, "Pakistan," http://www.acdi-cida.gc.ca/acdi-cida/acdi-cida.nsf/eng/jud-12916929-stl (accessed 14 January 2012); Campbell Clark, "Ottawa Bolsters Aid to Pakistan," *Globe and Mail*, 13 August 2009, http://www.theglobeandmail.com/news/politics/ottawa-bolsters-aid-to-pakistan/article4281763/ (accessed 14 November 2015).

16. David Carment and Yiagadeesen Samy, "Pakistan's Problems Now Ours," *Embassy*, 1 January 2010, http://embassymag.ca/page/view/pakistan-09-01-2010 (accessed 22 January 2012).

17. Ahmad Faruqui and Julian Schofield, "Pakistan: The Political Economy of Militarism," *Journal of Conflict, Security and Development* 2, no. 2 (2003): 5–23.

18. http://en.wikipedia.org/wiki/List_of_countries_by_income_equality (accessed 25 July 2014).

19. Interview, Louis Delvoie in discussion with the author, Montreal-Kingston, 23–24 January 2012; interview, Marie-Andrée Beauchemin in discussion with the author, Montreal-Italy, 27 January 2012; interview, David Collins in discussion with the author, Montreal-Kenya, 28 January 2012.

20. Duane Bratt, "Afghanistan: Why Did We Go? Why Did We Stay? Will We Leave?," in *Readings in Canadian Foreign Policy*, ed. Duane Bratt and Christopher Kukucha (Don Mills: Oxford University Press, 2011), 317, 321.

21. Johannes Braune, *Pakistan's Security Today and Tomorrow*, CSIS (22–23 January 2009), 11, http://publications.gc.ca/collections/collection_2013/scrs-csis/PS74-3-2009-eng.pdf (accessed 14 November 2015).

22. Dobell, "Canadian Relations with South Asia," 349, 351–52.

23. Gregory Chin, "Shifting Purpose—Asia's Rise and Canada's Foreign Aid," *International Journal* 64, no. 4 (Autumn 2009): 1004; interview, Louis Delvoie in discussion with the author.

24. Stephen Brown, "CIDA Under the Gun," in *Canada Among Nations 2007: What Room for Manoeuvre?*, ed. Jean Daudelin and Daniel Schwanen (Montreal: McGill-Queen's University Press, 2008), 172–207; Chin, "Shifting Purpose," 994.

25 Louis Delvoie, "Diplomacy at the Cold-Face: A Mission to Pakistan in the 1990s," in *Diplomatic Missions*, ed. Robert Wolfe (Kingston: Queen's University School of Policy Studies, 1998), 51.

26 Julian Schofield, "Pakistan's Strategic Trade with Afghanistan," *Sicherheit und Frieden* (Security and Peace), 4 (2010): 251–56; Julian Schofield, Brent Gerchicoff, and Jose Saramago, "Afghan Development Through Regional Trade," in *Afghanistan in the Balance: Counterinsurgency, Comprehensive Approach and Political Order*, ed. Hans-Georg Ehrhart (Montreal: McGill-Queen's University Press, 2011), 141–55; Julian Schofield, "Arms Races and War in the Indo-Pakistan Rivalry, 1947–1971," *Journal of South Asian and Middle Eastern Studies* 26, no. 3 (Spring 2003): 33–49.

27 Julian Schofield, "Diversionary Wars: Pashtun Unrest and the Sources of the Pakistan-Afghan Confrontation," *Canadian Foreign Policy Journal* 17, no. 1 (March 2011): 38–49.

28 Bill Gillespie, "Canadian's Terrorism Trial Points to Pakistani Double-Game," *CBC*, 11 June 2011, http://www.cbc.ca/news/world/story/2011/06/10/f-vp-gillespie-pakistan-headley.html (accessed 22 January 2012).

29 Julian Schofield and Jose Saramago, "Pakistani Interests in NATO's Afghanistan," in *Adaptation of NATO*, ed. Natalie Mychajlyszyn, 129–46, University of Manitoba Bison Papers Series 11 (Winnipeg: University of Manitoba Centre for Defence and Security Studies, 2008), 129–46.

30 Gerald Schmitz, *Canadian Policy Toward Afghanistan to 2011 and Beyond: issues, Prospects and Options* (Ottawa: Reference and Strategic Analysis Division, Parliamentary Information and Research Division, 2010), 7, 17.

31 Azmi, *Pakistan-Canada Relations 1947–1982*, 71; Chin, "Shifting Purpose," 990, 992–993, 1001, 1006.

32 Delvoie, "Diplomacy at the Cold-Face: A Mission to Pakistan in the 1990s," 43.

33 Justin Massie and Stephane Roussel, "Preventing, Substituting, or Complementing the Use of Force? Development Assistance in Canadian Strategic Culture," 3, unpublished manuscript, http://www.cpsa-acsp.ca/papers-2011/Massie-Roussel.pdf (accessed 22 January 2012); John W. Holmes, "Le Canada dans le monde," *Politiqueétrangère* 33, no. 4 (1968): 300; Joel J. Sokolsky, "Canada, the United States and NATO: A Tale of Two Pillars," in *North American Perspectives on European Security*, ed. Michael K. Hawes and Joel J. Sokolsky (Lewiston: Edwin Mellen Press, 1990), 213–15; Jennifer M. Welsh, *At Home in the World: Canada's Global Vision for the 21st Century* (Toronto: HarperCollins, 2004), 152; Delvoie, "Diplomacy at the Cold-Face," 43.

34 Brian Tomlin, Norman Hillmer, and Fen Osler Hampson, *Canada's International Policies* (Oxford: Oxford University Press, 2008), 156.

35 Massie and Roussel, "Preventing, Substituting, or Complementing the Use of Force? Development Assistance in Canadian Strategic

35 Culture," 9; Brown, "CIDA Under the Gun," 172–207.

36 Delvoie, "Diplomacy at the Cold-Face," 42; interview, Marie-Andrée Beauchemin in discussion with the author.

37 Delvoie, "Diplomacy at the Cold-Face," 42.

38 Junaid Ahmad, "Pakistan-Canada Economic Relations," MBA Thesis, Concordia University, 1976, 131.

39 Delvoie, "Diplomacy at the Cold-Face," 42.

40 Duane Bratt, *The Politics of Candu Exports* (Toronto: University of Toronto Press, 2006), 43, 201; Ahmad, "Pakistan-Canada Economic Relations," 138–39.

41 Ibid., 65–67, 140, 143, 153, 156–59, 162, 168.

42 Ibid., 207.

43 Massie and Roussel, "Preventing, Substituting, or Complementing the Use of Force? Development Assistance in Canadian Strategic Culture," 11, 12.

44 Interview, Marie-Andrée Beauchemin in discussion with the author; Ahmad, "Pakistan-Canada Economic Relations," 144, 154.

45 Jean-Philippe Therien, "Canadian Aid: A Comparative Analysis," in *Canadian International Development Assistance Policies: An Appraisal*, ed. Cranford Pratt (Montreal: McGill-Queen's University Press, 2004), 324–25.

46 Ahmad, "Pakistan-Canada Economic Relations," 161–62; David Morrison, "The Choice of Bilateral Aid Recipients," 132.

47 Azmi, *Pakistan-Canada Relations 1947–1982*, 89.

48 Duane Bratt, "Tools and Levers: Energy as an Instrument of Canadian Foreign Policy," in *Canada Among Nations 2008*, ed. Robert Bothwell and Jean Daudelin (Montreal: McGill-Queen's University Press, 2009), 224; Ahmad, "Pakistan-Canada Economic Relations," 137; Azmi, *Pakistan-Canada Relations 1947–1982*, 95.

49 Ahmad, "Pakistan-Canada Economic Relations," 139; Azmi, *Pakistan-Canada Relations 1947–1982*, 96.

50 Bratt, "Tools and Levers," 221–22; Azmi, *Pakistan-Canada Relations 1947–1982*, 109, 112.

51 Azmi, *Pakistan-Canada Relations 1947–1982*, 12, 35, 47, 90.

52 Massie and Roussel, "Preventing, Substituting, or Complementing the Use of Force? Development Assistance in Canadian Strategic Culture," 12.

53 Chin, "Shifting Purpose," 1003; interview, Marie-Andrée Beauchemin in discussion with the author.

54 CIDA, *Statistical Report on Official Development Assistance 2000–2001* (Ottawa: CIDA, 2002), 30, 33, 50–51; CIDA, *Statistical Report on Official Development Assistance 1998–1999* (Ottawa: CIDA, 2000), 32, 53; CIDA, *Statistical Report on Official Development Assistance 1999–2000* (Ottawa: CIDA, 2001), 30, 51.

55 Louis Delvoie, "Diplomacy at the Cold-Face," 44–45, 47.

56 Abdul Sattar, *Pakistan's Foreign Policy* (Karachi: Oxford University Press, 2007), 248.

57 Interview, Louis Delvoie in discussion with the author.

58 Global Humanitarian Assistance, *Briefing Paper: Pakistan: Country Aid Factsheet* (Somerset: August 2010), 2.

59 K. Alan Kronstadt, *Direct Overt U.S. Aid and Military Reimbursements to Pakistan, FY2002*-FY2011, prepared for the Congressional Research Service, using sources from the DoS, DoD, DoA, and USAID, 16 February 2010; Sattar, *Pakistan's Foreign Policy*, 247.

60 Global Humanitarian Assistance, *Briefing Paper: Pakistan: Country Aid Factsheet*, 1–2; Anis Cassar, *European Aid to Pakistan: Steadily on the Rise* (Paris: European Institute for Security Studies, December 2009), 2–4.

61 CIDA, *Statistical Report on Official Development Assistance 2003-2004* (Ottawa: CIDA, 2005), 30; Government of Canada, "Canada-Pakistan Relations," March 2012, http://www.canadainternational.gc.ca/pakistan/bilateral_relations_bilaterales/index.aspx?lang=eng&menu_id=10&menu=L&view=d (accessed 21 January 2012); Global Humanitarian Assistance, *Briefing Paper: Pakistan: Country Aid Factsheet*, 2.

62 Carl Meyer, "Missed Targets, Wild Optimism as Canada Heads Into the Final Stretch in Kandahar," *Embassy*, 18 May 2011, http://www.embassymag.ca/page/view/afpak-05-18-2011 (accessed 22 January 2012).

63 CIDA, *Statistical Report on International Assistance, 2009–2010* (Ottawa: CIDA, 2011), 4.

64 Carment and Samy, "Pakistan's Problems Now Ours."

65 Clark, "Ottawa Bolsters Aid to Pakistan."

66 CIDA, "Millennium Development Goals," http://www.acdi-cida.gc.ca/acdi-cida/acdi-cida.nsf/eng/JUD-13173118-GPM (accessed 1 February 2012).

67 Government of Canada, http://www.tbs-sct.gc.ca/dpr-rmr/2008-2009/inst/ida/ida01-eng.asp (accessed 22 January 2012).

68 Global Humanitarian Assistance, *Briefing Paper: Pakistan: Country Aid Factsheet*, 5.

69 Jonathan Kay, "Jonathan Kay on Pakistan: Why Is CIDA Sending Aid to de facto Enemy?", *National Post*, 1 December 2011, http://fullcomment.nationalpost.com/2011/12/01/jonathan-kay-pakistan-is-unworthy-of-ottawas-aid/ (accessed 18 January 2012).

70 Tom Hussain, "Foreign Aid to Pakistan is a Victim of Nepotism," *The National*, 5 July 2010), http://journal.probeinternational.org/2010/07/05/foreign-aid-to-pakistan-is-a-victim-of-nepotism (accessed 22 January 2012).

71 Lee Berthiaume, "Progress Slow on Canadian Post-Disaster Commitments in Pakistan, Haiti," *Postmedia News*, CAIDC-RCCDI, 13 Oct 2011, http://www.caidp-rccdi.ca/news/progress-slow-canadian-post-disaster-commitments-pakistan-haiti (accessed 22 January 2012).

72 Shahid Zahur, "No Benefit from US Aid?", *Pakistan Observer*, 22 January 2012, http://pakobserver.net/detailnews.asp?id=118118 (accessed 22 January 2012).

73 CIDA, Statistical Analysis and Reporting Section, *Canada's Statistical Report on International Assistance—Fiscal Year 2006–2007* (Gatineau: CIDA, 2009), 32–34, 40, 45.

74 Louis Delvoie, "Diplomacy at the Cold-Face," 46; interview, Louis Delvoie in discussion with the author; interview, Marie-Andrée Beauchemin in discussion with the author; interview, Doug Small in discussion with the author.

75 Louis Delvoie, "Diplomacy at the Cold-Face," 57. In 2011, there were just C$549 million in Canadian exports to Pakistan (of which 70 percent were vegetables, metals, and machinery), C$271 million in Pakistan exports (of which 70 percent were textiles and vegetables), and C$54 million in foreign direct investment into Pakistan. See "Pakistan," international.gc.ca; Statistics Canada/Industry Canada, http://www.ic.gc.ca/eic/site/tdo-dcd.nsf/eng/Home (accessed 28 October 2011).

76 Alexandre Gauthier and Simon Lapointe, *Canadian Trade and Investment Activity: Canada-Pakistan* (Ottawa: Parliamentary and Information Service, 2010), 2–4; Government of Canada, "Pakistan," http://www.international.gc.ca/world/embassies/factsheets/Pakistan-FS-en.pdf (accessed 21 January 2012); Asia Pacific Foundation of Canada, "Canada's Merchandise Trade with Pakistan," http://www.asiapacific.ca/statistics/trade/bilateral-trade-asia-product/canadas-merchandise-trade-pakistan (accessed 1 February 2012); Economy Watch, "Pakistan Exports, Imports and Trade," http://www.economywatch.com/world_economy/pakistan/export-import.html (accessed 1 February 2012); interview, Louis Delvoie in discussion with the author; interview, Marie-Andrée Beauchemin in discussion with the author.

77 Asia Trade Hub, "Pakistan," http://www.asiatradehub.com/pakistan/trade.asp (accessed 1 February 2012); interview, Louis Delvoie in discussion with the author; interview, David Collins in discussion with the author.

78 Mohiuddin Aazim, "Top Ten Trading Partners," *Dawn*, 16 January 2012, http://www.dawn.com/2012/01/16/top-ten-trading-partners.html (accessed 1 February 2012).

79 W. M. Dobell, "Canadian Relations with South Asia," 358.

80 Government of Canada, "Canada-Pakistan Relations," http://www.canadainternational.gc.ca/pakistan/bilateral_relations_bilaterales/canada_pakistan.aspx?lang=eng (accessed 17 November 2015).

81 Parliament of Canada, "Wajid Kahn," http://www.parl.gc.ca/parlinfo/Files/Parliamentarian.aspx?Item=97fa4cf0-c7f7-4b3e-8d59-905a0c93a8d6&Language=E&Section=ALL (accessed 1 February 2012); Tomlin, Hillmer, and Hampson, *Canada's International Policies*,

297; Delvoie, "Diplomacy at the Cold-Face," 53.

82 Interview, Louis Delvoie in discussion with the author; interview, David Collins in discussion with the author.

83 Interview, anonymous DFAIT employee in discussion with the author, Montreal-Ottawa, 31 January 2012.

84 Interview, Marie-Andrée Beauchemin in discussion with the author.

85 Asia Pacific Foundation, "Opportunity to Market Canadian Education in Pakistan," 21 December 2011, http://www.asiapacific.ca/news/opportunity-market-canadian-education-pakistan (accessed 22 January 2012).

86 Asia Pacific Foundation, "Study Permit Applications Approved to Applicants from Asia," http://www.asiapacific.ca/statistics/immigration/education/study-permits-issued-applicants-asia (accessed 1 February 2012).

87 Asia Pacific Foundation, "Asia Pacific Visitors to Canada," http://www.asiapacific.ca/statistics/immigration/tourism/asia-pacific-visitors-canada (accessed 1 February 2012).

88 Interview, Louis Delvoie in discussion with the author; Massie and Roussel, "Preventing, Substituting, or Complementing the Use of Force? Development Assistance in Canadian Strategic Culture," 13.

89 Interview, Louis Delvoie in discussion with the author.

90 Interview, Louis Delvoie in discussion with the author.

91 Interview, Marie-Andrée Beauchemin in discussion with the author; interview, David Collins in discussion with the author; interview, Doug Small in discussion with the author.

92 Dobell, "Canadian Relations with South Asia," 355.

93 Azmi, *Pakistan-Canada Relations 1947–1982*, 38.

94 Dernd Debusmann, "Pakistan and the Questions of Foreign Aid," *Reuters*, 13 May 2011, http://blogs.reuters.com/bernddebusmann/2011/05/13/pakistan-and-questions-over-foreign-aid (accessed 22 January 2012); Swaran Singh, "Sino-Pak Defence Co-operation: Joint Ventures and Weapons Procurement," *Peace Initiatives* 5, nos. 3–4 (May–December 1999), 12; Wren Elhai and Molly Kinder, "Pakistan Aid Facts," *Rethinking US Foreign Policy Assistance Blog*, 26 August 2010, http://blogs.cgdev.org/mca-monitor/2010/08/pakistan-aid-facts.php (accessed 22 January 2012).

95 John Meehan and David Webster, "From King to Kandahar: Canada, Multilateralism and Conflict in the Pacific, 1909–2009," in *Canada Among Nations 2008*, ed. Robert Bothwell and Jean Daudelin (Montreal: McGill-Queen's University Press, 2009), 279.

96 Azmi, *Pakistan-Canada Relations 1947–1982*, 28–29.

97 Azmi, *Pakistan-Canada Relations 1947–1982*, 33.

98 Louis Delvoie, "Taming the South Asian Nuclear Tiger: Causes and Consequences, and Canadian Responses," in *A Big League Player?*, ed. Fen Osler Hampson, Martin Rudner, and Michael Hart (Oxford: Oxford University Press, 1999), 233–52, 244–45.

99 CBC, "Baird Vows Support for Afghan Women at Bonn Summit," 5 December 2011, http://www.cbc.ca/news/politics/story/2011/12/05/pol-baird-bonn.html (accessed 22 January 2012).

100 Interview, Doug Small in discussion with the author.

101 Louis Delvoie, "Diplomacy at the Cold-Face," 45.

102 Saman Kelegama, *EU Trade Policy and Democracy Building in South Asia* (Colombo: Institute of Policy Studies of Sri Lanka, 2010), 7, 16–17.

103 Contrary to the views of these authors, see Delvoie, "Diplomacy at the Cold-Face," 47, 50; Louis Delvoie, "Taming the South Asian Nuclear Tiger," 247; Kanti Bajpai, "India and Canada: Moving Ahead," in *Canada Among Nations 2009–2010*, eds. Fen Osler Hampson and Paul Heinbecker (Montreal: McGill-Queen's University Press, 2010), 161.

CHAPTER 7

BOSNIA:
From Failed State to Functioning State

Duane Bratt

Introduction

The concept of failed states originated with a 1992 article in *Foreign Policy* by Gerald Helman and Steven Ratner.[1] One of the countries that Helman and Ratner explicitly identified as a failed state was Bosnia in the early 1990s. After declaring its independence in April 1992, Bosnia was the scene of the most vicious of the wars in the former Yugoslavia. By the end of the war in late 1995, Bosnia's population had decreased, through death and migration, from 4.3 million to less than 2 million.[2] Moreover, the tactics of the combatants were especially odious. Both sides targeted civilians through city sieges and ethnic cleansing. However, the Bosnian case is not just an example of a failed state; it is also an example of how, with the help of the United Nations (UN) and the North Atlantic Treaty Organization (NATO), a failed state can be turned back into a functioning state.

This chapter has two objectives. First, it briefly describes, and assesses the success of, the UN peacekeeping operation that was deployed in Bosnia from February 1992 until the summer of 1995, when it was replaced by NATO. Second, this chapter analyzes Canada's contribution to the UN

Figure 1: Map. (Credit: Marilyn Croot)

peacekeeping operation, and explores how the Bosnian mission reflected a fundamental shift in Canadian foreign policy. Although Canada participated in a multilateral fashion, its participation in the Bosnian peacekeeping operation was important in several respects. Canadians held several senior leadership positions. For example, General Lewis MacKenzie was the first commander of the United Nations Protection Force (UNPROFOR) in Bosnia and led the critical task of re-opening the Sarajevo airport in the summer of 1992. Canada was also one of the largest troop contributors to UNPROFOR, with a peak contribution of 2,400 soldiers.

Canada's participation in UNPROFOR also represented a fundamental break from its past practices and policy preferences. First, it showed support for the dissolution of a federation. Leery of establishing a precedent

Figure 2: Canadian Major-General Lewis MacKenzie commanded the UN Protection Force charged with keeping Sarajevo's airport open and humanitarian aid flowing. He is shown here with Colonel Michel Forestier of the French Army, who was responsible for airport security. (Credit: DND Photo e011160351/LAC)

that might weaken its position with separatist forces in Quebec, Canada had previously supported the maintenance and unity of ethnically mixed countries. Second, it illustrated a willingness to support greater intervention into the internal affairs of states. In Bosnia (as well as Somalia and other operations in the early 1990s), Canada used its own military contribution on the ground and encouraged its coalition partners to move beyond the traditional concepts of peacekeeping—consent, impartiality, and limited use of force—to more forceful styles of peacekeeping. Early, or first generation, peacekeeping involved the UN interpositioning troops between two countries to monitor ceasefires. Later, or second generation, peacekeeping drew the UN into internal conflicts and greatly expanded its tasks to include monitoring/conducting elections, demobilizing troops, protecting humanitarian convoys, monitoring no-fly zones, and protecting designated "safe areas."[3] Finally, the ultimate success of the Bosnian case provided an example of turning a failed state into a functioning state, encouraging Canada and its allies to intervene militarily in other failed states.

The Bosnian Conflict

Modern-day Yugoslavia was created at the end of World War II by Marshall Josip Broz Tito, the leader of the Yugoslav partisans. Yugoslavia was a federation of six republics: Serbia, Croatia, Slovenia, Bosnia-Herzegovina, Macedonia, and Montenegro. Although the boundaries of these republics were based on ethnicity, each republic contained substantial minority groups with strong ethnic identities. This was particularly true of Bosnia. Under Tito's highly centralized, dictatorial Communist government, these ethnic nationalisms were held in line.

This changed during the 1980s. As Yugoslavia's economy started to collapse, Croatia and Slovenia, the economic powers, demanded ever greater autonomy. This was granted, gradually turning Yugoslavia into a decentralized state. However, nationalist stirrings were not confined to Croatia and Slovenia. A key moment in the lead-up to Yugoslavia's disintegration was the 1987 rise of Slobodan Milošević to the Serbian Presidency. Part of Tito's unification strategy had been to keep Serbian nationalism controlled, a feeling that was summed up by Serbian nationalists with the phrase "a weak Serbia makes a strong Yugoslavia."[4] Milošević capitalized on this simmering Serbian nationalism by attempting to speak for all Serbs, no matter where they lived.

The catalyst for the war in Bosnia was a crisis in Kosovo, an autonomous province in Serbia of mainly Albanian ethnicity, but with a Serbian minority. A series of incidents in Kosovo in the late 1980s—dissolving the Kosovo Assembly, restricting the Albanian language, and repressing the Kosovar Albanians—revived old fears of Serbian nationalism and spurred the independence movements in the other republics. As a constitutional crisis erupted and dragged on for much of 1989–91, Yugoslavia slowly unravelled. Croatia and Slovenia formed their own armies, while paramilitary groups were organized by Serbians in the Krajina region of Croatia. All sides were preparing for the inevitable civil war. Finally, on 25 June

1991, Croatia and Slovenia declared themselves independent. The Serbs, backed by the Yugoslav National Army (JNA), responded with force, and the Yugoslav conflict had officially begun.

The first Yugoslav war pitted Serbia against Slovenia. It lasted only a week before the JNA, which was controlled by Serbia, gave up and allowed Slovenia to secede. There were two major reasons why the war in Slovenia was so short. First, Slovenia was the most homogenous republic, with a population that was over 90 percent Slovene. Thus, there was no large ethnic minority in Slovenia attempting to keep it in Yugoslavia. Second, Slovenia did not share a common border with Serbia, which was the republic most determined to keep the federation united.

The second war, between Croatia and the JNA and Serbia, was much more violent. Its first six months were hard-fought and bloody, climaxing in the siege of Dubrovnik. In addition, there were several instances of "ethnic cleansing" during the early stages of the war. Ethnic cleansing can be defined as "the elimination, by the ethnic group exercising control over a given territory, of members of other ethnic groups." In practice this included "harassment, discrimination, beatings, torture, rape, summary executions, expulsions, shelling of civilian population centres, relocation of populations by force, confiscation of property, and destruction of homes and places of worship and cultural institutions."[5] By January 1992, it appeared that the two sides had agreed to a ceasefire.

Conflict in the former Yugoslavia, however, was not over. Rather, Croats and Serbs trained their eyes on Bosnia. Each planned on helping their respective compatriots inside Bosnia to create a Greater Croatia or a Greater Serbia. Bosnia, nicknamed "little Yugoslavia" because its ethnic mix was similar to that of the country as a whole, faced a dilemma. The Bosnian government, with the exception of the Bosnian Serb component, wanted to remain part of a united Yugoslavia. However, after Croatia and Slovenia left, the Bosnian government decided that it had no choice but to secede as well. A referendum on independence was held on 1 March 1992 and passed overwhelmingly. Bosnia was recognized as a sovereign state by the European Community, the United States, and Canada in April 1992, and was accepted into the United Nations in May.

Bosnian Serbs, who made up 31 percent of the population, boycotted the referendum and launched an attack against the Muslim-dominated Bosnian government. The Bosnian Serbs were also supported by elements of the JNA. At the beginning of the war there was an alliance between the Muslims and the Bosnian Croats against their common enemy, the Serbs. In fact, a formal defence treaty had been signed by the president of Bosnia-Herzegovina, Alija Izetbegović, and the president of Croatia, Franjo Tuđman. However, by the spring of 1993 this alliance had collapsed and the war had turned into a three-way fight with the Bosnian Croats joining the Bosnian Serbs in their attacks on the Muslims. The fighting between Bosnian Croats and Muslims ended with the signing of a ceasefire and the formation of the Bosnian Federation on 23 February 1994.[6]

The war in Bosnia led to a frightful humanitarian tragedy. By 21 April 1992, the conflict had resulted in over 230,000 displaced persons.[7] This number would continue to grow, so that by the end of the first year and a half of fighting there were 150,000 killed, 150,000 missing, and about two million refugees—all from a pre-war population of 4.3 million.[8] However, it was the nature of the suffering that grabbed the world's attention. The ethnic cleansing that had first begun in Croatia became even more widespread in Bosnia. Helsinki Watch asserted that genocide was being committed in Bosnia, particularly by the Bosnian Serbs.[9] The most arresting images emerged from the siege of Sarajevo. Sarajevo, which is the capital of Bosnia and inhabited by all three ethnic groups, came under siege on 4 April 1992. This led to severe rationing of food and gas. It was as a result of the dire humanitarian situation in Bosnia, which seemed to take on greater importance because it was in Europe's backyard, that UNPROFOR was deployed.

There were essentially three combatants in the Bosnian civil war, although there were also many additional paramilitary groups beyond the control of the three command structures. First, there were the Bosniacs, who were almost exclusively Muslim. The Bosniacs were led by Alija Izetbegović, who had been elected president of Bosnia in 1990. According to the last pre-war census in 1991, the Muslims represented 44 percent of Bosnia's 4.3 million inhabitants.[10] Although the Bosniacs in power quite rightly referred to themselves as the Government of Bosnia (there was some minor representation in the cabinet from the two non-Muslim ethnic groups), it was essentially a Muslim organization. Izetbegović was infamous for his "Islamic Declaration" of 1970, which called for "the creation of a united Islamic community from Morocco to Indonesia."[11] Izetbegović subsequently recanted this idea and promised a pluralistic Bosnia, though many Bosnian Serbs and Bosnian Croats feared that he was trying to turn Bosnia into an Islamic, rather than a secular, state.

Second, there were the Bosnian Serbs. Led by Radovan Karadžić and the Serbian Democratic Party of Bosnia-Herzegovina, they constituted 31 percent of the population. The Bosnian Serbs formed their own "parliament" in Pale and desired a union or close association with Serbia. Karadžić insisted that "it is impossible for Serbs to live together with other peoples in a unitary state."[12] The relationship between the Bosnian Serbs and Serbia, as events would later show, was not always cordial, nor were their war aims congruent. While many in the international community believed that Milošević could control Karadžić, it was soon apparent that Karadžić had his own goals and objectives.

Third, there were the Bosnian Croats, representing 17 percent of the population. The major Bosnian Croatian organization was the Croatian Defence Council led by Mate Boban, who wanted to form an autonomous Bosnian Croat republic with some type of association with Croatia proper. In fact, some observers considered Boban to be simply a puppet of Tuđman, and there were divisions among the Bosnian Croats, with some groups supporting an independent and unified Bosnia. These divisions led to the conflicting strategies that the Bosnian Croats pursued throughout the war, particularly in their tenuous alliance with the Bosniacs.

Several points need to be made when describing the pre-war ethnic composition of Bosnia. In contrast to the situation in Croatia, Bosnia's ethnic communities did not live in clusters but were distributed across its territory. This made the option of partition very difficult. Of Bosnia's 112 administrative units, Bosniacs held a majority in 37, Serbs in 32, Croats in 13, and 30 contained no majority at all. Moreover, there was plenty of intermarriage among the ethnic groups during the pre-war years. This meant that over 16 percent of Bosnian children in 1991 were from mixed marriages.[13] The situation was further complicated by the tendency of Bosnian Serbs, when they did live together, to congregate on the western side of Bosnia, the part of the country most removed from Serbia, which bordered the east. Thus, a critical strategic goal of the Bosnian Serbs was to secure a land route between Serbia and the west region of Bosnia.

Bosnia's ethnic dimensions led to one final consideration for the international community. There was great concern about the potential for intervention by neighbouring states. Keeping Serbia and Croatia from continuing their war in Bosnian territory was, of course, a prime consideration, but there were also great fears that the war could spread throughout southern Europe.[14] These fears were expressed by United States Secretary of State Lawrence Eagleburger in late August 1992: "I think there's a real chance that this conflict can spread. It's what has terrified us all from the very beginning. It's been nothing but one escalation after another."[15]

The Bosnian conflict constituted a humanitarian crisis with accusations, from all sides, of ethnic cleansing, systematic rape, and even genocide. These atrocities were the catalyst for action from the international community. The conflict was being fought by three distinct, and unequal, ethnic groups: the almost wholly Muslim Bosniacs, who controlled the internationally recognized Bosnian government, but possessed few arms and had no regional sponsor; the Bosnian Serbs, who lacked recognition, but were well-armed and were receiving logistical support from Serbs in Belgrade; and the Bosnian Croats, who also lacked recognition, but were receiving assistance from Croats in Zagreb.

The unequal footing of the combatants, which turned the weaker Bosniacs into the clear victims, also divided the great powers. The Europeans, particularly the British and the French, viewed the conflict as a civil war. Although they acknowledged that Serbia was assisting its ethnic cousins in Bosnia, the Europeans correctly argued that the conflict was fought almost exclusively by Bosnians. Americans, however, insisted that the war was a simple case of Serbian aggression against Bosnia. In Washington's eyes, it was 1990 and Iraq's invasion of Kuwait all over again. Finally, efforts at conflict resolution were complicated because the nature of the ethnic distribution meant that partition without war was seen as an unlikely situation. Thus, UNPROFOR was deployed, in an internal conflict which had the potential of spreading, in order to prevent humanitarian suffering.

UNPROFOR in Bosnia

The UN's first presence in Bosnia arrived before the war had officially begun. The UN established the headquarters of UNPROFOR, which was responsible for monitoring the conflict in Croatia, in Sarajevo on 26 March 1992. The decision to place the headquarters of UNPROFOR in the

Bosnian capital was controversial. The UN hoped that its mere presence in Sarajevo would prevent conflict from erupting in Bosnia. However, the military leadership of UNPROFOR worried that "once we put the UN flag up in front of our headquarters, it will be a lightning rod for every problem in and around Sarajevo; yet we'll have neither mandate nor resources to deal with inevitable requests for help."[16]

The UN commanders were right—the establishment of UNPROFOR's headquarters in Sarajevo was a major error. This decision not only caused logistical difficulties for the Croatian operation but also failed to stop the conflict in Bosnia from igniting. Moreover, the UN's Sarajevo headquarters soon became a target for all sides in the Bosnian conflict. With no mandate in Bosnia, the UN was powerless to act and eventually had to transfer its civilian workers back to Zagreb. As the UN secretary-general noted in a report to the Security Council, "the establishment of UNPROFOR's headquarters in Sarajevo has not prevented a savage conflict from breaking out there."[17]

The UN was gradually creeping toward establishing a separate peacekeeping operation in Bosnia.[18] The UN judged that the fighting in Bosnia was due to the "concerted effort by the Serbs of Bosnia-Herzegovina."[19] It was also determined that the Bosnian Serbs were being assisted by Serbia. On 15 May 1992, the UN adopted Security Council Resolution 752, demanding "that Bosnia-Herzegovina's neighbours take swift action to end" all forms of interference "and respect the territorial integrity of Bosnia-Herzegovina."[20] Two weeks later, after the brutal shelling of a Sarajevo breadline, the Security Council, acting under Chapter VII of the UN Charter (the UN's enforcement mechanism), imposed comprehensive economic sanctions on Serbia because of its involvement in the Bosnian conflict.[21]

Resolution 752 also asked Secretary-General Boutros Boutros-Ghali to "review the feasibility of protecting international humanitarian relief programmes ... and of ensuring safe and secure access to Sarajevo airport."[22] The Sarajevo airport agreement was a major milestone for both the establishment of a peacekeeping operation in Bosnia and the role Canada would play in the conflict. Responding to this initiative, the secretary-general suggested that the UN could "provide armed protection for convoys of humanitarian supplies en route from Sarajevo Airport to distribution centres within that city." However, he warned that this type of mission would not only be "extremely difficult and expensive" but also "could make it more difficult to secure the cooperation" that UNPROFOR needed in Croatia.²³ The Security Council, in Resolution 757, requested that Boutros-Ghali work with the Bosnian parties to achieve a "security zone encompassing Sarajevo and its airport," in order to "ensure unimpeded delivery of humanitarian supplies" throughout the city.²⁴

On 5 June 1992, after three days of negotiations between Cedric Thornberry, the director of civil affairs for UNPROFOR, and the three Bosnian factions, an agreement was reached to re-open the airport. The deal gave UNPROFOR full responsibility for the functioning and security of the Sarajevo airport.²⁵ Canadian Major-General Lewis MacKenzie, who led the largest contingent in Sarajevo, was named UNPROFOR commander.

Implementing the airport agreement, which involved supervising the withdrawal of anti-aircraft weapons and the concentration of heavy weapons at agreed locations throughout Sarajevo, was not easy. Word of the airport agreement had led to renewed fighting between the Bosniacs and the Bosnian Serbs. As General MacKenzie noted, "this is a characteristic of peacekeeping assignments throughout the world: anytime there is a chance that UN action will freeze the status quo on the ground, the parties to the conflict go on a last-minute offensive to make as many territorial gains as possible before the appointed time for the ceasefire arrives."²⁶ Accordingly, each Bosnian party made additional demands that were not part of the original agreement. The Bosnian Serbs had effective control of the airport and did not want to give it up. Karadžić proposed that the Bosnian Serbs operate the airport for the UN, while the Bosniacs demanded that all heavy artillery be moved twenty kilometres outside of Sarajevo.²⁷ Although three of the basic conditions of the June 5 agreement were not yet established—a ceasefire, the complete concentration of heavy weaponry under UNPROFOR supervision, and the establishment of security corridors to allow for the delivery of humanitarian aid—UNPROFOR was taking strides to re-open the airport.²⁸ These efforts were aided by a surprise visit from French President Francois Mitterrand on 28 June. Finally, five days later, the Sarajevo airport was reopened, secured by Canadian and French troops, and nine planes full of humanitarian aid landed. This was a major achievement.

After the opening of the Sarajevo airport, UNPROFOR's mandate evolved to include additional tasks. First, it established a peacekeeping

Figure 3: The war in Bosnia demanded a more robust form of peacekeeping and troops equipped with heavy firepower. A Cougar armoured personal carrier is shown patrolling the winter roads of Bosnia. (Credit: DND Photo CFJIC ISC93-20060-23)

operation, solely for Bosnia, which was responsible for protecting humanitarian aid convoys.[29] Second, it created a no-fly zone over Bosnia and enlisted NATO to enforce the ban.[30] Third, it declared six safe areas in cities throughout Bosnia: Sarajevo, Tuzla, Zepa, Goražde, Bihac, and Srebrenica. These safe areas, as UN Security Council Resolution 819 put it, "should be free from any armed attack or any other hostile act."[31] Fourth, it agreed to monitor the February 1994 ceasefire agreement between the Bosniacs and the Bosnian Croats.[32]

UNPROFOR's mandate officially expired on 20 December 1995, when it transferred its authority to the NATO Implementation Force (IFOR). However, UNPROFOR's role as a peacekeeping operation effectively ended much earlier, when NATO's Operation Deliberate Force was launched on 29 August 1995. For several weeks, NATO used its superior air power to target Bosnian Serb ammunition and fuel depots, radar and communications sites, and command posts across Bosnia. The use of air strikes was a clear move away from peacekeeping and toward peace enforcement.

According to one Western diplomat, the strikes were also successfully to "bomb [the Bosnian Serbs] to the negotiating table."³³ A temporary agreement was reached with the Bosnian Serbs on 14 September 1995, and the air strikes were ended. This interim agreement led to intense, high-level peace negotiations brokered by US diplomat Richard Holbrooke, which culminated in the Dayton Agreement of 21 November 1995.³⁴ Integral to the Dayton Agreement was the decision to implement it with sixty thousand NATO troops, a third of whom would be American.³⁵

Assessing UNPROFOR's Success

There are four principal ways to measure the success of UNPROFOR.³⁶ The first indicator is whether UNPROFOR effectively fulfilled its four-part mandate. Though UNPROFOR had multiple tasks, it must be concluded that it was moderately successful. Despite being subject to frequent closure due to attacks or threat of attack, UNPROFOR reopened Sarajevo's airport, which handled more than 150,000 tons of humanitarian relief between 3 July 1992 and 30 May 1995. The UN force was more successful in enforcing the no-fly zone and monitoring the ceasefire between the Bosniacs and the Bosnian Croats. Crucially, however, UNPROFOR was unable to protect the humanitarian convoys that delivered aid from the airport, nor could it protect the safe areas. UNPROFOR was powerless to prevent the siege of Sarajevo and other cities. The situation was even worse in Srebrenica where, despite the presence of a thousand Dutch peacekeepers, the safe haven was overrun by Bosnian Serb forces in July 1995. It is estimated that around seven thousand civilians were killed in Srebrenica.

The success of UNPROFOR can be assessed by the extent to which it facilitated conflict resolution. The Dayton Agreement ended the war in 1995, but UNPROFOR's role in shaping that accord was limited. It was the combination of NATO air power and US political strength that led to the signing of the peace settlement. Some Western diplomats and UN administrators have argued that UNPROFOR was "invaluable" to the continuation of political negotiations in Bosnia by its efforts to constrain the fighting.³⁷ As one UN peacekeeping official argued, "without UNPROFOR there would be no agreement to reach. Everyone would have died in the fighting."[38] However, the Bosniacs and their supporters argue otherwise, contending that UNPROFOR's presence prevented an earlier resolution of the conflict and, instead, helped prolong the fighting.[39] This less favourable view of UNPROFOR's ability to facilitate conflict resolution in Bosnia is the more accurate. UNPROFOR was deployed in Bosnia for almost four years, but a peace agreement was only reached when the mission was, for all intents and purposes, taken out of their hands. As Professor Michael Wesley has concluded, UNPROFOR was "worse than ineffectual"; they acted "as impediments to the termination of the conflict."[40]

Was UNPROFOR successful at containing the conflict? There was great fear in many Western capitals that the fighting in Bosnia would spread throughout the region, but, in fact, the conflict remained in Bosnia. Military experts state that without the constraining presence of UNPROFOR, the Bosnian Serbs would have captured all of Bosnia.[41] This might have led to either the spread of war throughout the Balkans or Croatian intervention. Either of these consequences would have led to a larger war, possibly involving regional or great power intervention. However, UNPROFOR's failure in important parts of its mandate led NATO countries to deploy 60,000 troops to Bosnia. The arrival of that many troops from North America and Western Europe could hardly be seen as containing the conflict.

Finally, was UNPROFOR successful at limiting casualties? While UNPROFOR was moderately effective at limiting factional fighting and protecting Bosnian civilians from shelling and sniper fire, it failed to stop the widespread ethnic cleansing that took place on its watch. Admittedly, ethnic cleansing had begun in Bosnia with the start of the war in April 1992, a month before UNRPROFOR arrived in Sarajevo. Moreover, the peacekeepers' role was limited to that city until their mandate was expanded in September to embrace the entire country. Over the next three years, however, the force proved unable to stop the killing; the Srebrenica Massacre provides especially painful evidence that UNPROFOR was powerless to stop ethnic cleansing in Bosnia.

UNPROFOR was ultimately a failed peacekeeping operation. The only area where UNPROFOR received even a partial passing grade was in its mandate performance, and even there its inability to protect designated safe areas represented a deep stain on its mission. Meanwhile, under every other indicator of success—facilitating conflict resolution, conflict containment, and limiting casualties—UNPROFOR failed.

Why did UNPROFOR fail? The UN Secretariat argued that UNPROFOR "has not, of course, ended the war in that strife-torn country, but it has been neither mandated nor equipped to do that."[42] UNPROFOR was deployed as a half-measure because the Security Council members were not initially prepared to commit to a large-scale operation in Bosnia, but neither could they ignore the crisis. Thus, a humanitarian peacekeeping operation was created to alleviate civilian suffering while negotiations to end the conflict proceeded. As one Bosniac official correctly stated, "the UN redefined the conflict to meet their solution."[43] The underlying truth was that peacekeeping was "used as a palliative, an alibi, an excuse to cover the lack of political will to confront the reality of the war in Bosnia-Herzegovina."[44]

Assessing Canada's Contribution to UNPROFOR

Canada was one of the largest troop contributors to UNPROFOR, supplying over 6 percent of UNPROFOR's maximum strength of 40,000. At its peak, Canada supplied 2,400 troops plus unarmed military observers and civilian police officers, and at critical junctures, such as June–July 1992, Canada was the single largest, most equipped, and best trained contingent. Canada also arrived early and stayed late. Its first troops arrived in April 1992 and stayed until the end of the UN mission in December 1995.[45] Only the British and French supplied more troops than Canada to UNPROFOR over its lifetime.

Although the Canadian contingent performed many different tasks in Bosnia, it filled two roles that were very important: opening the Sarajevo airport and protecting the safe area of Srebrenica. The first task, carried out in July 1992, was a major accomplishment for UNPROFOR, as it created a crucial corridor with the outside world to bring in humanitarian relief supplies. As force commander Lewis MacKenzie recalled twenty years later, "for 30 days, commencing July 2, Canadian soldiers led by Lieutenant-Colonel Michel Jones and operating in an extremely dangerous environment facilitated the delivery of approximately 300 tonnes of food and medical supplies a day to a city that was short of both. Soldiers risked their lives rescuing Sarajevans who were wounded and exposed to sniper fire."[46] To complete the assignment, the 850-strong Canadian battle group, a combination of the Royal Canadian and Royal 22nd regiments, brought in some heavy firepower: a hundred armoured personnel carriers, anti-tank missile systems, and high-explosive ammunition. They also expanded the rules of engagement to allow for the use of force to protect the mission. In both of these instances, MacKenzie was violating the existing rules for UN peacekeeping.[47]

The second task was protecting the safe area of Srebrenica. In March 1993, a 330-strong Canadian company was dispatched through Bosnian Serb–occupied territory to Srebrenica with a multi-pronged agenda: establish observation posts in the city, facilitate the delivery and distribution of humanitarian aid, disarm the Bosniacs inside the city, and protect the city from the Bosnian Serb forces. This was a dangerous mission and the Canadians were often under fire, but they were relatively successful in establishing Srebrenica as a safe area. The city was still under threat from Bosnian Serb attacks, and the surrounding countryside was being ethnically cleansed. Srebrenica was, as Canada's External Affairs Minister Barbara McDougall described, like "living in a ghetto or in a fortress. There is no freedom of movement, no freedom of economic activity."[48]

The Canadians remained in Srebrenica until March 1994, when they were replaced by a Dutch contingent. While the Canadians were largely successful in protecting Srebrenica, the same could not be said of their replacements. In July 1995, one thousand Dutch peacekeepers were forced to evacuate the city under threat from the Bosnian Serbs, led by General Ratko Mladić, who had a substantially larger force massed on its outskirts. When the peacekeepers fled, Mladić's forces entered the city and separated the military-aged men from the women, children, and elderly. The men were murdered and many of the women were raped. Over seven thousand people were massacred. Mladić would later be indicted by the International Criminal Tribunal for the Former Yugoslavia for his part in the Srebrenica massacre. He is currently on trial in The Hague with a decision expected in 2016.

Shift in Canadian Foreign Policy

The Bosnian operation illustrated a major shift in Canadian foreign policy. It supported Bosnian independence from the former Yugoslavia and even took military action to defend Bosnia from external, as well as internal, actors who wished to partition the country. Traditionally, Canada had always supported the unity of federal states. This was due to the spectre of Quebec separatism in Canadian domestic politics. The fear of nationalism, and its potential to break up the federation, was one of the sources of commonality that Canadian diplomats often brought up with their Yugoslav counterparts during the Cold War era.[49] Even when Yugoslavia started to collapse in the late 1980s, Ottawa initially favoured keeping the country united.[50] Yet, by the early 1990s, Canada was supporting the self-determination of the breakaway Yugoslav republics. When Slovenia and Croatia announced their independence on 25 June 1991, Canada, following the lead of Germany, officially recognized the new states on 16 January 1992. Progressive Conservative Prime Minister Brian Mulroney explained that "the Yugoslav federation as we have known it no longer exists and cannot be reconstituted by force."[51] Canada extended diplomatic recognition to Bosnia on 8 April 1992, a month after a referendum—boycotted by the Bosnian Serbs—overwhelmingly affirmed Bosnian independence.

It is important to note that Canada recognized these secessionist states in the midst of a major national unity crisis back home. The Meech Lake Accord, designed to convince Quebec to sign the 1982 Canadian Constitution, was unravelling, while support for separation spiked in Quebec. The federal cabinet was in full disarray. A prominent minister and close Mulroney confidant, Lucien Bouchard, bolted from Cabinet and formed the Bloc Québécois, a new nationalist party. When the Parti Québécois formed the provincial government in 1994, it immediately launched plans for a second referendum on Quebec sovereignty. Although the 1995 referendum was narrowly defeated, the spectre of Canada breaking apart could not be separated from Ottawa's support of Bosnia's secession from Yugoslavia. Canadian officials maintained that secession was permissible in failed states, such as Yugoslavia, but not in highly developed democratic states such as Canada.

The second major shift was to support greater intervention, including military intervention, into the internal affairs of states. This was a fundamental break from Canada's previous policy of non-intervention in failed states. Even in cases of humanitarian crises, such as Biafra in the 1960s, and Bangladesh and Cambodia in the 1970s, Canada was a firm believer in Article 2.7 of the UN Charter, which stated that "nothing contained in the present Charter shall authorize the United Nations to intervene in matters which are essentially within the domestic jurisdiction of any state or shall require the Members to submit such matters to settlement under the present Charter; but this principle shall not prejudice the application of enforcement measures under Chapter VII."

But Canada reversed this historic policy in the case of Bosnia. In the spring of 1992, Mulroney pleaded for "the UN and its member states" to "intervene earlier and stronger in the future to prevent such disasters.... What kind of signal does it send when the world turns a blind eye to the carnage?" Bosnia "followed the rules established by the UN" and "they took the world's word, but they were left to fend for themselves against heavily armed opposition." The result has been "a disgrace for humanity."[52] A year later, McDougall further emphasized this point. "We have to reconsider the UN's traditional definition of state sovereignty," she argued. "I believe that states can no longer argue sovereignty as a licence for internal repression, when the absolutes of that sovereignty shield conflicts that eventually could become international in scope." There should be "no protection to those guilty of breaches of the common moral codes enshrined in the Universal Declaration of Human Rights."[53]

As the conflict in Bosnia escalated, despite the presence of UN peacekeepers, Canada began advocating, both at the UN and in NATO, for greater military intervention. Canada wanted to expand the rules of engagement for the troops on the ground (including the Canadian contingent), give more authority for NATO warships in the Adriatic (which included the Canadian destroyer HMCS *Iroquois*) to enforce the arms embargo, and authorize the use of air strikes. This support for more aggressive rules of engagement was a direct consequence of MacKenzie's experience in changing UN Chapter VI rules, which limited peacekeepers to light arms and to shooting only in self-defence, to more robust rules of engagement in order successfully to defend the Sarajevo airport. This meant, as MacKenzie explained, "if those bastards fired at the aircraft when it was landing, unloading or taking off, then we could take them out."⁵⁴ In other words, the UN's rules of engagement shifted from permitting individual self-defence to allowing "self-defence" of the mission. This reconceptualization of self-defence would later be used for much of UN-PROFOR's mandate—for example, in protecting the UN's designated safe areas. Demanding, and in many cases using, greater degrees of force did not come without consequences. UN peacekeepers, including Canadians, were sometimes taken hostage by the much larger Bosnian Serb army. For example, in November 1994, fifty-five Canadian peacekeepers were taken hostage, and again, in May 1995, video footage of Canadian Captain Patrick Rechner handcuffed to a pole in Pale was transmitted across the globe. More tragically, twenty-three Canadians lost their lives in Bosnia.

What explains this significant shift in Canadian policy, which was seen in Bosnia, as well as in other failed states like Somalia and Cambodia? First, the end of the Cold War allowed the concept of state sovereignty to be reconfigured. Studies of UN behaviour during the Cold War revealed a strong commitment to the non-intervention doctrine,⁵⁵ but the early years after the end of the Cold War provided an opportunity for intervening in internal conflicts that had been fuelled by the American-Soviet rivalry.⁵⁶ The end of the Cold War also ended the stalemate between the Americans and the Soviets on the Security Council. With fewer vetoes, or threats of vetoes, the Security Council could make bolder and bolder decisions. UN Secretary-General Boutros Boutros-Ghali pronounced that "the time of absolute and exclusive sovereignty . . . has passed; its theory was never matched by reality."⁵⁷ Between 1988 and 1994, the UN sent peacekeeping missions to Angola, Namibia, Nicaragua, El Salvador, Western Sahara, Cambodia, Croatia, Somalia, Macedonia, Mozambique, Haiti, Liberia, Rwanda, Chad, and Tajikistan, as well as to Bosnia. Canada also accepted this new conception of sovereignty. Prime Minister Mulroney announced in a major speech in 1991 that Canada was receptive to "re-thinking the limits of national sovereignty in a world where problems respect no borders."⁵⁸

Second, Ottawa policymakers placed increasing importance on human rights in international relations. The severe humanitarian crisis in Bosnia, which included concentration camps, city sieges, refugees and internally displaced people, ethnic cleansing, civilian massacres, and the organized raping of women, required a strong response. Philosophers had been developing the concept of humanitarian intervention for centuries. Michael Walzer, one of the key modern advocates of humanitarian intervention, argued that it was "justified when it is a response (with reasonable expectations of success) to acts 'that shock the moral conscience of mankind.'" As Walzer further noted, "when a people are being massacred, we don't require that they pass the test of self-help before coming to their aid. It is their very incapacity that brings us in."[59] This sentiment was repeated by McDougall in a speech to the UN General Assembly on 25 September 1991. McDougall argued that "a collapse of effective governmental authority in Yugoslavia, if it continues, could . . . endanger peace and security in neighbouring countries. So the concept of sovereignty must respect higher principles, including the need to preserve human life from wanton destruction."[60]

Third, Ottawa was influenced by the successful use of military force in the Gulf War, where a US-led, but UN-authorized, taskforce forcibly removed Iraq from Kuwait. The Gulf War showed Canada, which supported the operation both politically and militarily, the effectiveness of force in international relations. It also proved to Canadian policymakers that Canada did not have to restrict itself solely to UN peacekeeping operations but could participate in a range of military activities. When discussing Canada's military role in the Gulf War, External Affairs Minister Joe Clark cited its previous military action in Korea—and also foreshadowed future operations in Kosovo, Afghanistan, and Libya—when he said that "Canada will continue as a peacekeeper and we will continue as a peacemaker."[61]

Conclusion

Bosnia is significant for a number of reasons. First, it was, along with Somalia, one of the first failed states of the post–Cold War era. Second, it was the site of a large UN and NATO intervention. While the UN peacekeeping operation of 1992–95 was a failure, it did set the stage for a subsequent humanitarian intervention led by NATO that produced peace in Bosnia. Bosnia is an example of a failed state becoming a functioning state. From a Canadian viewpoint, Bosnia represented a major military and diplomatic initiative. Canada put a large number of troops on the ground for a sustained period of time, and Prime Minister Mulroney took a personal interest in the operation, which saw him work the phones of other UN and NATO leaders. More significantly, Bosnia illustrated a fundamental shift in Canadian foreign policy in terms of dealing with secessionist states and doctrines of intervention. These shifts reflected the experiences of Canadian soldiers on the ground in Bosnia, as well as new strategic thinking in Canada by government officials in the Prime Minister's Office, External Affairs, and National Defence. More importantly, these shifts may have originated within the Mulroney government, but they have been adopted by successive Canadian governments led by Jean Chrétien, Paul Martin, and Stephen Harper. Concepts such as human security and the responsibility to protect, and military operations in more recent failed states such as Kosovo, Afghanistan, and Libya, can all be traced back to the principles enunciated during the Bosnian conflict.

Notes

1. Gerald B. Helman and Steven R. Ratner, "Saving Failed States," *Foreign Policy* 89 (Winter 1992–93): 3–20.
2. United Nations High Commissioner for Refugees, *Information Notes on the Former Yugoslavia* (July 1994), 11.
3. For a good description of these changes, see William J. Durch, ed., *The Evolution of UN Peacekeeping: Case Studies and Comparative Analysis* (Washington: Henry L. Stimson Center, 1993).
4. Mihailo Crnobrnja, *The Yugoslav Drama* (Montreal: McGill-Queen's University Press, 1994), 99.
5. United Nations Department of Public Information, *The United Nations and the Situation in the Former Yugoslavia* (May 1993), 25.
6. United Nations document (hereafter UN doc), S/1994/291, Annex, 11 March 1994.
7. UN doc, S/23836, 24 April 1992.
8. Crnobrnja, *The Yugoslav Drama*, 178.
9. Helsinki Watch, *War Crimes in Bosnia-Hercegovina*, vols. 1–2 (New York: Human Rights Watch, 1992). Also see *New York Newsday* foreign correspondent Roy Gutman's 1993 Pulitzer Prize–winning series of articles on "ethnic cleansing" in Bosnia. Roy Gutman, *A Witness to Genocide* (New York: MacMillan, 1993).
10. All census figures about Bosnia are from United Nations, *The Blue Helmets: A Review of United Nations Peace-Keeping*, 3rd ed. (New York: UN Department of Public Information, 1996), 487.

11 Quoted in John Zametica, *The Yugoslav Conflict*, Adelphi Paper 270 (London: International Institute for Strategic Studies, Summer 1992), 38.

12 Quoted in Helsinki Watch, *War Crimes in Bosnia-Hercegovina*, vol. 1, 46.

13 Crnobrnja, *The Yugoslav Drama*, 23.

14 Kosovo and Macedonia were thought to be the next sites for the growing wars in the former Yugoslavia. In addition, all seven of the former Yugoslavia's neighbours—Italy, Austria, Hungary, Romania, Bulgaria, Greece, and Albania—had interests in the Bosnian conflict. Also showing interest in the conflict were Russia and Turkey. For an analysis of the international dimension to the Bosnian conflict, see Zametica, *The Yugoslav Conflict*, 46–74.

15 Quoted in *New York Times*, 22 August 1992, A3.

16 Major-General (Retired) Lewis MacKenzie, *Peacekeeper: The Road to Sarajevo* (Vancouver: Douglas and McIntyre, 1993), 106–7.

17 UN doc, S/23900, 12 May 1992.

18 There had been forty military observers deployed to Mostar in April 1992 to monitor an initial ceasefire, but these observers were withdrawn a couple of weeks later.

19 UN doc, S/23900, 12 May 1992.

20 UN doc, S/Res/752, 15 May 1992.

21 UN doc, S/Res/757, 30 May 1992.

22 UN doc, S/Res/752, 15 May 1992.

23 UN doc, S/24000, 26 May 1992.

24 UN doc, S/Res/757, 30 May 1992.

25 For the full text of the Sarajevo Airport Agreement, see UN doc, S/24075, Annex, 6 June 1992.

26 MacKenzie, *Peacekeeper*, 204.

27 Ibid., 209–20.

28 UN doc, S/24263, 10 July 1992.

29 UN doc, S/Res/776, 14 September 1992.

30 UN doc, S/Res/816, 31 March 1993.

31 UN doc, S/Res/819, 16 April 1993. Also see S/Res/824, 6 May 1993 and S/Res/836, 4 June 1993.

32 UN doc, S/Res/908, 31 March 1994.

33 *Globe and Mail*, 31 August 1995, A1.

34 UN doc, A/50/790—S/1995/999, 21 November 1995.

35 UN doc, S/Res/1031, 15 December 1995.

36 This methodology is adapted from Duane Bratt, "Assessing the Success of UN Peacekeeping Operations," *International Peacekeeping* 3, no. 4 (Winter 1996): 64–81. For a more elaborate mechanism, see Paul F. Diehl, *Evaluating Peace Operations* (Boulder: Lynne Rienner Publishers, 2010).

37 Confidential interviews, New York, 8–16 November 1994.

38 Confidential interview, New York, 14 November 1994.

39 Confidential interview with Bosniac officials, New York, 15 November 1994.

40 Michael Wesley, "Blue Berets or Blindfolds? Peacekeeping and the Hostage Effect," *International Peacekeeping* 2, no. 4 (Winter 1995): 458.

41 Confidential interviews, New York, 8–16 November 1994.

42 UN doc, S/1994/300, 16 March 1994.

43 Confidential interview, New York, 15 November 1994.

44 Confidential interview, New York, 16 November 1994.

45 When NATO replaced the UN in Bosnia in December 1995, Canada remained in the country in varying numbers (the peak was 1,000 soldiers) and in several capacities. The last Canadian soldier did not leave Bosnia until 2010.

46 Lewis MacKenzie, "Coming to the Aid of Sarajevo," *Globe and Mail*, 3 July 2012.

47 Carol Off, *The Lion, the Fox, and the Eagle* (Vintage: Toronto, 2000), 190–91.

48 Quoted in Nicholas Gammer, *From Peacekeeping to Peacemaking: Canada's Response to the Yugoslav Crisis* (Montreal: McGill-Queen's University Press, 2001), 160.

49 Ibid., 47–49.

50 Ibid., 56.

51 Quoted in ibid., 126.

52 Quoted in ibid., 98.

53 Quoted in ibid., 101.

54 Quoted in Off, *The Lion, the Fox, and the Eagle*, 191.

55 See Hugh Miall, *The Peacemakers: Peaceful Settlement of Disputes since 1945* (New York: Palgrave Macmillan, 1992) and N. A. Pelcovits and Kevin L. Kramer, "Local Conflicts and UN Peacekeeping: The Uses of Computerized Data," *International Studies Quarterly* 20, no. 4 (December 1976): 533–52.

56 Lori Fisler Damrosch, ed., *Enforcing Restraint: Collective Intervention in Internal Conflicts* (New York: Council on Foreign Relations, 1993).

57 Boutros Boutros-Ghali, *An Agenda for Peace: Preventive Diplomacy, Peacemaking and Peace-keeping* (New York: United Nations Department of Public Information, 1992), 9.

58 Office of the Prime Minister, "Notes for an address by Prime Minister Brian Mulroney on the occasion of the centennial anniversary convocation," Stanford University, 29 September 1991.

59 Michael Walzer, *Just and Unjust Wars: A Moral Argument with Historical Illustrations* (Basic Books: New York, 1977), 106–7.

60 Quoted in Tom Keating and Nick Gammer, "The 'New Look' in Canadian Foreign Policy," *International Journal* 48, no. 4 (Autumn 1993): 725.

61 Quoted in Gammer, *From Peacekeeping to Peacemaking*, 69.

CHAPTER 8

SIX YEARS IN KANDAHAR:
Understanding Canada's Multidimensional Effort to Build a Sustainable Afghan State[1]

Stephen M. Saideman

Introduction

In Afghanistan, Canada faced its most severe challenge with a contemporary failed state—trying to develop order and good governance in an extremely hostile and impoverished environment. The simple phrases used to define the key "pillars" of the effort—security, governance, and development—are more than a little deceptive, as they gloss over the reality that Afghanistan lacked the ability to provide any core function of government. While the entire country faced, and continues to face, incredible difficulties after thirty years of war, the history, geography, and demography of the southern province of Kandahar made it an exceptionally hard place to build "state capacity."[2]

For most of Canada's time in the province, its agents largely ran the international state-building effort in Kandahar, testing the Canadian government's capacity to coordinate its civilian and military efforts, and its

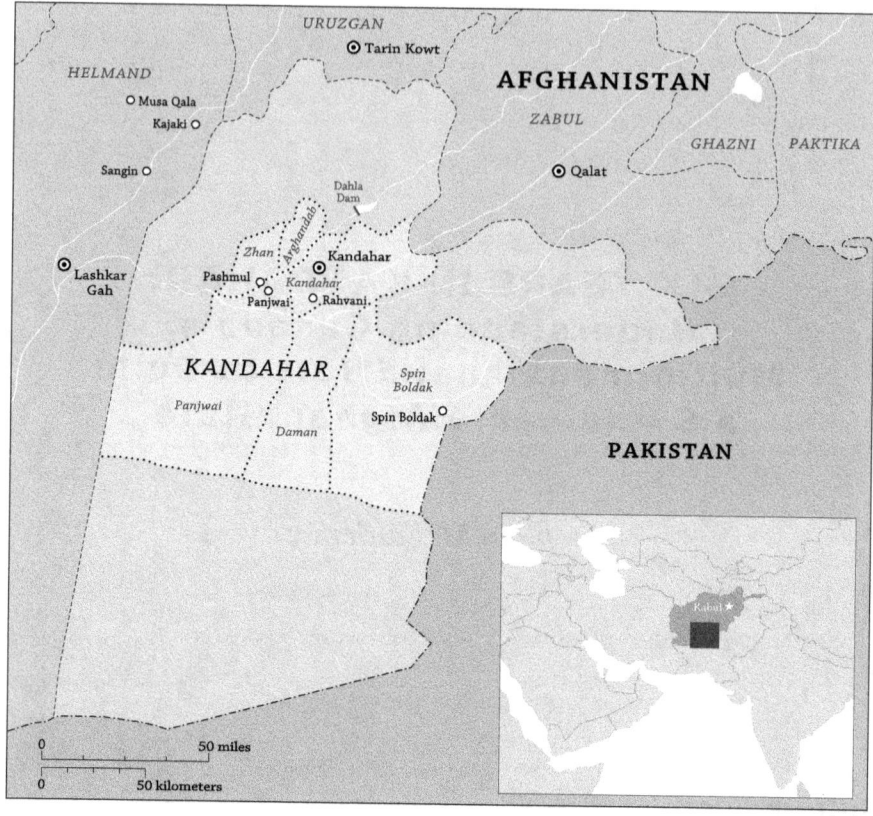

Figure 1: Map. (Credit: Marilyn Croot)

willingness to dedicate sufficient resources to the work. The combination of limited means and challenging environment was daunting enough. Managing the Afghan mission was made even more difficult since the intervention occurred during an unusual time in Canadian history—one of minority government. Successive Liberal and Conservative governments had a hard time generating enough support in Ottawa and in the rest of the country to maintain the effort. Indeed, the bipartisan manoeuvring through which the mission was extended in 2008 also ensured its ending—imposing an arbitrary deadline of 2011. Consequently, Canada had only six years to "fix" one of the most failed regions of one of the most failed countries in the world.

Given the context and the constraints imposed by Canada's limited capabilities and domestic politics, any evaluation of the effort must be a relative one. No international campaign was going to transform Kandahar into a functional, democratic, stable, productive, responsible, and sustainable success story in so little time. However, Canada's relative success in Kandahar, even if only for a short period, suggests that Canada has the potential to play a positive state-building role in other failed and failing states. In Afghanistan, as this chapter contends, Canada did make a difference, albeit a limited one that is likely to be of only temporary impact.

The Challenge of Kandahar

Afghanistan is a largely traditional society with very low literacy rates, an almost entirely agrarian economy, a history of decentralized political authority, and tribal divisions so complicated that outsiders brought in anthropologists to understand the complexities of local ties. The Soviet Union's invasion in December 1979 plunged the country into war, with nearly continuous fighting ever since. The successful fight against the Soviet occupiers and the internecine wars among the victorious factions that followed were extraordinarily brutal. Peace, relative and temporary, came in 1996 at a high price—a very repressive Taliban government, whose Islamic fundamentalist leaders aimed to destroy most of the country's surviving institutions and practices.[3]

The defeat of the Taliban in 2001-2 by the United States, working with the existing power brokers (warlords) in the northern corners of the country, provided only a temporary respite. The US and its allies defeated the Taliban quickly but responded slowly in rebuilding Afghan institutions. Other than anointing Hamid Karzai as the Taliban's heir apparent, the US did little in the early 2000s to reconstruct the country, since such efforts seemed akin to nation-building, a policy that was anathema to American President George W. Bush and Secretary of Defense Donald Rumsfeld.[4] Only in 2005-6 did NATO move outside Kabul to support the Afghan government as it sought to extend its authority beyond the capital and into the countryside.

Historic underdevelopment, decades of war, and the relatively slow Western response after 2001 have meant that Afghanistan consistently ranks near the top in any measure of state fragility or state failure. Indeed, that any country other than Somalia might be more "failed" than Afghanistan is stunning.[5] Despite efforts by NATO to stabilize the country, Afghanistan remains one of the world's largest producers of refugees. Indeed, the NATO strategy focused on providing growing bits of order in concentrated areas—the "ink spots" approach to counter-insurgency. This reveals precisely how limited the reach of the Afghan government was—to where NATO troops were standing and not much further. Indeed, since responsibility for security has transitioned from the International Security Assistance Force to the Afghan National Security Forces, we have seen the ink spots shrink, with the reach of the Afghan government decreasing and the zones of disorder becoming larger.

NATO's efforts to build the sound governing institutions required by a self-sustaining country have been constrained by the Afghan government itself. In contrast to the situation in Bosnia, where international stakeholders via the Office of the High Representative could remove recalcitrant politicians, the Afghan government was largely immune to outside interference. President Hamid Karzai appointed government officials from the highest levels to the lowest office, and his focus was not always on good governance. In Kandahar, Canadians were often frustrated, not just with the governors and bureaucrats appointed by Karzai but also with the region's key power broker: Ahmed Wali Karzai, brother of the president.[6]

Within this badly failed state, Kandahar stands out as one of the most challenging parts of the country.[7] The province sits astride key trading routes between Pakistan and the poppy-rich province of Helmand. The Arghandab river provides not only irrigation but, potentially, electrical power for the region. The city of Kandahar is one of the largest in the country, and the closest population centre to the Taliban's safe havens in Pakistan. These features provide tremendous opportunities for whoever controls this area, which has most recently been the home of the Taliban. The Islamic movement emerged from Kandahar, where it was based on the strength of key tribes in the province. Any attempt by the government of Afghanistan to extend its authority into this region, even with the support of its international backers, could expect to face intense resistance. And it did.

The Canadian Effort

In 2005, Canadian politicians decided to deploy the Canadian Forces to Kandahar to support the Provincial Reconstruction Team (PRT), which was staffed by Canadian military advisors, officials from Foreign Affairs and CIDA, and individuals from various police forces and Corrections Canada. A NATO innovation to concentrate local governance and development efforts, most PRTs were led by a single country, which largely followed its own agenda. The Kandahar PRT drew the Canadian Forces and the rest of the Canadian political system to the southern Afghan province.[8]

To support the PRT, Canada sent a battle group to Kandahar to deter and thwart the Taliban. This decision has become quite controversial in Canada, with some arguing that the Canadian military duped its civilian partners and cabinet overseers.[9] The evidence, however, indicates that the decision was made by Liberal prime minister Paul Martin with the encouragement of both General Rick Hillier and the Canadian Forces, and the various civilian agencies.[10] While Foreign Affairs may not have had a clear corporate position, key elements within it advocated in favour of Kandahar as the choice for Canada's Afghanistan deployment as it would represent a more visible and, hopefully, influential effort.[11] CIDA considered Kandahar to be a place of maximum need, perhaps overlooking the reasons why it was so underdeveloped in the first place.[12]

Regardless of the blame casting, Canadian politicians knowingly sent a "whole of government" team to one of the most inhospitable and difficult regions in Afghanistan to help build a self-sustaining Afghan government, hopeful that they would make a difference. This represented a far more extensive effort than previous interventions in Somalia and Bosnia, since the PRT was developed not only to provide security but also to facilitate good governance as well as economic and social development.

Though Canadian agencies and departments often talked a good game of harmonious inter-agency cooperation, that effort was not co-ordinated and "synced." Unfortunately, each government agency brought its own baggage (standard operating procedures, bureaucratic tendencies, expectations) to the effort, and only the enormous political gymnastics and administrative changes required to have the mission extended in 2008

Figure 2: Canadian Master Bombardier Clint Godsoe, Kandahar Provincial Reconstruction Team (PRT) patrols Kandahar in August 2008 on the way to deliver supplies to a local school. (Credit: ISAF Photo by Staff Sgt. Jeffrey Duran)

produced a relatively integrated effort. The sections below examine each major departmental role and assess the success of the "whole of government" approach to fragile states.

The Canadian Forces: Victory Despite Failure

Perhaps the best indicator of how the Canadian Forces feel about the Kandahar experience is the fact that nearly every commander of the Task Force has been promoted.[13] This is striking when compared to popular Canadian attitudes toward the effort in Kandahar—that the mission failed.[14] While the CF bore the brunt of the burden in the province, with over 150 killed in action and many more wounded, as an institution its prestige rebounded sharply from the "decade of darkness" that followed the deep post–Cold War cuts to its budget in the 1990s and the reduction of its standing in Canada.[15] Why? Because Canada "punched above its weight," fighting hard in an unusually dangerous environment and contributing far more than larger and wealthier allies, most notably Germany.

Some analysts have argued that the CF effort was aimed largely at ending the peacekeeping myth that constrained Canadians' imagination of what the CF could do.[16] There is doubtless some truth in the charge that the CF had grown frustrated by the popular Canadian view of the armed forces as peacekeepers and not warriors.[17] The mission did see the CF fight differently than in the recent past, as commanders in Ottawa gave commanders in the field far more operational discretion.[18] The CF went on the offensive in 2005 and afterward, moving far afield, including into Uruzguan and Helmand to help out the Dutch and British respectively.

There are two very different ways to measure the CF's impact in Kandahar. On the one hand, one might ask if the Canadian military prevented the Taliban from winning. Or, one could ask, to what extent were the CF able to create a safe and secure environment to facilitate the rest of the state-building project? There is little doubt that Canadian troops prevented the Taliban from seizing Kandahar. Operation Medusa in the summer of 2006, for instance, thwarted a large-scale Taliban campaign to force the Canadians to flee the province.[19] Failing to take the city through direct combat, the Taliban had to rely on roadside bombs, suicide bombers, and assassinations to pressure NATO forces and the Afghan government. While such tactics would not win the hearts and minds of the people of Kandahar, they stopped the CF and NATO from meeting their stated goal of providing a safe and secure environment for the reconstruction of the failed Afghan state.

The CF faced real limitations on its capacity to operate in Kandahar. Most importantly, there were simply not enough troops on the ground, given the size of the population and of the territory they were supposed to pacify.[20] Indeed, the unsatisfactory ratio of counter-insurgents to population, far short of the 1:20 cited in the doctrine manuals, was a key part of a presentation by Brigadier-General Denis Thompson when he spoke in Montreal after his tour as commander of Task Force Kandahar.[21] Lacking troops, the Canadians needed others to help out, and the CF were forced to focus considerable attention on training and equipping the Afghan National Army (ANA) and Afghan National Police (ANP) to bolster their numbers. This met the short-term goal of improving the numbers fighting against the insurgents, and eventually helped address the long-term objective of building Afghan security capacity. However, until the American troop surge of late 2009 led to a significant reinforcement in the province, the Canadians simply did not have enough troops to build a safe and secure environment. They could *clear* the insurgents in keeping with the counterinsurgency strategy of "*clear, hold, build,*" but they could neither *hold* nor *build*. Until 2010, the Canadian operation in Afghanistan's most dangerous province might be characterized as simply "mowing the lawn" or "serving as a fire brigade"—having a significant but temporary impact, which did not extend the control of the Afghan government beyond the city of Kandahar.

Training the ANA and ANP not only provided a supply of counterinsurgents, but also formed a critical part of the struggle to "un-fail" Afghanistan. Canada, with the rest of NATO, made a significant effort to restore and reinforce Afghan capacity in the area of rule of law. Years before outside actors focused on improved training for the ANP, NATO took seriously the task of training the ANA. Early success with the Afghan army encouraged many NATO officials to suggest that the police would experience a similar trajectory upward. In numbers of trained personnel and resulting improvements in policing the populated areas of Afghanistan, insisted the optimists, the ANP were just a few years behind the ANA. However, this assumes that police training and policing are rather similar to army training and army tasks. A corrupt army does not necessarily impact people very directly, but a corrupt police force undermines the government every single day.

Various measures indicate considerable success in training the ANA, which has continued to attract significant numbers of new recruits. Almost certainly, the ANA improved as a result of Canadian mentoring. However, reports on performance, especially in battle, remain mixed. So far, the ANA has fought hard despite serious losses, although civilian casualties have increased. The real test, of course, is occurring only now, after most NATO forces have withdrawn. Will the ANA perform well? Will the ANA hold together? The unhappy experience of the reconstructed Iraqi army in the face of the insurgent Islamic State during 2014 hardly fills one with optimism.

DFAIT and the Challenges of Governance

The endeavour to build modern governance institutions confronted even greater challenges than those faced by the Canadian military. Canada's foreign ministry had little experience in mounting expeditions of this kind and facilitating governance. Moreover, its putative partner and target, President Hamid Karzai's Afghan government, had little interest in reforming and developing itself. It was not an especially happy or productive partnership.

Canada's political operations were set back significantly soon after they started, when Glyn Berry, the head of the PRT, was killed by a roadside bomb in January 2006. This prompted Ottawa to withdraw most Canadian civilians from Kandahar for a time. The mission was restarted a few months later with a small team including five DFAIT staff. However, by the time the Canadian effort peaked in 2010–11, the PRT had almost sixty civilians, including nearly twenty DFAIT officials.[22] While there is much discussion online and in government reports about priorities (security, basic services, humanitarian assistance, border relations, national institutions, and reconciliation) and signature projects (the Dahla dam, polio eradication, and fifty schools), DFAIT's main job was to engage the Afghan political community in Kandahar to facilitate these various projects and to improve the quality of local governance.

The results were uncertain. Canadian diplomats made much progress in facilitating the work of other departments, but headway on governance and governing institutions was limited. Foreign Affairs officials assisted CIDA in developing and funding a variety of aid projects, in helping police and Corrections Canada officials build Afghan security and justice capacity, and in advising the Canadian Forces as they engaged with both local and international actors. Indeed, all of the various projects undertaken by Canadian agencies in Kandahar were possible only with DFAIT personnel managing the politics. This was especially true after March 2008, when Ottawa appointed diplomat Elissa Golberg as its first Representative of Canada in Kandahar (RoCK), enhancing the mission's capacity to coordinate inter-agency relations. Golberg and her successors played a tremendous role in coordinating civilian and military efforts, and working as the primary point of contact with senior Afghan officials in

Kandahar. Similarly, all development activities and funding depended on DFAIT easing the way.

DFAIT's success as a coordinating body in Kandahar contrasts sharply with its limited progress in improving governance in the province. Two basic, interrelated problems sharply constrained how much DFAIT officials, or anyone else, could improve governance: the reality that provincial governors, and key officials further down the chain of command, were appointed and replaced by President Karzai; and the fact that informal power brokers held great sway. Because the key officials in Kandahar were beholden to Karzai in Kabul, they were not as focused on making improvements in Kandahar, where the local population's satisfaction did not come into play. Indeed, when Canadian foreign minister Maxime Bernier publicly expressed Canada's frustration with Governor Asadullah Khalid, the embarrassing incident actually delayed the governor's departure.[23] Annoyance with the series of Kandahar governors was part of a larger problem—that the real power broker during Canada's time in Kandahar was Ahmed Wali Karzai, head of the provincial council. AWK, as he was known, said all the right things, but was associated with corruption, crime, and the US Central Intelligence Agency, and working with him tainted the Canadian effort. Yet, to get anything done, one needed to work with those who held power, and no one could wish away this difficult reality.

This speaks to a broader challenge for liberal democracies when faced with state failure or the prospect of intervening in a country after civil war. Conflict and intervention generally reward the most powerful actors—the people who destroyed the state and won the civil war battles.[24] State fragility often requires and empowers people who are corrupt and adept at surviving in difficult circumstances. It should not be surprising, then, that Canada faced some difficult challenges in Kandahar, as previous decades of violence had generated actors who were among the least inclined to facilitate transparency and good governance. Working around these inappropriate partners or forcing them from power would have required a much greater commitment of resources and willingness to bear significant costs than Canada was prepared to make.

CIDA and Developing from Ground Zero

Given the realities on the ground in Kandahar, CIDA, too, was compelled to shed its traditional operating procedures and aid priorities, and develop new expertise. Rather than supporting long-term development projects managed by intermediaries, it began to manage the processes itself and had to shift its focus from familiar Africa to Afghanistan. Suddenly, it was operating in an Asian conflict zone and required to organize development projects. This was a big change from its normal way of operating: funding international organizations and non-governmental organizations in national capitals. This section will explore how CIDA fared in making this transition by examining the most traditional project it backed—the Dahla dam. CIDA's Ottawa-centric approach and the agency's amazing opacity also erected barriers to success in Afghanistan.

The most high-profile of Canada's signature projects in Kandahar was CIDA's promise to rehabilitate the Dahla dam and Arghandab irrigation system. This involved spending close to $50 million to improve the flow of water to the Kandahar area, hiring vast numbers of contractors to dig out silt and reshape five hundred kilometres of canals, and paying guards to protect the workers.[25] It also included training farmers in irrigation maintenance and other related tasks. The dam project raised expectations and morale, but local farmers do not seem to be that much better off. The Canadian government's final reports and the more critical newspaper accounts contradict each other on how extensive the improvements have been.[26] Given that this kind of project has the most measurable of outputs—flows of water—it is disturbing that the results and assessments of this project are as unclear as they are.

CIDA also invested heavily in other aspects of Kandahar's development. Educational efforts focused on building schools and training teachers, while health care initiatives involved polio vaccinations and training health care workers. CIDA also sought to develop the regional economy through improving the marketplace. All these efforts represented a radical shift away from traditional CIDA activities, which previously had focused on longer-term projects and been aimed at poverty alleviation rather than supporting the Canadian Forces, who were focused on short-term, quick-impact projects. This, of course, met with significant resistance within the agency and between the agency and the development community.

Figure 3: The repair of the Dahla Dam and the Arghandab Irrigation Rehabilitation Project was a key Canadian priority, which aimed to create jobs, transfer knowledge, build capacities, and ensure sustainability in water allocation and agricultural development for Kandaharis. (Credit: CIDA/Lisa Vandehei)

One of the greatest, yet least obvious, challenges for CIDA was that as a bureaucracy it operated very differently from the Canadian Forces. The CF increasingly delegated authority for key decisions to the commanders on the ground, best exemplified by Brigadier-General Jonathan Vance's "model village" program, which focused its efforts on a much smaller area.[27] CIDA, on the other hand, remained highly centralized, with senior managers in Ottawa making most key decisions. This traditional decision-making model might work well for long-term projects, but adaptation to conditions in Afghanistan required more local decision making than CIDA could manage.

Over-centralization also created problems for CIDA as it struggled to inform Canadians about its work and marshal domestic backers. CIDA posted a significant volume of information on its Kandahar projects on its website but denied its field officers permission to speak to the media. This is one reason, observed journalist Murray Brewster, why reporters working in the province spent little time covering development work—Ottawa-based reporters could get the same story just as easily.[28]

Moreover, CIDA faced the most common challenge associated with working in all failed states—corruption. Just as it was almost inevitable that DFAIT personnel encountered bent officials and powerful warlords, CIDA worked in murky environments where public and private realms were often mixed and inseparable, co-existing uneasily with large pools of development funding. This presented a series of difficult trade-offs that had to be faced and finessed rather than denied and ignored.[29] Simply put, in places like Kandahar, there was no way to avoid dealing with corrupt actors and the diversion of some money from development projects. Failed states will not be as squeaky-clean and transparent as Norway or Canada when it comes to public administration. Surely it is no coincidence that among the world's most corrupt states are many of the most fragile and failed ones.[30] The question becomes not so much whether to tolerate corruption but which forms ought to be tolerated. Is it better to get a road built with kickbacks, or not at all? Future efforts will have to figure out ways to limit the ability of the local partners to divert resources, such as providing soldiers' pay via direct deposit rather than giving cash to superiors.

Whole of Government?

For most observers, Ottawa's enthusiastic talk of Whole of Government or Three D (diplomacy, defence, and development) approaches to state failure was unconvincing. It was always clear that the various Canadian agencies in Afghanistan were not cooperating as much as they should have been. Furtive leaks and open finger pointing made it apparent that the elements of the Canadian government were not "synced." The innovations propelled by the Manley Panel (see below) made a difference, mostly by empowering the RoCK and by creating a deputy minister–level position in the Privy Council Office to coordinate an interdepartmental Afghanistan Task Force to manage the mission. However, basic differences in priorities and management styles meant that significant friction remained.

The best example might be one of the government's signature projects—constructing fifty schools in Kandahar. The scheme envisioned providing better access to education, especially to girls, by building these schools throughout the province. In 2008, officials in Ottawa drew up a list of locations where the schools would be built. But when American troops surged into Kandahar, the Canadian Forces were no longer required to provide security for the entire province and were asked to cover just a few specific areas. Brigadier-General Vance focused on a handful of model villages, but some of the schools built within them did not count against the list of fifty developed in Ottawa. At the same time, the CF were no longer in a position to provide security for CIDA's schools outside their areas of responsibility, and the schools project foundered.[31] With agencies adopting different priorities and different processes for making decisions, friction was inevitable.

Minority Government, the Manley Panel, and Mixed Outcomes

Nearly the entire mission in Afghanistan took place during an unusual period in Canadian politics—one of minority government. "Un-failing" a failed state is tough enough, but it was made much harder as two of the three opposition parties—the Bloc Québécois and the New Democratic Party—were firmly against the mission, whilst the Liberal Party was ambivalent. Frankly, it is surprising that Canada was able to stay in Afghanistan as long as it did. At any point, the minority Liberal government of Prime Minister Paul Martin or Prime Minister Stephen Harper's Conservative government could have faced a no-confidence vote. Because the opposition parties could not unite around specific policy demands and because they often wanted to avoid elections when they felt unprepared, the mission was extended twice. The first extension occurred in 2006, soon after the Conservatives replaced the Liberals, who had initially agreed to the Kandahar deployment. This made it difficult for the Liberal Party to oppose the mission. Within two years, the balance of domestic opinion had begun to shift, and Prime Minister Harper recognized that renewal in 2008 would be much more contentious. Seeking political cover, he organized an elite, non-partisan commission, the Manley Panel, to study the Kandahar effort and make recommendations.

The panel was led by a retired Liberal cabinet minister and prominent businessman, John Manley, and included a former Conservative minister, Jake Epp, a journalist, and two former high-profile public servants. It engaged in serious research, conducted hundreds of interviews, travelled to Afghanistan, and developed a comprehensive set of recommendations. These shaped the course of Canada's mission. The panel recommended extending the mission, but only if the following conditions were met:

- NATO allies must provide more help in the form of an additional battalion;
- the Canadian Forces must receive helicopters and drones;
- Canada must improve its Whole of Government approach;
- aid must be better focused on Kandahar and distributed directly rather than through multilateral institutions;
- the government must improve its reporting to the Canadian people.[32]

These recommendations were largely followed. The Americans sent a battalion to Kandahar to meet the first condition in 2008 before sending several more military units when President Obama's troop surge kicked in a year later. The Canadian Forces leased new helicopters and bought used ones to meet creatively the commission's second recommendation. David Mulroney, the forceful associate deputy minister of foreign affairs, was handed a deputy minister–level appointment as head of the interdepartmental Afghanistan Task Force charged with coordinating the activities and policies of the various Canadian agencies working in Kandahar.[33] The RoCK was also empowered with more authority over CIDA and DFAIT officials, who had been micro-managed from Ottawa.[34] The RoCK was also authorized to allocate a small but significant portion of CIDA funds.

Unfortunately, the panel's findings led Canadian departments and agencies to emphasize signature projects that could be featured in quarterly reports to Parliament. These projects concentrated Canadian investments in an effective way—a good thing—but also limited flexibility as the situation changed on the ground. Fifty schools throughout Kandahar Province might have made for good reporting back home in Canada, since voters can easily count that high, but whether those schools were staffed, maintained, and operating was not always as clear. Fewer schools in better locations where the Canadian Forces remained active would have been more sustainable.

Significantly, the Harper government ignored one key recommendation from the Manley Panel. Though the commission could have specified an end to the mission, it chose not to do so, suggesting that the mission ought to be evaluated as the conflict unfolded. Instead, in the spring of 2008, Prime Minister Harper shrewdly tabled a resolution in the House of Commons that called for the withdrawal of Canadian combat troops from Kandahar in 2011. With popular support for the war quickly eroding, this was a politically expedient compromise that put the mission on the sidelines of national politics and removed it as a potential election issue. The Conservative motion was also expedient for the Liberals, who were divided over the prospect of continuing the dangerous mission. With the Manley stamp of approval *and* a time limit, the Liberals could safely rally behind the mission. Consequently, Canada withdrew from Kandahar in July 2011, with the CF undertaking safer and less controversial training missions and the civilian agencies changing their focus to Kabul-based activities. The departing Canadians left behind them much unfinished business: a dam not yet complete, schools built but without teachers, partially trained police, and an uncertain security environment.

Implications

It is difficult to draw broad conclusions from the Canadian experience in Kandahar; so many factors were arrayed against it. History and geography and regional stakeholders and NATO allies with different interests and perspectives, as well as corrupt local officials, all made it exceptionally challenging indeed. But none of these conditions are unique to Afghanistan. In any failed state, outside interveners are unlikely to agree entirely on how to proceed. Locals will have a different outlook, too, as well as their own conflicting interests, with some individuals willing to profit at the expense of their society. History will always be a challenge. Why? Because the dynamics that cause a state to fail do not dissipate when interveners show up. Also, the interveners will bring the same baggage they carry every time they intervene.[35] Agencies that normally do not get along are not going to cooperate very well when pressure and responsibility increase.

There are other lessons worth drawing from Canada's experience in Afghanistan that may be applicable the next time Canada intervenes in a failed or failing state. Indeed, the importance of learning lessons is the first lesson to learn. In contrast to Canada's earlier interventions in failed states, the government's civilian agencies have worked hard at the kind of "lessons learned" exercises that the military does as a matter of course.[36] Indeed, the Stabilization and Reconstruction Task Force (START) was created to institutionalize these lessons within the Department of Foreign Affairs, with Elissa Golberg, an early RoCK and an advisor to the Manley Panel, serving as its first director.[37]

It is worth acknowledging, too, that success in failed or fragile states can be hard to quantify. Afghanistan reminds Canadians that they should expect this problem to continue in future interventions. Schools built, children vaccinated, and water pumped are measurable outputs, but it is not clear how counting these connects to the larger goals associated with "un-failing" a fragile state. State failure is fundamentally a political problem. When governments cannot provide services or domestic security, citizens will develop strategies to overcome their society's paralysis. Distrust, corruption, and the emergence of militias and warlords are all logical reactions to state failure. Canadians, policymakers, and voters alike must recognize that it is impossible to reverse such processes quickly. Our focus must be on modestly ameliorating, not radically transforming, fragile states.

Reducing expectations makes it easier to see that Canada did make a difference in Afghanistan. The Canadian Forces denied the Taliban control of Kandahar City and helped to keep most of the violence in the outlying districts. DFAIT personnel did much to mitigate the worst instincts of the local politicians. CIDA project officers did fund much development, including the Dahla dam, as well as roads, schools, and health care. Canadian police and corrections officers helped to improve the treatment of prisoners. But Canada's ability to extend good governance and offer development aid was limited. Canada made a difference only in areas where Canadian troops worked and only for as long as those forces were present. The struggle is now almost entirely in Afghan hands.

Notes

1. This chapter borrows heavily from my latest book, *Adapting in the Dust: Lessons Learned from Canada's War in Afghanistan* (Toronto: University of Toronto Press, 2016).

2. Barnett R. Rubin, *The Fragmentation Of Afghanistan: State Formation and Collapse in the International System* (New Haven: Yale University Press, 2002).

3. Gilles Dorronsoro, *Revolution Unending: Afghanistan, 1979 to the Present* (New York: Columbia University Press, 2013).

4. There has been much written on the early desire to avoid nation building. A good start on this is Rajiv Chandrasekaran, *Little America: The War Within the War for Afghanistan* (New York: Alfred A. Knopf, 2012).

5. See *Foreign Policy*'s *Failed States Index*, http://www.foreignpolicy.com/articles/2010/06/21/2010_failed_states_index_interactive_map_and_rankings (accessed 17 January 2012).

6. AWK, as he was known, was assassinated just as Canada's mission in Kandahar ended in July 2011.

7. Just using the simple measure of coalition troops killed in action, Kandahar is second only to Helmand: two-and-a-half times more were KIA in Kandahar than in the next province. See Operation Enduring Freedom, http://www.icasualties.org/OEF/ByProvince.aspx (accessed 17 January 2012).

8. Kenneth Holland, "The Canadian Provincial Reconstruction Team: The Arm of Development in Kandahar Province," *American Review of Canadian Studies* 40, no. 2 (2010): 276–91; and Kimberly Marten, "From Kabul to Kandahar: The Canadian Forces and Change," *American Review of Canadian Studies* 40, no. 2 (2010): 214–36.

9. Janice Gross Stein and J. Eugene Lang, *The Unexpected War: Canada in Kandahar* (Toronto: Viking Canada, 2007).

10. Murray Brewster, ed., *The Savage War: The Untold Battles of Afghanistan* (Mississauga, ON: Wiley, 2011). Also see Matthew Willis, "An Unexpected War, A Not-Unexpected Mission: The Origins of Kandahar 2005," OpenCanada.org, 8 January 2013, http://www.opencanada.org/features/an-unexpected-war-a-not-unexpected-mission/ (accessed 14 November 2015); and David J. Bercuson and J. L. Granatstein, with Nancy Pearson Mackie, *Lessons Learned? What Canada Should Learn from Afghanistan* (Calgary: CDFAI, 2011). I discuss this question at greater length in Chapter 3 of Saideman, *Adapting in the Dust*.

11 Interview, former Ambassador Chris Alexander in discussion with the author, 24 July 2013, Ottawa; interview, Wendy Gilmour, former DFAIT director general, in discussion with the author, 15 August 2013, Ottawa; interview, David Mulroney in discussion with the author, 18 July 2013, Ottawa.

12 Nipa Banerjee wrote the CIDA evaluation comparing Herat and Kandahar provinces. Interview, Nipa Banerjee in discussion with the author, 17 May 2013, Ottawa.

13 I discovered this in the course of interviewing nearly every Canadian who commanded in Afghanistan. Interviews in Ottawa, Montreal, and Edmonton, 2007–11.

14 It was not only Canadians who felt that efforts in Kandahar were a failure, as Rajiv Chandrasekaran's controversial book asserts. See Chandrasekaran, *Little America*.

15 Former chief of defence staff Rick Hillier made this quite clear in his memoir: see Rick Hillier, *A Soldier First: Bullets, Bureaucrats and the Politics of War* (Toronto: HarperCollins, 2010).

16 Eric Wagner, "The peaceable kingdom? The national myth of Canadian peacekeeping and the Cold War," *Canadian Military Journal* 7, no. 4 (2006–7): 45–54.

17 Hillier, *A Soldier First*.

18 For an extensive treatment of this evolution, see Saideman, "Canadian Forces in Afghanistan: Generational Change While Under Fire," in *Military Adaptation and War in Afghanistan*, ed. Theo Farrell, Frans Osinga, and James Russell (Palo Alto: Stanford University Press, 2013), 219–41.

19 Bernd Horn, *No Lack of Courage: Operation Medusa, Afghanistan* (Toronto: Dundurn Press, 2010).

20 Chandrasekaran notes the shortage and cites an American general as saying that the Canadians did not want to be reinforced in Kandahar; see Chandrasekaran, *Little America*, 62. This conflicts with everything I heard from Canadian officers, not to mention the public pressures represented by the Manley Panel and the parliamentary debate about the extension in 2008.

21 Brigadier-General Denis Thompson, "The Struggle for Kandahar: Canadian Soldiers Making a Difference in Afghanistan," presentation, 24 March 2009, Montreal.

22 Canada, Canadian Engagement in Afghanistan, http://www.afghanistan.gc.ca/canada-afghanistan/kandahar/kprt-eprk.aspx?view=d (accessed 16 May 2012). Also, informal information from DFAIT officials.

23 "Kandahar Governor Set To Leave Until Bernier Spoke, Says Afghan Official," *CBC News*, 22 April 2008, http://www.cbc.ca/news/world/story/2008/04/22/afghan-cda.html (accessed 17 May 2012).

24 Peter Andreas, *Blue Helmets and Black Markets: The Business of Survival in the Siege of Sarajevo* (Ithaca: Cornell University Press, 2008).

25 *Canadian Engagement in Afghanistan 14th and Final Report*, 2012, 17, http://www.afghanistan.gc.ca/canada-afghanistan/assets/pdfs/docs/r06_12-eng.pdf (accessed 16 May 2012). Alas, these

26 See CIDA's project browser page: http://www.acdi-cida.gc.ca/cidaweb/cpo.nsf/projEn/A033627001 (accessed 18 July 2012); Paul Watson, "Canada's Afghan Legacy: Failure at Dahla Dam," *Toronto Star,* 14 July 2012, http://www.thestar.com/news/world/article/1226412--canada-s-afghan-legacy-the-failure-at-dahla-dam (accessed 18 July 2012).

27 Brian Hutchinson, "Assignment Kandahar: Interview with Jonathan Vance, Canada's Top Commander in Kandahar," *National Post,* 13 August 2010, http://news.nationalpost.com/2010/08/13/assignment-kandahar-interview-with-jonathan-vance-canadas-top-commander-in-kandahar/ (accessed 11 October 2014).

28 Brewster, *The Savage War.*

29 In late 2007, I was part of a group of Canadian scholars who were given a tour of Kabul and Kandahar by NATO and by the Canadian Forces. The CIDA advisor in Kandahar seemed unwilling to face this trade-off in our conversation.

30 Transparency International, Corruption Perceptions Index 2011, http://cpi.transparency.org/cpi2011/results/ (accessed 24 July 2012).

31 Based on interviews with Canadian officers.

[The text before note 26 reads:] reports are no longer easy to find as the government of Canada has archived the relevant websites.

32 Hon. John Manley, Derek H. Burney, Hon. Jake Epp, Hon. Paul Tellier, and Pamela Wallin, *Independent Panel on Canada's Future Role in Afghanistan* (Ottawa: Minister of Public Works and Government Services, 2008).

33 Interviews with military officers and civilians seem to indicate that the Canadian Forces were least enthusiastic about being coordinated from on high. CIDA does such a good job of restricting access to its employees that it is difficult to determine how unhappy they were about being managed by Mulroney. Mulroney was replaced by Greta Bossenmaier when he became ambassador to China in 2009.

34 Interviews with two RoCKs: Ben Roswell in discussion with the author, 17 May 2011, Waterloo, ON; and Elissa Golberg in discussion with the author, 7 June 2011, Ottawa.

35 Séverine Autesserre, *Peaceland: Conflict Resolution and the Everyday Politics of International Intervention* (Cambridge: Cambridge University Press, 2014).

36 Alas, the lessons learned effort by the Privy Council Office has been buried so deep that members of the government have not seen the report, let alone pesky academics filing Access to Information requests.

37 Interview, Golberg.

CHAPTER 9

CANADA AND FRAGILE STATES IN THE AMERICAS

Jean Daudelin

A number of states in the Americas are overwhelmed by the security, social, and economic challenges that they confront, while others have such limited capacities that any significant test would prove them wanting. Those states can be understood as "fragile" because their political order is already shaky or because they risk being broken under any significant stress.

State fragility can represent an international security threat. A weak state's limited and brittle capabilities often imply the existence of spaces where political or criminal groups can gather, train, and accumulate resources to challenge other states. The instability associated with fragility may also lead to population movements that upset nearby countries and even destabilize whole regions. More broadly, fragility matters for development as fragile states are unable to provide the infrastructure and institutional environment required to generate economic investment and to function efficiently. The challenges of fragility, international security, and development, in other words, are deeply intertwined.

This chapter examines Canada's policy toward fragile states in the Americas, asking if that policy makes sense given the nature and scale of the problem and Canada's capacity to have a significant impact on the situation. The chapter focuses on the adequacy of the policy from the standpoint of the region's fragile states, deliberately leaving out policy determinants and the intricacies of the decision-making process(es). Moreover, this assessment is not based on an examination of particular projects, formal policies, or specific aid delivery mechanisms. Rather, it examines the resources transferred by the Canadian government to those countries since 2000, the weight of such transfers in the broader context of Canadian assistance, the nature, channels, and declared purposes of those transfers, and the evolution of these variables.

Five questions structure the chapter's enquiry: What is state fragility? Which states are fragile in the Americas? What kind of aid have they received from Canada? How adequate is that assistance, given the characteristics of the challenge these states confront and Canada's technical and political capacity to help? And how sustainable is the current effort, given the economic, security, and political implications of fragility in those states for Canada and its government?

The chapter has three sections: the first outlines the conception of fragility underlying the analysis and identifies those states of the region that qualify as fragile; the second looks at Canadian assistance to these countries; and the third section assesses it. A conclusion discusses the scope and limits of the analysis.

In sum, this analysis argues that (1) four groups of American states qualify as fragile: a group of one, made up of Haiti, whose capabilities are so limited that they are overwhelmed by every significant challenge; Central America's Northern Triangle (El Salvador, Honduras, and Guatemala), where significant but limited state capacity confronts an onslaught of drug-related violence that these states are unable to manage; a subset of Caribbean states endowed with significant capacities but which are nonetheless unable to tackle extremely high levels of criminal violence; and finally one South American country (Venezuela), where a surprising discrepancy has emerged between huge capabilities but even larger challenges; (2) Canada's efforts have been concentrated on Haiti, the West Indies and, increasingly, Central America's Northern Triangle; and (3) the policy over the last ten years is well suited to the challenges of fragility in the region and appears to be politically sustainable.

State Fragility in the Americas

As David Carment, Stewart Press, and Yiagadeesen Samy have shown in exquisite detail,[1] current conceptualizations of the nature, determinants, and consequences of state fragility are extremely varied, with emphases on a wide range of factors, from the broad structural conditions that constrain effective political rule to the political "will" of governments.[2] Most studies, however, focus on the state's administrative and military capabilities and on state legitimacy.

This study adopts a minimalist approach, focusing strictly on the capacity of the state and its rulers to manage in a sustainable manner the pressures exerted on them. Reaching back to Max Weber's classic intuition about the core characteristics of states, it will focus on the ability of those "political organizations with continuous operations" to "successfully claim the monopoly of the legitimate use of physical force in the enforcement of [their] order."[3] The ultimate test of a state's capacity, in other words, lies in its ability to enforce a sufficient modicum of order in the territory it claims.

To assess that capacity, the analysis considers only the material and administrative resources that states can mobilize to produce and guarantee order. Some measure of legitimacy or social recognition of a state's capacity certainly matters; otherwise it would constantly be called upon to use that capacity, disrupting the very order it intends to uphold. But like Weber, the chapter will not assume that such legitimacy necessarily implies support for, or subjective agreement with, the nature and characteristics of the order the state enforces, as this is only one of the possible foundations of the practical recognition by subjects of the validity of the particular rule to which they submit.[4] For these reasons, the complex problem of legitimacy will be collapsed into the much easier one of material and administrative capabilities.

An assessment of the extent to which such capabilities are sufficient must take into account the challenges that each state confronts. Imposing order on a huge and populous country like Brazil or the Democratic Republic of the Congo (DRC) calls for an immense amount of resources. Brazil clearly has them, but the DRC does not. Similarly, the intensity of the competition over resources or markets affects the scale of the demand for order that a state confronts. The discovery of alluvial diamonds and oil, for instance, played a central role in turning weak but relatively stable political orders in West and Central Africa into chaotic messes.

Finally, some or even most of those challenges may come from the outside, either as a result of pressure from a neighbour—think of Ukraine—or simply because a state's territory happens to be a key link in a long criminal value chain—a problem that afflicts Afghanistan as well as several states of the Americas.

Obviously, a rigorous and comprehensive assessment of state fragility combining these two sets of issues is well-nigh impossible. This chapter, therefore, uses an impressionistic selection methodology based on a broad range of data. All the countries of the Americas were assessed, with particular attention given to four widely used classifications of state fragility: Carleton University's Country Indicators for Foreign Policy; the latest editions of the "Failed States Index" (now called "Fragile States Index"); the Center for Systemic Peace's "State Fragility Index"; and the World Bank's "Worldwide Governance" indicators.

I have adopted none of these indices wholesale, in part because of the sometimes patently absurd results that their methods have generated (e.g., the "Failed States Index" portrays Colombia as more fragile than any country of the region but Haiti; and Brazil is defined as more fragile than El Salvador in the "State Fragility Index"). Instead, I have focused on the existence of a significant discrepancy between a state's capacity and the challenges it confronts, a relative measure that is not used by these indices' methodologies. For that purpose, I have incorporated data from the World Development Indicators and, for crime and violence, have used statistics from the United Nations Office on Drugs and Crime (UNODC). Table 1 presents the dimensions of both challenges and capabilities, as well as the indicators I have used to assess them.

Table 1: Analytical Framework

	TYPES	INDICATORS
Challenges	Economic	• Sustained recession • High inflation • International insolvency • High dependence on foreign donors
	Military	• Foreign occupation • Invasion or long-distance attack or credible threat thereof • Presence and activity of domestic anti-government forces • Civil war between sub-components of society
	Political	• Mostly peaceful anti-government mobilizations by domestic social movements or organizations
	Environmental	• Major negative climatic change • Large-scale and/or frequent extreme weather events • Large-scale and/or frequent geological events
	Criminal	• Presence and activity of large criminal organizations • High levels of homicide and other violence crimes

	DIMENSIONS	INDICATORS
State capabilities	Economic	• Access to revenue (tax base, revenues from state corporations or investments, royalties, foreign assistance) • Stability of that access
	Political	• Stability of the government • Ability to command respect for its laws and regulations without the use of force
	Military and police	• Human and material resources available for territorial control and public order

	Administrative	• Human, material, and organizational resources available for the
		    - provision of public services
		    - regulation of economic activities
		    - management of major natural disasters

Table 2: Fragile States in the Americas

	Economic	Military	Political	Environmental	Criminal
Belize			X		xxx
El Salvador					xxx
Guatemala			X		xxx
Guyana		X	Xx		xx
Haiti	xxx		X	xx	x
Honduras			Xx		xxx
Jamaica					xxx
Suriname			Xx		xx
Venezuela	xx	X	xx		xxx
West Indies					xx/xxx

Using the data sources listed above, and building on a broad overview of the region's recent economic and political history to combine the two sets of parameters, I propose the picture of fragility painted in Table 2. The presence of one, two, or three Xs identifies challenges that over the last ten to fifteen years have overwhelmed government capabilities, as well as the degree to which they have done so (low, medium, high). The table includes all the countries that currently appear fragile in at least two of the five categories or that have high levels of fragility in any one of them. Obviously, the "calculations" involved here are highly approximate and most of the indicators on which they rely are impressionistic. This approach has been chosen mainly for reasons of expediency: the paper assesses Canadian policies toward fragile states in the Americas, it does not propose a theory to explain fragility in the hemisphere. Still, I would contend that the results presented here are not any less compelling, and arguably more so, than those arrived at by using supposedly "precise" proxies to reach clear but sometimes absurd results, like the rankings of Brazil or Colombia mentioned above.

The diagnosis summarized in Table 2 has a number of key features. Criminal challenges represent the most important determinant of fragility in the Americas, as they often overwhelm, sometimes massively, the capabilities of the region's governments.[5] In almost all cases, some of this violence is tied to drug markets, local, regional, and global.

Figure 1: Homicide Rates in the Americas in 2010 (per 100,000, for countries whose rate is larger than 10 per 100,000)

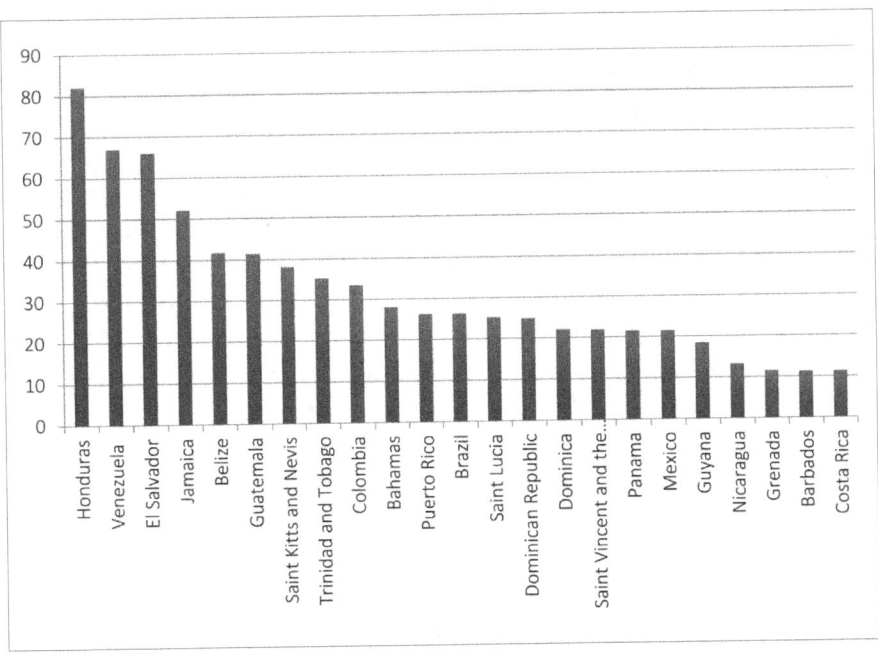

The region's staggering number of homicides represents the most shocking expression of those challenges: between 145,000 and 150,000 murders annually in recent years, totalling over a million deaths in the last decade.[6] Because of the sheer size of their respective countries, most of the victims are Brazilian (50,000), Mexican (15,000), and Colombian (15,000). However, with the exception of Venezuela, it is in the region's smaller countries that homicide rates reach their highest levels (cf. Figure 1): using Canada's homicide rate of about 1.5 per 100,000 as a yardstick, consider that in 2010, Honduras, Venezuela, El Salvador, Jamaica, and Belize had rates hovering between 25 and 50 times higher. While homicide rates are often poor proxies for general levels of criminality, such high levels of violence imply a terrible climate of insecurity that profoundly disturbs and damages people's everyday lives. Moreover, while violence is almost always extremely concentrated in particular regions or neighbourhoods, national homicide rates of over 30 per 100,000 are never associated with low levels of crime. Basic physical insecurity affects whole societies through its impact on social relations, economic activities, and political discussions.

Political dynamics are the second locus of fragility in the Americas. While all states of the region but Cuba have held regular democratic elections for almost twenty years—with recent "hiccups" in Honduras and Venezuela—the political system in a number of these countries is pervaded by deep divisions: ethnic (Guyana, Suriname), social (Haiti, Honduras, Venezuela), and political (Venezuela again). Political fragility lies in the inability of these states to channel social demands and manage the competition for power between ethnic groups, social classes, or broad political movements, pushing elites to coup conspiracies, ordinary people to the streets, and social movements toward challenging the legitimacy of the political systems themselves. The relative political stability of the last twenty years has not been accompanied by a broad re-legitimation of political institutions. Legislatures, in particular, continue to meet with profound cynicism from electorates, which results in highly personalized struggles for executive power and in the confrontational exercise of that power. Such arrangements limit the state's ability to muster the capacity needed to tackle challenges, beginning with tax collection and ending with the provision of basic public order and justice.

The economy remains a challenge for parts of the region. Despite two "golden" decades of growth in what remains a commodity-dependent region, some of its richest countries (Venezuela, for instance) are in a critical economic position, with high inflation, poor growth rates, deteriorating infrastructure, declining domestic and international investment, and limited access to global financial markets. Again, Haiti is uniquely situated because of its dependence on foreign aid from Western donors and cheap oil from vulnerable Venezuela, and because of the chronic inability of its government to establish a self-sustaining basis for long-term growth.

Beyond these prominent themes, one should also draw attention to the remarkable geographic concentration of fragility in the Americas. All the weakest and most fragile states are located in the Caribbean Basin, and all but Venezuela are among the small republics of Central America and the West Indies. Size matters.

A brief overview of key individual cases completes this portrait. Haiti and Venezuela are the worst cases of severe multidimensional fragility. It is a profound paradox that the poorest and one of the best-endowed countries of the region find themselves at the top of our fragility ranking. Haiti owes its place to a tragic mixture of very poor material endowments, secular social and educational under-investment, a history of political mismanagement, chronic and acute administrative deficiencies, extreme social inequalities, and severe geological, environmental, and climatic vulnerabilities. From any angle and by almost any measure the country is a developmental and human security disaster.

By contrast, Venezuela has no good reason for its high fragility ranking. It was already one of the best-educated countries in the hemisphere by the end of the 1950s (along with pre-Castro Cuba, Argentina, and Costa Rica). It has few deep ethnic fractures and it enjoyed remarkable political stability during the region's troubled 1960s and 1970s, when it benefited immensely from the global oil crisis and played a leading role in the establishment of OPEC.

Problems started to emerge only in the 1980s, when the price of oil dropped violently and the government proved unable to adjust its policies to the country's shrinking bounty. Corruption of the political parties that had dominated Venezuela since the 1950s, mismanagement of public finances, ever more severe inequality, and growing popular discontent paved the way for the eventual rise to power of President Hugo Chavez in 1999. Using state programs, price controls, and administrative recruitment to build and consolidate support among the poor, Chavez was able substantially to reduce both poverty and inequality. Corruption and economic mismanagement have worsened under his successor, Nicolás Maduro, threatening those gains. Inflation is at an all-time high, economic growth has stalled, and the country, which has some of the largest oil reserves in the world, remains heavily dependent on imported refined gasoline and diesel. To make matters worse, public security has deteriorated drastically. The military and well-armed party militias do not always see eye-to-eye, and the opposition appears unable to harness popular discontent, prompting some of its members to seek extra-constitutional routes to power. Collapsing oil prices since 2014 have added fuel to this explosive mix.

The absence of Brazil, Colombia, and Mexico from this portrait warrants a comment. In all three cases, the levels of violence are very high (homicide rates of 26, 33, and 21 per 100,000 respectively in 2010) and, in the case of Colombia, two anti-government guerrilla movements are still active in the country. However, government capacity in these states is extremely high and is not overwhelmed by these challenges. Public safety aside (Colombia's guerrillas should be seen today primarily as a public order issue), none of these states confront very significant challenges, notwithstanding a lagging economy in Brazil and Mexico.

Canadian Assistance to Fragile States in the Americas

This section, detailing the allocation of Canadian aid to fragile states, is divided into four subsections. First, it considers the overall character of that aid and its main hallmarks. Specifically, it addresses the relative weight of the region's weakest states in Canadian aid flows to the Americas, as well as its channels (bilateral, regional, or multilateral). Second, this section explores the sub-regional allocation of aid flows, beginning with Haiti, and moving to the fragile states of Central America, the Caribbean, and South America. Third, the examination moves to country allocation and, fourth, to sectoral allocations for fragile states as a whole, for sub-regional groupings, and for the largest individual recipients.

The data comes from the website of the former Canadian International Development Agency (CIDA) and covers all Canadian transfers to developing countries between fiscal year (FY) 2000–2001 and FY 2012–13, including military and police assistance, when the data are available.[7]

Overall Picture

Total assistance to the fragile states of the region, as identified in Section 1 of the chapter, was worth C$3.64 billion between FY 2000–2001 and 2012–13. Three basic features dominate the overall official flows of Canadian aid to the region's fragile states: their small size in Canada's total aid envelope, their remarkable concentration in Haiti, and the dominance of bilateral over multilateral disbursements.

Including all transfers and loans, as well as contributions to regional programs and multilateral banks, total outflows to fragile states in the Americas represented just 5 percent of all Canadian aid since FY 2000–2001. Once the spike that followed the 2010 earthquake in Haiti is excluded, fragile states capture only about 40 percent of Canadian assistance to

Figure 2: Canadian Assistance to Fragile States of the Americas

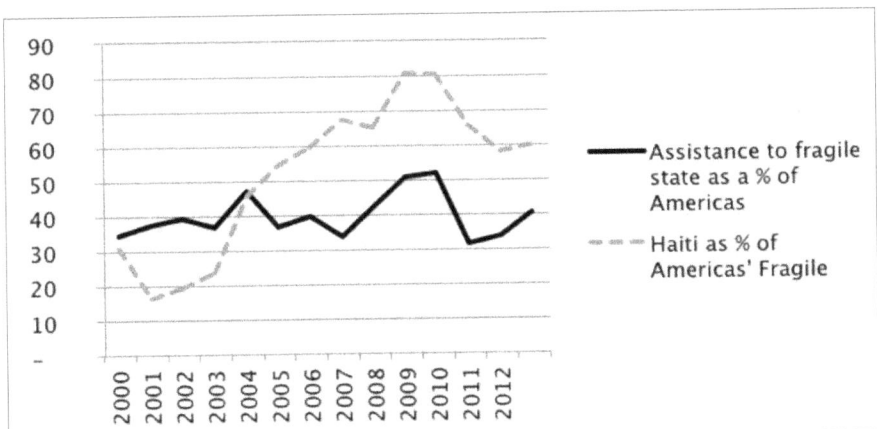

Source: International Assistance Reports, DFATD

the Americas (Figure 2). Beginning around 2004, more than half of that aid went to Haiti, reaching a peak of about 80 percent in FY 2009–10 and FY 2010–11, when a terrible earthquake devastated the country. Canada's fragile state policy in the Americas is essentially a Haiti policy.

The relatively small weight of the Americas in Canada's assistance envelope comes as no surprise. All countries of the region, including fragile ones but excepting Haiti, have "graduated" from the ranks of the least developed countries (LDC), making it difficult to justify sending significant assistance to them. Still, the fact that about 60 percent of Canada's total assistance in the region goes to countries that are neither LDCs nor fragile points to an allocation that, for the Americas at least, is clearly driven by motives other than tackling fragility or extreme poverty.

Assistance to fragile states is primarily channelled through bilateral programs. Overall, in fact, the proportion of aid going through multilateral channels has declined over the decade, although this decline is driven by assistance to Haiti, which is overwhelmingly bilateral. Even when assistance to that country is factored out, about two-thirds of fragile state assistance still flows through bilateral channels.

Figure 3: Preferred Channels for Assistance to Fragile States in the Americas

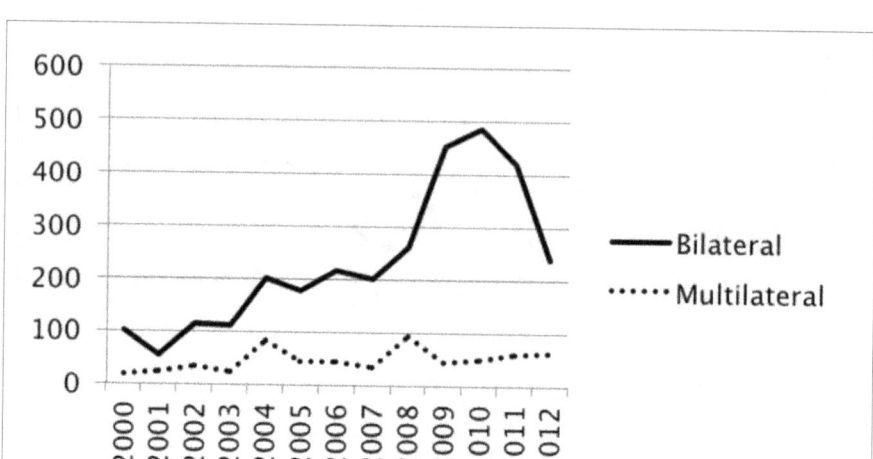

Sub-Regional Allocation

The list of fragile states proposed in Section 1 lends itself logically to a four-part classification. Haiti stands as a unique case, with massive challenges and extremely limited capabilities. Venezuela, too, is in a class by itself, blessed with immense resources but overwhelmed by political, institutional, and criminal challenges. Central America's so-called "Northern Triangle" of El Salvador, Honduras, and Guatemala—lower-middle-income states plagued with extreme violence tied to drug trafficking—make up the third group. The countries of the West Indies also confront formidable levels of violence. But Jamaica, Trinidad and Tobago, the Bahamas, and their smaller neighbours have higher revenues, much higher levels of education, and better public administrations, and represent a fourth subset of regional fragility. Belize, Guyana, and Suriname will be considered a part of this group, as historical, cultural, and sociological traits make them very similar to the British Caribbean islands, though their institutional and economic situations are somewhat closer to Central America's Northern Triangle.

Breaking down Canadian assistance among these groups shows Haiti grabbing 50 percent, clearly the largest share. The rest is captured by

Central America's Northern Triangle (19 percent), the West Indies (16.5 percent), and the Caribbean Regional Fund (13.5 percent). Troubled and much bigger Venezuela gets less than one percent of the total.

Sectoral Allocation

Canadian aid takes a wide variety of forms, which are now carefully specified in the government's statistical reports (see Annex 2 for a full breakdown of the twenty-three distinct categories that were used in FY 2012–13). Four groupings are especially relevant to state fragility: (1) development assistance controlled by CIDA, which has a broad mandate to focus on the poorest countries, covers four of the twenty-three categories; (2) the bilateral and multilateral assistance extended by the former Department of Foreign Affairs and International Trade (DFAIT), which pursues policies linked to commercial and security objectives, falls into two categories; (3) the bilateral programs of the Department of National Defence (DND), which focuses on military training, constitute one category (from 2004 to 2012); and (4) the bilateral programs of the Royal Canadian Mounted Police (RCMP), which finances capacity building for the police, also form one category (from 2006).

These four groupings represented 86 percent of Canadian assistance to fragile states from 2000 to 2013. CIDA's development aid alone accounted for 76 percent of the total.

Development Aid (CIDA Funding)

Beginning in FY 2003–4, Haiti has dominated development assistance flows to fragile states in the Americas, capturing about half of this type of aid in "normal times." Figure 4 appears to suggest that the proportion of aid going to the West Indies has slowly declined, relative to the amounts received by Central America. This is, however, something of an illusion, as the islands get a substantial share of the Caribbean regional funding.

Foreign Affairs

Foreign Affairs funding clearly has broader objectives, and fragile states have received only about half of the aid allocated by the Department to the Americas since FY 2000–2001. It contributed a modest 5.9 percent of

Figure 4: Development Assistance (CIDA) to Fragile States in the Americas

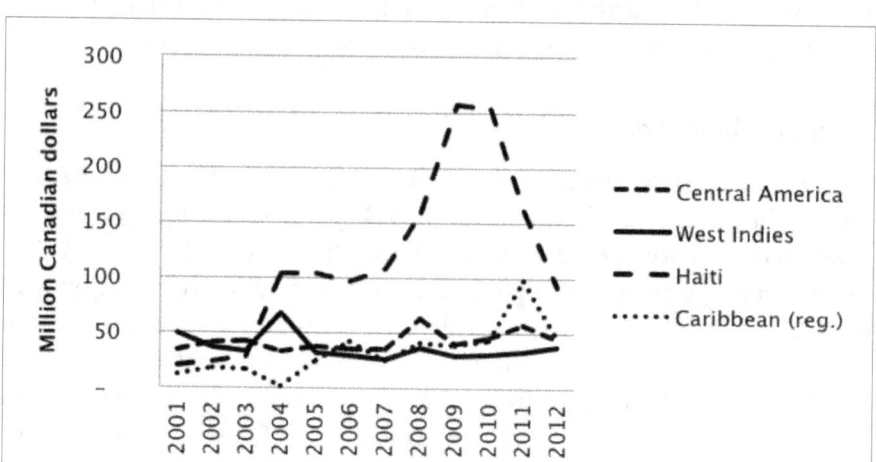

the fragile state assistance envelope for the period. Although Haiti once again received the lion's share of those funds (60 percent), the evolution of disbursements highlights a significant reorientation toward Central America. Its allocation, beginning in 2010, was growing as fast as Haiti's was declining: by FY 2012–13, both Haiti and the three Central American republics were receiving about C$17 million annually.

DND and RCMP Assistance

Canadian military and police assistance to fragile states is minute, both in absolute terms (C$144 million over the whole thirteen-year period) and as a proportion of the total flows of government aid to these countries (1.5 percent and 2.5 percent respectively). For the period covered by CIDA's dataset, only three countries have received assistance from DND (Haiti, Jamaica, and Nicaragua) and two from the RCMP (Haiti and Guatemala). Again, Haiti receives the lion's share of this help, with more than 99 percent of the funds provided to the entire Americas, including non-fragile states. This represents about 40 percent of all Canadian aid from these two envelopes.

How Adequate and Sustainable is Canada's Aid?

It is a sad statement on the limitations of public policy analysis that the questions of adequacy and sustainability, so central to assessing or designing policies, remain fiendishly difficult to answer. The material on which this assessment is based makes the challenge even more formidable, as it does not include an analysis of individual programs or projects, focusing instead on broad patterns of scale and allocation. However, to the extent that scale matters when tackling relative state capabilities, as do broad allocations of funds, which are less volatile than program or project spending, there is much to learn from those broad patterns.

Table 3: Parameters of Adequacy and Sustainability

Adequacy	Target truly fragile?
	Large-enough amount of assistance?
	Allocation consistent with challenges?
Sustainability	Consistency of engagement with broadly shared view of Canada's interests?
	Domestic support for the size of the aid package?

Adequacy will be assessed by answering two questions: Are funds going to states that confront severe challenges to their ability to provide order in their societies, and on a scale that is sufficient to make a difference? And does the general allocation of the assistance—between countries, among channels, and by sector—make sense in terms of the characteristics of the destination countries' challenges?

Fragility is a truly structural predicament, and attempts to tackle it should not only have a proper scale but also be made over a significant time period. The sustainability of an assistance policy toward fragile states is thus crucial. Once again, two questions will guide this assessment: given Canada's security and economic interests and domestic political incentives, can the scale of current investments be maintained over time? And is the allocation of funding among countries politically sustainable?

Adequacy of Scale and Allocation

At face value, a fragility policy in the Americas that focuses primarily on Haiti is on the right track. That country is by far the most vulnerable on the continent and it is the only one that ranks among the truly fragile states of the planet. The amount of aid provided is also significant at C$1.8 billion over thirteen years, an average of $140 million per year, or between $12 and $20 per capita annually. This may look puny, but one should consider that Canada is just one of many sources of assistance to Haiti. Taken together, the total weight of official development assistance (ODA) in the country's gross domestic product (GDP), hovering around 10 percent, is so large that it radically alters the incentive structure of its rulers. Indeed, with government revenues tied to aid and thus disconnected from the performance of the economy, Haitian rulers have little reason to focus their efforts on the latter. Along with Afghanistan, in other words, Haiti stands as the poster child for the "aid curse," and large flows of assistance are probably one of the reasons why it remains stuck with fragility.[8] In other words, while the focus on Haiti is probably justified, the scale of the effort, for which admittedly Canada is only partly responsible, may well be too large for Haiti's own good.[9]

Given their challenges, the presence of Central America's Northern Triangle countries and the West Indies among recipients of Canadian assistance makes a lot of sense from a fragility perspective. The scale of the investment in the Caribbean (C$600 million since FY 2000–2001) looks reasonable enough at about C$6.00 per capita. With significantly larger GDP and government tax revenues than Haiti, as well as more capable public administration, these countries need less external support and are unlikely to be "cursed" by the amounts they receive from Canada and their other foreign supporters.

Central America's Northern Triangle is a much different proposition. These countries are among the most violent in the hemisphere and are clearly overwhelmed by the challenges posed by criminal networks. Yet, Canadian aid, totalling C$690 million over thirteen years, or barely C$2.40 per capita in FY 2012–13 (even after a substantial increase in FY 2010–11), remains small. Despite substantial institutional and political problems, these states could easily absorb much larger amounts of aid.

Sectoral allocation of Canadian aid looks adequate. The profound and multidimensional character of the challenges confronting Haiti, the main target country, justifies the kinds of broad-based development programs that CIDA favours. Still, and despite the small sums involved, DND and the RCMP might have a more powerful impact were more of their investments directed to Central America, and especially Caribbean military and police forces.

Adequacy over time matters, too. Investments to tackle fragility must have a long time horizon. While the short period covered here makes an assessment of that variable difficult, the volatility of aid flows in that timeframe is worrying. Investments in Haiti exploded after the fall of Jean-Bertrand Aristide and—more understandably—collapsed two years after the earthquake. Similarly, the Northern Triangle seems to have been discovered only in 2010, though it had already been racked by extreme violence for at least a decade. By contrast, Canada's presence in the West Indies seems to have a stronger, more stable footing.

In sum, Canada's approach looks adequate in Haiti and the West Indies, while a stronger push in Central America would clearly be warranted. In addition, the kind of long-term commitment that one sees toward the Caribbean would be a welcome addition to increased funding for Central American programming.

Political Sustainability

Aid and foreign policy advocates invariably try to ground assistance in the "hard" interests of donors. Indeed, nothing anchors a long-term policy toward a country like sizeable investments and trade flows, significant security threats, or a mobilized diaspora community that commands significant political influence. These are the conditions that make for strong, long-term international commitments.

From this perspective, the fragile states of the Americas fare rather poorly. None of them is a significant trade partner. And while more than two-thirds of Canadian investments in Latin America and the West Indies sit in a handful of Caribbean tax havens (the Bahamas, Barbados, Bermuda, and the Cayman Islands), the security of those investments relies less on peaceful and stable governments than on the possibility of transferring them to other shores at the flip of a switch.

Similarly, within low-crime Canada, it is difficult to argue successfully that the criminal violence in the urban peripheries of Central American or Caribbean cities justifies a significant investment of Canadian aid. Nor is domestic pressure in Canada likely to change this. The sizable diasporas from Haiti, the West Indies, and Central America in Canada are poorly organized and (except in a single Montreal federal riding with a large Haitian community) their political influence is diluted in Canada's large immigrant population.

One traditional driver of Canadian foreign policy, however, brings a degree of stability to Canada's presence in the Caribbean. The United States is sensitive to instability in countries that sit on its southern maritime border. American policymakers worry about the region's role in the drug value chains that end up on its territory. Haiti is a particular concern. It is a source of illegal immigrants, and the sizeable Haitian diaspora communities in New York City and Miami have considerable political clout. Canada's long presence in the region and the fact that many of its diplomats, police agents, and soldiers are francophone make it one of Washington's most useful and reliable regional partners. Brazil and its South American neighbours have taken a prominent role in the UN mission in Haiti, but they have few good reasons to linger. In contrast, Canada is likely to remain in Haiti even if Washington's interest in Canada's Caribbean policy hardly provides Ottawa policymakers with a compelling rationale for a prolonged effort to tackle local fragility.

A sustained and sizeable investment in the fragile states of the Caribbean rests on a weak interest foundation, a situation even more dismal in the case of Central America's Northern Triangle. Canada's policy toward those states will likely depend on political expediency and the entrepreneurship of committed public servants and civil society organizations. With due respect for their work over the last decade, this does not constitute the strong and sure footing that is required to confront the many challenges facing the region's fragile states.

Conclusion

This chapter has examined Latin American and Caribbean cases as part of a broad assessment of Canada's fragile states policy. While detailed case studies on Haiti[10] and on such thematic issues as drugs do exist,[11] a systematic assessment of Canadian policy in the whole region has not yet been done. This essay fills that gap by assessing foreign aid, broadly conceived, as a proxy for Canadian policy.

The chapter clearly demonstrates that Haiti is the primary focus of Canada's fragile states policy in the Americas and that the Canadian presence there is broad-based and significant. Large investments have also been made in the West Indies and Central America. Venezuela, despite of the scale of its problems, is simply not on Canada's fragility radar screen.

Overall, Canadian aid flows appear to be too large in Haiti, despite its daunting challenges. More measured investments in the Caribbean seem adequate, while Central America's vast needs are poorly addressed. Sustainability is probably the main risk to Canada's policy toward those countries, as Canadian economic, security, and political interests in the region appear insufficient to justify investments on the scale needed and for the timeframe required.

Annexes

Annex 1: Channels of Canadian Assistance to Fragile States of the Americas (Minus Haiti)

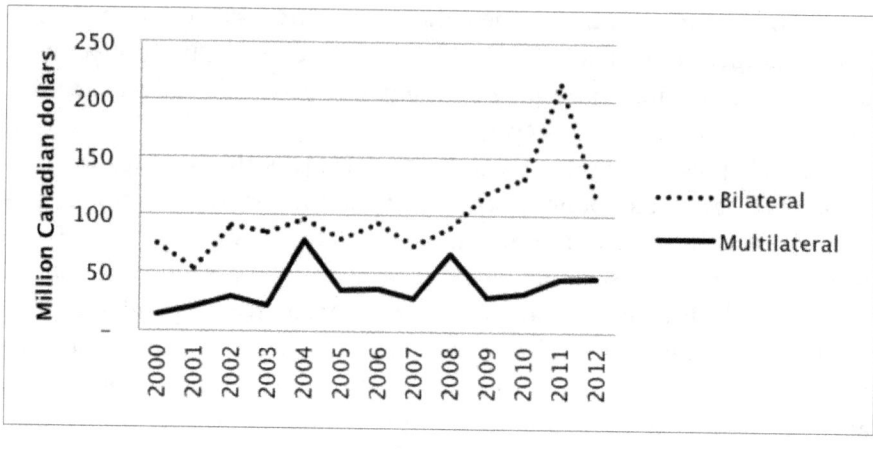

Annex 2: Canadian Government Breakdown of Foreign Assistance

Canadian International Development Agency	Country and Regional Programs	Bilateral Aid
	Canadian Partnership Programs	Bilateral Aid
	Multilateral Programs	Bilateral Aid
		Multilateral Aid
	Other (Bilateral Aid)	Bilateral Aid
Other Sources	Department of Foreign Affairs and International Trade	Bilateral Aid
		Multilateral Aid
	Finance Canada	Bilateral Aid
		Multilateral Aid
	Environment Canada	Bilateral Aid
		Multilateral Aid
	Royal Canadian Mounted Police	Bilateral Aid
	Department of National Defence	Bilateral Aid
	International Development Research Centre	Bilateral Aid
	Export Development Canada	Bilateral Aid
	Health Canada	Multilateral Aid
	Public Health Agency of Canada	Multilateral Aid
	Parks Canada	Bilateral Aid
	Employment and Social Development Canada	Bilateral Aid
	Natural Resources Canada	Bilateral Aid
	Industry Canada–ITU	Multilateral Aid
	Canada Post–UPU	Multilateral Aid
	Province of Quebec	Bilateral Aid
		Multilateral Aid
	Other Provinces	Bilateral Aid
	Municipalities	Bilateral Aid
	Imputed Aid (Bilateral)	Bilateral Aid
Loan Repayments	Canadian International Development Agency	Bilateral Aid
		Multilateral Aid
	Export Development Canada	Bilateral Aid

Notes

1. David Carment, Stewart Press, and Yiagadeesen Samy, *Security, Development and the Fragile State: Bridging the Gap Between Theory and Policy* (New York: Routledge, 2010), 20–76.

2. Sebastian Ziaja and Javier Fabra Mata, *State Fragility Indices: Potentials, Messages and Limitations* (Bonn: Deutsches Institut für Entwicklungspolitik, 2010).

3. Max Weber, *Economy and Society* (Berkeley: University of California Press, 1978), 54.

4. Weber's extensive discussion of legitimacy is best summarized in Guenther Roth's introduction to the English edition of *Economy and Society*: "men act as they do because of belief in authority, enforcement by staffs, a calculus of self-interest and a good dose of habit." Weber, *Economy and Society*, xxxv.

5. United Nations Development Program, *Human Development Report for Latin America 2013–2014. Citizen Security with a Human Face: Evidence and Proposals for Latin America* (New York: United Nations Development Program, 2013).

6. UNDP, *Human Development Report for Latin America 2013–2014*.

7. All channels, all allocation types, all GDNP categories, all DAC ODA and non-ODA, all concentrations, all expenditure types, all Caricom, all Commonwealth, and all Francophonie. Canada, Department of Foreign Affairs, Trade and Development, "Statistical Report on International Assistance—by Country Spending," http://www.acdi-cida.gc.ca/acdi-cida/acdi-cida.nsf/eng/CAR-616135752-P3Q (accessed 4 October 2014).

8. Simon Djankov, Jose G. Montalvo, and Marta Reynal-Querol, "The Curse of Aid," *Journal of Economic Growth* 13, no. 3 (2008); Jean Daudelin and Yiagadeesen Samy, *In Praises of Taxes? Fiscal Pacts, Development Policy and Conflict Risk*, CSDS Working Paper 07 (Ottawa: Centre for Security and Defence Studies, 2008).

9. David Carment and Yiagadeesen Samy, "A Marshall Plan for Haiti? Think Again," *Globe and Mail*, 19 February 2010.

10. Yasmine Shamsie and Andrew S. Thompson, eds., *Haiti: Hope for a Fragile State* (Waterloo, ON: Wilfrid Laurier University Press, 2006); Stephen Baranyi, "Canada and the Travail of Partnership in Haiti," in *Fixing Haiti: MINUSTAH and Beyond*, ed. Jorge Heine and Andrew S. Thompson (Tokyo: United Nations University Press, 2011).

11. Jean Daudelin, "A New Drug Warrior?," in *The State and Security in Mexico: Transformation and Crisis in Regional Perspective*, ed. Brian Bow and Arturo Santa-Cruz (New York: Routledge, 2012).

CHAPTER 10

CORPORATE SOCIAL RESPONSIBILITY IN FRAGILE AND STABLE STATES:
Dilemmas and Opportunities in South Sudan and Ghana

Hevina S. Dashwood

Introduction

This chapter asks whether corporate social responsibility (CSR) can be a means for fostering socio-economic development through a comparison of Ghana (a stable state) and South Sudan (a fragile state), two resource-rich countries in Africa. To address this question, developments in global thinking on the role of the private sector in international development, together with the challenges of CSR implementation in the Global South, will be examined within the broad context of Canadian government policy toward the activities of Canadian extractive companies operating abroad.

The notion that private actors can provide services and development assistance through CSR initiatives runs up against the common perception of multinational companies engaged in resource extraction as being the *causes* of the violent conflicts and human rights abuses associated with resource-rich fragile and failed states. The strong association between resource abundance, major companies engaged in oil, gas, and mineral extraction, and state fragility, derives from the role of natural resources in providing both a motive and financial support for armed conflict.[1] Ian Smillie, for example, has extensively documented the role of the diamond trade in fuelling violent conflict in countries such as Sierra Leone and Angola.[2] Despite these challenging realities, major donor states and international development organizations, such as the World Bank, are increasingly emphasizing the role of the private sector in fostering economic growth and development in the developing world. The growing attention paid to CSR initiatives reflects an understanding that, regardless of the negative role ascribed to major companies engaged in extraction in developing countries, there is potential for the private sector to play a positive role in promoting sustainable socio-economic progress. In both fragile and stable states such as South Sudan and Ghana, major extractive companies have found that in order to gain long-term success they must engage with local communities and attempt to meet their development needs.

While there is considerable debate as to what CSR does or should entail, it can be defined as the obligations companies have toward society in the environmental, social, and economic realms.[3] CSR needs to be understood as an *obligation*, as opposed to the "discretionary" activities often associated with CSR through companies' charitable or philanthropic activities. These obligations need not be legally required, but they exist because corporations' economic activities affect the social and ecological systems in which they are embedded.[4]

Various components of the institutional context, such as the type of government, government capacity, the regulatory regime surrounding extraction, interdepartmental coordination, and social customs, among other factors, all play a very important role in shaping the types of CSR activities undertaken by private sector actors.[5] Weak government capacity and lack of funding in the developing country context, for example, puts pressure on companies to provide schools, clinics, and basic infrastructure—"public goods" typically provided by governments in advanced industrialized economies. Questions abound about the appropriateness of CSR initiatives that take on government functions, as in the long term these initiatives risk absolving local and central governments of responsibility for the provision of social services.[6] Local communities, however, often expect this of companies operating nearby, in part to fill the gap left by government, and in part to capture some of the benefits of extraction, even if such benefits may not be sustainable over the long term.

Among developing countries in Africa, what is possible or expected in terms of CSR will vary depending on where the country sits on the fragile-state-to-stable-country continuum. By comparing CSR in Ghana, one of the most politically stable and democratic countries in Africa, and South Sudan, one of the continent's most fragile and unstable states with widespread poverty, violent conflict, and extremely weak or non-existent state institutions, the impact of institutional context on CSR's potential becomes readily apparent. For example, in Ghana CSR activities have increasingly turned to sustainable livelihood projects that support broader socio-economic development goals. In fragile states such as South Sudan, the vulnerability of the fixed assets of extractive companies to attack necessarily places a premium on ensuring security in a manner consistent with international human rights norms.

In keeping with global developments, the Canadian government has placed considerable emphasis on the role the private sector can play in developing countries and has developed a supportive framework for CSR through its "Building the Canadian Advantage" strategy, revised in November 2014.[7] Ghana has long been a "country of focus" under Canada's official development assistance (ODA) program, and South Sudan was added to the list of countries of focus in June 2014.[8] Canada has invested considerable diplomatic and humanitarian capital in South Sudan over the years, most recently through the Stabilization and Reconstruction Taskforce (START) program housed in the Department of Foreign Affairs, Trade and Development.[9] This newly independent country is rich not only in oil and gas but also in mineral reserves such as gold, and is of significant interest to Canadian companies engaged in oil and gas or mineral extraction (although this interest has not yet translated into actual investments). Similarly, there is a strong Canadian investment presence in Ghana's mineral sector (primarily gold), and significant interest in Ghana's offshore oil-and-gas fields, which came into commercial production in 2011. Both Ghana and South Sudan, key recipients of Canadian ODA, are important to Canada's foreign political and economic interests.

There is a role, and indeed an obligation, for the private sector to promote conditions conducive to socio-economic development and respect

Figure 1: Ed Fast, Minister of International Trade, announcing the appointment of Jeffrey Davidson as Canada's CSR Counsellor for the extractive sector at the annual convention of the Prospectors and Developers Association of Canada in March 2015. (Credit: DFATD)

for human rights in host countries. The challenges, however, are complex and cannot be resolved through CSR alone. Even in a "star" country such as Ghana, the potential benefits of resource extraction do not seem to materialize at the local community level where extraction takes place.[10] In South Sudan, *effective* natural resource governance is of vital importance to the stabilization, reconstruction, and eventual sustainable development of that country. Yet these very attributes are least likely to be found in fragile states. Therein lies one of the paradoxes of relying on CSR as a means to promote development—in fragile states, resource exploitation can exacerbate conflict and inflict harm on local communities. Even where the relatively more robust institutional framework of Ghana would lead one to expect more promising outcomes, the perception of local communities is that few, if any, of the benefits of mining have reached them. To be effective, therefore, CSR initiatives must be supportive of state capacity building and in sync with broader national development objectives, an insight that drives the mandate of the Canadian International Resources and Development Institute (CIRDI), funded by the Department of Foreign Affairs, Trade and Development.[11]

The Evolution of Canadian Government Policy on CSR

The Canadian economy has a major stake in the global extractive sector and Canadian extractive companies have growing investments in Africa's oil-and-gas and mineral sectors. Furthermore, Canada is a repository of significant legal, technical, and financial expertise for the global mining industry. Although CSR, by definition, entails self-regulation on the part of the private sector, it is appropriate briefly to account for the Canadian government's role and examine how it intersects with the Canadian extractive sector and CSR. The Canadian government has a longstanding record of favouring "voluntary" approaches to corporate responsibility, as opposed to a regulatory role. The preference for voluntary approaches to CSR respecting the performance of Canadian extractive companies abroad is maintained in the government's revised CSR strategy, released in November 2014.[12] Canadian mining activities around the world have expanded significantly since the early 1990s. As the number and value of Canadian investments in foreign countries increased, critics directed growing attention to the activities of Canadian oil-and-gas and mining companies abroad. In 1999, the activities of Talisman Energy Incorporated, an oil-and-gas company based in Calgary, Alberta, became the source of considerable embarrassment for Prime Minister Jean Chrétien's Liberal government and its foreign minister, Lloyd Axworthy, when reports surfaced alleging that the company was implicated in human rights abuses in Sudan. The government commissioned a report by lawyer John Harker, who alleged that Talisman had been complicit but not a direct participant in those violations.[13] Despite intense national NGO and global pressure on the Canadian government to force Talisman to divest from Sudan, and after difficult internal debates that Axworthy lost, the government decided not to act against Talisman.[14] That company's decision to divest from Sudan in 2002 was ultimately precipitated by pressure from the American government and institutional investors.[15]

The reluctance of the Canadian government to act against Talisman led to greater efforts on the part of civil society to bring Canadian mining companies to account. In 1999, for example, the NGO Mining Watch Canada was founded with a mandate to monitor the activities of Canadian mining companies in Canada and abroad. As NGOs such as Mining Watch Canada and the Halifax Initiative took advantage of new information technologies to widely disseminate information about the bad practices of Canadian mining companies, the Canadian government came under growing pressure to regulate the activities of Canadian extractive companies operating abroad. The significant increase in Canadian investment in developing countries' extractive sectors was concomitant with media reports of environmental devastation and human rights abuses involving Canadian companies.

A particularly significant development was the tabling, in June 2005, by the Parliamentary Standing Committee on Foreign Affairs and International Trade (SCFAIT) of a report on *Mining in Developing Countries and CSR*. The report was the culmination of several years of hearings before the SCFAIT Subcommittee on Human Rights and International Development on the activities of Canadian companies in developing countries. The report noted that mining activities in some countries had adverse effects on local communities and the environment in a context where regulatory capacity was weak or not enforced. The report singled out as a case study the activities of Canadian mining company TVI Pacific in the Philippines, accusing it of abusing the indigenous and human rights of local inhabitants. It noted that smaller companies like TVI Pacific often lacked the resources, knowledge, or incentives to address issues arising from the social, cultural, political, or environmental contexts in which they operated, and expressed concern at the lack of Canadian laws to regulate the activities of Canadian mining companies. The parliamentary committee called for legislation to hold companies accountable for their activities overseas.[16]

In its response to the SCFAIT report, the Liberal government, headed by former businessman and finance minister Paul Martin, agreed to a number of the recommendations but shied away from enacting legislation that would entail the extraterritorial application of Canadian law in foreign jurisdictions.[17] Instead, the government launched a major series of roundtable consultations with industry associations, NGOs, Indigenous peoples, and academic experts, as well as company and government representatives, to discuss the issues raised in the report. The national roundtables on Corporate Social Responsibility and the Canadian Extractive Sector in Developing Countries entailed public consultations in four major cities across Canada throughout 2006.

Although the roundtable process was deemed successful in bringing together various stakeholders, the outcome has been disappointing. NGOs, in particular, were upset because the government continued to resist enacting legislation that would regulate the activities of Canadian companies abroad. Instead, in March 2009, Prime Minister Stephen Harper's Conservative government, which explicitly promoted private sector and free market solutions, announced its strategy for promoting CSR in the Canadian extractive sector. Called "Building the Canadian Advantage," the government set out various initiatives to promote CSR in the extractive sector, including the alignment of Canadian policy with emerging global norms and initiatives concerning the activities of international business abroad.[18] The revised CSR strategy released in November 2014 adopts a similar approach, expanding the list of global initiatives to which Canadian mining companies are expected to adhere. Notwithstanding continued efforts by NGOs and other interested parties to push the government into regulating the activities of Canadian extractive companies abroad, there is no expectation that the government will move away from supporting "voluntary" initiatives.[19] In light of the importance of these initiatives to the global and Canadian extractive sectors, the following section elaborates on their development.

The Emergence of CSR as a Norm Informing Business Practice

The rapid expansion of investment by multinational companies in the Global South over the past two decades has drawn attention to the environmental, labour, and human rights practices of foreign investors. The proliferation of global "voluntary" standards reflects the difficulty of regulating foreign companies in a globalized economy, the weak regulatory regimes in developing countries, and the growing societal expectations about standards of appropriate behaviour (norms) on the part of global companies. In some sectors, such as mining, private business has been a key force behind the development of standards in order to address reputational concerns stemming from widely publicized environmental disasters, human rights abuses, and NGO activism.[20]

Over the past fifteen years, the evolution of global CSR norms—defined as collective understandings of appropriate behaviour—has led to the development of a number of global standards that address specific activities of direct relevance to the extractive sector. Some, such as the Global Reporting Initiative (GRI), are considered "voluntary" because companies may choose to adopt them. However, such voluntary standards are often required by industry associations as a condition of membership, as is the case with the International Council on Mining and Metals, whose members are required to report against the environmental, social, and economic indicators of the GRI. Others, such as the International Finance Corporation's (IFC) Environmental and Social Performance Standards, are quasi-voluntary in the sense that private companies may or may not adopt them, but they are required of companies that seek IFC funding for projects in developing countries. Given the capital-intensive nature of investment in the extractive sector, the need for funding from a consortium of private banks and public institutions such as the IFC means that the performance standards are effectively a regulatory requirement. It should be further noted that many of the "voluntary" initiatives the Canadian government now supports, such as the Voluntary Principles on Security and Human Rights and the Extractive Industries Transparency Initiative (EITI), are not strictly speaking voluntary, because they combine governmental with NGO and industry oversight.[21]

The Extractive Industries Transparency Initiative was launched in 2002 by British Labour Prime Minister Tony Blair to promote greater transparency and accountability in the payment of governments and reporting by extractive companies of taxes and royalties. As is the case with the Voluntary Principles, the EITI has a board of directors composed of representatives from governments, NGOs, and companies.

A significant recent state-led initiative is the development of the United Nations Framework for Business and Human Rights, under the leadership of John Gerard Ruggie.[22] A prominent international relations scholar, Ruggie served as Special Advisor to the UN Secretary General during the lengthy consultation process, drafting the framework and its subsequent operationalization guidelines.[23] Ruggie's UN framework document, *Protect, Respect and Remedy: A Framework for Business and Human Rights*,[24] calls on international business to respect global human rights norms while placing responsibility on states for protecting human rights. To fulfill their social obligation to respect human rights, companies are expected to exercise due diligence by taking steps to become aware of, prevent, and address adverse human rights impacts.[25] The Guiding Principles, as they are now commonly referred to, also require firms to consider (1) the specific country context in which they operate, (2) the human rights activities of companies within that context (for example, in their capacity as producers, service providers, employers, and neighbours), and (3) whether they may contribute to abuse through the relationships connected to their activities (such as supply chains or state agencies).[26] As part of their responsibility to exercise due diligence, companies are expected to adopt human rights policies, conduct human rights impact assessments, develop an internal company culture of commitment to human rights, and track and report on performance.[27]

An important multi-stakeholder initiative in keeping with the UN's Guiding Principles is the Organisation for Economic Co-operation and Development's (OECD) "Due Diligence Guidance for Responsible Supply Chains of Minerals from Conflict-Affected and High-Risk Areas." The guidance provides recommendations to assist companies that source minerals or metals from conflict-affected and high-risk areas to help them respect human rights and avoid contributing to armed conflict. These two global initiatives aim to help extractive companies avoid precisely the situation Talisman found itself in almost two decades ago, and are supported under the government's revised CSR strategy.

Taken together, the range of CSR standards through industry self-regulation, collaborative global governance arrangements, and state-led initiatives constitute a global normative framework for acceptable business practice. It is within the context of this emerging global normative framework that all Canadian actors—the government, extractive companies, and NGOs—operate. They seek to compensate for the "governance gaps" that arise from the activities of global companies, which are especially acute in fragile states, and inform the CSR practices of individual extractive companies.

State Fragility, the Resource Curse, and the Private Sector

Effective governance in resource-rich countries is widely recognized as essential to the realization of the potential of resource wealth and to counter the effects of the "resource curse." The "resource curse," or "paradox of plenty," refers to the association between heavy state and economic dependence on the extractive sector for revenues and foreign exchange earnings, and the resulting political instability and outright conflict, high levels of corruption, and the neglect of other sectors of the economy. The resource curse literature is extensive, and dates back to the early 1990s, as systematically accumulated empirical evidence suggested that developing countries endowed with natural resources tend to turn in poorer economic performances than their resource-poor counterparts,[28] to experience limited democratic progress,[29] and to be more likely to suffer violent conflict or war.[30]

There is a strong association in the literature on fragile states between the possession of abundant natural resources and the proclivity for violent conflict.[31] Paul Collier and Anke Hoeffler, who have written extensively on poverty, economic development, and the resource curse, found in their research that in countries where natural resources accounted for 26 percent or more of GDP, there is a 23 percent probability of civil conflict, compared to a 0.5 percent probability in countries with limited resources.[32] Access to valuable diamonds has been shown to have fuelled and prolonged violent conflict in Sierra Leone and Liberia.[33] In Nigeria, often considered the classic example of the resource curse in Africa, the abundance of oil and gas has distorted political and economic incentive structures away from providing for the public good in favour of personal wealth accumulation and other forms of corruption.[34]

Within this broad reality, however, there is important variation. Not all fragile states in Africa possess an abundance of natural resources, and not all resource-rich African countries are failed or fragile states. Botswana and Ghana, for example, have to date been able to govern their mineral resources within the context of stable economic and politically democratic structures. Developing country governments are keen to attract foreign direct investment to develop their economies' extractive sectors. The allure of royalties and tax revenue holds the promise that governments can invest their resource wealth to promote broad-based economic development. Global extractive companies are in a position to transfer skills and technology, foster greater innovation, provide more affordable financing, and deliver high-quality products and services. Resource-rich fragile states, it is argued, stand to benefit from foreign investment that otherwise might not take place in view of the high-risk investment environments that such countries represent.[35] In resource-rich developing countries, given the extensive capital and technical requirements of the industry, the private sector is composed primarily of foreign extractive multinationals. Locally based entrepreneurs lack the capital and expertise to engage in exploration and extraction activities on a large scale. The liberalization of developing countries' extractive sectors and the resulting privatization of state-owned companies means that oil-and-gas and mineral wealth is exploited by foreign companies.

The prominent role played by major extractive companies in the economies of resource-rich developing countries helps to explain the emphasis placed on CSR as a mechanism for the promotion of socio-economic development. The potential role of CSR can be understood as a reflection of the increasing emphasis placed by donor states on the important role of the private sector in promoting economic growth together with development, as reflected in the "Busan Declaration" of the OECD member states.[36] It is now widely recognized that effective state institutions are necessary in order for the private sector to play a positive role. As noted by the House of Commons Standing Committee on Foreign Affairs and International Development (SCFAID) 2012 report, "without strong public institutions, economic growth will either be inhibited and/or proceed in a way that does not benefit most members of a society."[37] CSR as practised by private investors is increasingly looked to as a means to compensate for state fragility and the absence of appropriate institutional supports and policies.

However, two challenges emerge when analyzing the growing emphasis on the private sector and CSR in the context of state fragility and resource-rich African countries. First, the ability of private sector actors to contribute to development and natural resource governance appears to be linked to the quality of domestic institutions;[38] and second, reliance on the major extractive companies to provide public goods can be a conceptual stretch in the face of well-documented instances of the human rights harms and proclivity for violent conflict associated with their presence.[39] Where the institutional framework surrounding extraction is weak or non-existent, the likelihood that extractive companies can play a constructive role is diminished, but not always. Research has shown that extractive companies can serve as the "functional equivalent of the state"[40] as long as there are incentives for profit-oriented companies to act in a manner that is not merely asset-depleting. As will be seen below, South Sudan exhibits many traits of both the *resource curse* and state fragility, though that does not preclude socially responsible behaviour on the part of multinationals engaged in extraction.

Conceptualizing CSR in the Developing Country Context

Most understandings of CSR recognize that organizations have a greater responsibility to society beyond generating economic returns. As recently as ten years ago, much of the writing on CSR was based on research in the context of advanced industrialized economies. As noted above, CSR in the context of developed countries is informed by markedly different institutional contexts as compared to developing countries. Stakeholder theory in the business literature now acknowledges that firms have obligations toward a range of stakeholders, including employees, the environment, local communities, suppliers, and governments, which, while not always legally mandated, move beyond the realm of discretionary voluntarism.[41] CSR therefore takes on different forms, and in developing countries requires a greater degree of responsibility toward the communities affected by extractive activities and to the larger society.[42]

Much of the extractive activity in Africa takes place in rural communities. These are often heavily populated—unlike in Canada—and have historically been neglected by central governments in terms of the provision of social services, yet bear most of the negative impacts of extraction. To meet expectations of local communities, major companies' CSR generally includes the provision of employment in places where jobs are extremely scarce, the provision of social services such as roads, electricity, sanitation, schools, and clinics, the promotion of sustainable livelihood initiatives in support of socio-economic development, and the preservation of the environment for people whose livelihoods depend on the land and water. In the case of extraction, a company's commitment to CSR may be assessed against the extent to which it pays attention to local economic development challenges and thereby moves beyond the mere business of asset-stripping to value addition through forward and backward linkages and economic growth.[43] The emerging literature on CSR in the developing country context demonstrates that local communities expect companies to contribute to sustainable socio-economic growth and progress. In Africa, CSR relates to the role and responsibility of oil-and-gas and mining companies in the socio-economic development and security of the continent and its people.[44]

While companies can and should be expected to contribute more effectively to socio-economic development, there are limits to what CSR can accomplish.[45] Mining companies alone cannot promote sustainable development, and they cannot and should not take on the role of government. The extent to which companies can enhance social and economic value in the countries where they operate depends on the enabling or disabling dynamics resulting from a range of interactions with actors outside the boundaries of the company.[46] These challenges aside, companies are expected to add economic, social, and ecological value to the communities in which they operate.[47]

Challenges of CSR Implementation in Stable and Fragile Contexts

As the above discussion suggests, practicing CSR in the African context means addressing and compensating for weak institutional contexts, as well as proactively contributing to sustainable socio-economic development in situations of extreme poverty. The range of activities will vary depending on whether one is looking at fragile/conflict states, post-conflict states, or stable states.[48] Strategies appropriate for a stable country such as Ghana would be different from those required in a conflict-prone, fragile state setting such as South Sudan. However, even institutionally more robust countries such as Ghana face serious difficulties in addressing the challenges posed by resource extraction. By the same token, although the situation in South Sudan would appear especially inauspicious for CSR, that does not rule out the potential for CSR to make a positive difference. The discussion now turns to Canada's engagement with Ghana and South Sudan, and the potential impact of CSR initiatives in these countries.

Canada in Ghana and South Sudan

Canada has long been engaged with Sudan. It has provided humanitarian assistance, diplomatic backing for negotiations to resolve the North–South conflict, and material support for the African Union (AU) mission in Darfur, as well as the UN mission in South Sudan. The Canadian government has expended substantial diplomatic capital in South Sudan, in contrast to Canada's involvement in Ghana, which has largely been confined to development assistance and private sector investment in the extractive sector. There are about a dozen Canadian companies, ranging from junior mining firms (e.g., Asanko Gold) to major multinationals (key among these are Golden Star Resources and Kinross), operating in Ghana. The West African country has been relatively stable since transitioning to multi-party democracy in 1992 and has enjoyed impressive average annual GDP growth of 10 percent over the past five years.[49] Following the departure of Talisman from Sudan in 2002 after allegations of complicity in severe human rights abuses, Canada's corporate presence in Sudan has disappeared, for the most part. Indeed, Indian and Chinese companies are the dominant players in Sudan—and, now, South Sudan—and, notwithstanding Canadian private sector interest, there are no Canadian companies operating in South Sudan at the time of writing.[50] Given Talisman's withdrawal and the Canadian government's lead with respect to relations with South Sudan, the potential role of CSR through the Canadian private sector is largely hypothetical. Nevertheless, it is instructive to consider what, if any, incentives there might hypothetically be for Canadian companies to adhere to CSR in a fragile country such as South Sudan.

Ghana: The Evolution of CSR

Until the early 1980s, the practice of CSR in Ghana was a moot point, because the mining sector was almost entirely state-owned. Prolonged political instability and a deteriorating economy resulted in Ghana coming under intense pressure by the International Monetary Fund and World Bank to introduce market-based reforms. In 1983, Ghana's Provisional National Defence Council launched an economic recovery programme of structural adjustment that led in 1986 to the reform of Ghana's mining law, the liberalization of the mining sector, and the opening of the moribund, state-owned extractive sector to foreign direct investment. The 1990s witnessed the rapid expansion of surface mining, as foreign-owned multinational corporations obtained generous concessions from the Ghanaian government. This led to the establishment of seven surface mining companies in the mineral-rich Wassa West district in western Ghana alone. Although the purpose of this section is not to analyze the performance of individual Canadian mining companies operating in Ghana, illustrative examples of Canadian companies will be used to highlight points made in the discussion. (For a more detailed discussion of Canadian corporate performance, readers are encouraged to consult reports prepared by Mining Watch Canada, as well as the sources cited in the next paragraph.)

Rapid expansion of surface mining in areas where the primary economic activity is farming often leads to conflict over land use, and in Ghana it resulted in human rights abuses and environmental degradation.[51] The human rights abuses that were identified in the report of the

Figure 2: The granting of large mining concessions to foreign companies in Western Ghana displaced farmers and attracted artisanal miners (known as 'Galamsey'/illegal miners in Ghana), who engage in dangerous and environmentally damaging practices to earn a living. (Credit: Hevina Dashwood)

Commission on Human Rights and Administrative Justice include involuntary displacement and the loss of livelihoods through the elimination of farmlands, inadequate compensation for relocated farmers, destruction of sacred and cultural sites, police and mine security brutality in the mining communities, air and water pollution, and health problems related to water and airborne diseases.[52] Canada's Golden Star Resources (GSR), for example, experienced poor community relations in the early 2000s, in part because of a negative mining legacy inherited from the past, but also because of allegations of poor environmental performance and human rights abuses related to the reliance on state security personnel adjacent to the mine.[53]

By the late 1990s, international NGOs, together with Ghanaian NGOs such as the Third World Network and the Wassa Association of Communities Affected by Mining, had begun to exert pressure on the major mining companies and their home country governments to improve their practices. Institutional help from the Environmental Protection Agency, established in 1994 to protect Ghana's natural environment, and legal protections under the 1992 Constitution, which enshrines human and economic rights in Ghana, have proven to be weak when it comes to defending communities affected by mining. Given the traditional tendency of the central government to neglect rural areas, local communities typically turn to the major mining companies for redress and the provision of social services.

The range of CSR initiatives has evolved since they were first introduced in the late 1990s and early 2000s, when mining companies began to take small steps to address community concerns. There has been considerable learning on the part of the mining industry concerning what CSR initiatives are most appropriate. Initially, CSR projects included the construction of boreholes to provide clean water when rivers and streams became polluted, the provision of funding for school supplies, the delivery of preventive medical services for employees and their families, the construction of schools and clinics, and scholarships for children of employees. These efforts, while laudatory, tended to take place with minimal consultation with local communities, and some initiatives, such as alternative livelihood programs, were inappropriate to local needs.[54]

Mining companies keen to foster good relations with local communities learned from their mistakes, and from the mid-2000s to the early 2010s, they began to engage more systematically with local communities. Rather than just providing public goods, they consulted more and sought to work with community leaders to better learn about their needs and priorities. Major and mid-tier mining companies, such as GSR, established community relations departments and put in place structures for regular consultation with local communities and for airing grievances. Moreover, mining companies started to partner with development-oriented NGOs in order to develop more appropriate and viable sustainable livelihood programs. GSR, for example, established an oil palm plantation initiative for the benefit of resettled farmers, in a context where there is a strong market for oil palm fruits.[55]

These developments can be understood as part of a larger reality for mining companies operating in developing countries—the need to obtain a "social license to operate."[56] A major challenge for companies engaged in mining and oil-and-gas extraction is that the benefits of mining do not reach grassroots communities, where endemic unemployment and chronic poverty lead to resentment and conflict. The reasons for this are varied, complex, and not fully the responsibility of extractive companies. However, when communities suffer the negative effects of extraction, including pollution, ill health, and displacement, without realizing any of the benefits, their anger and resentment is directed at the highly visible companies in their midst.

Beginning in the early 2010s, businesses began to move away from a heavy focus on the traditional "bricks and mortar" approach to CSR. The major mining companies have been engaged in CSR activities long enough that many of the communities where they operate have reached a saturation point when it comes to the construction of new schools, clinics, and community centres. Increasingly, major companies are focusing their CSR efforts on human capital development through business skills training, assistance with locally appropriate trades, and greater efforts to maximize local procurement. Since mining companies are not set up as development organizations, they have increasingly turned to multi-stakeholder partnerships with development-oriented NGOs and local governments to build this capacity. This emerging approach to CSR recognizes that companies are not the only agents of development, that supplanting government authority and responsibility for the provision of public goods needs to be avoided, and that initiatives need to be sustainable and capable of surviving beyond the life of the mine. Rio Tinto Alcan, for example, worked with World University Service Canada (WUSC) to improve the quality and governance of education in schools near its operations.[57] One important benefit of multi-stakeholder partnerships is that they have the potential to expand benefits to a larger population beyond the immediate catchment area of the mines.[58] Mining companies typically restrict their CSR initiatives to the communities in the vicinity of their mine operations. While this approach makes sense in terms of maintaining their "social license to operate," the approach is limiting from a developmental perspective. For CSR initiatives to be lasting, they have to extend beyond the immediate confines of a mining company's catchment area.

If they are well designed, multi-stakeholder partnerships have the potential to reach a broader area and to join local initiatives with regional and national development priorities and planning. For example, while controversial in Canada, CIDA funding of three "cross-sectoral" partnerships with Canadian extractive companies made it possible for participating NGOs to expand the reach of their activities.[59] If CSR is to be relied upon as one part of the drive for sustainable socio-economic development, then expanding its scope is an important means to overcome CSR's limitations from a developmental perspective.[60] Such activities are possible in relatively stable countries but are very difficult to achieve in fragile and violence-prone states like South Sudan.

South Sudan

Hany Besada, who has extensive expertise on the role of the private sector in fragile states, has noted that even in situations of complete social, economic, and political collapse as a result of brutal civil wars, these conditions need not militate against prospects for recovery. Citing Susan Woodward, Besada argues that a breakdown of the old institutional order after civil war can provide the potential for a fresh start.[61] At one level, this has taken place in South Sudan, which emerged from the North–South civil war as an independent country on 9 July 2011. Independence from the repression and brutalization of the government in Khartoum does entail an important break for South Sudan and represents the realization of a longstanding goal of the Sudanese People's Liberation Army under the leadership of the late John Garang.

After four years, however, it has become clear that not enough of the old order was cast aside. Longstanding ethnic and personal allegiances have impeded the building of consensus around a viable political order, resulting in President Salva Kiir's ousting of Vice-President Riek Machar in 2013 and the outbreak of civil war. From the outset, the inherited economic structure, including an overwhelming dependence on oil for government revenues (98 percent) and export earnings and no means to get the oil to market except via a pipeline running through Sudan, has proven to be highly destabilizing. As Uwafiokun Idemudia has documented in the case of Nigeria, the government cannot extract or exploit oil on its own, so there is a complete dependence on multinational corporations (MNCs) for oil extraction.[62] In South Sudan, these oil multinationals are preponderantly Indian and Chinese. Already there is evidence of significant plundering of government revenues, estimated to be in the order of $4 billion.[63] In early 2014, the major oilfields of Bentiu were overrun by rebels and several hundred civilians were killed in a mosque, causing oil production to come to a halt and demonstrating the continuing role of extraction as both cause and effect of conflict.

In short, South Sudan exhibits many of the worst traits of the resource curse. One criticism of the 2005 Comprehensive Peace Agreement that brought an end to the conflict between Sudan and South Sudan is that it was silent on how properly to confront the severe structural imbalances in South Sudan's economy. The failure to address this has meant there was insufficient groundwork laid to ensure adequate oversight knowledge within government departments and agencies, or to ensure sufficient capacity in the negotiation of oil contracts. It meant, too, that the government was unable to overcome administrative weaknesses in decision making, undermining the country's ability to develop a cohesive, integrated approach to natural resource management.[64] Furthermore, the instability has hindered renewed efforts of the South Sudanese government to promote an orderly regulatory regime around exploration activities in the country's rich mineral sector, long neglected because of the civil war.

With oil production reduced to a fraction of its 2013 levels, what role, then, is there for CSR? Although Canada currently does not have an investment presence in South Sudan, it is instructive to consider under what conditions CSR might contribute to positive outcomes for local communities. Research by Tanja Börzel, Jana Hönke, and Christian Thauer convincingly demonstrates that, even in situations of civil war, given the right incentives, individual companies will provide public goods through CSR.[65] Extractive companies, wherever they operate, require a "social license to operate." Even in relatively stable countries such as Ghana, local communities can seriously disrupt company activities through protests, demonstrations, road blocks, and the destruction of infrastructure.[66] The costs incurred by companies through sabotage, destruction of equipment, and, in extreme cases, forced site closure provide strong incentives for extractive companies to fill the governance gaps.[67] Since investment must take place where the minerals or oil and gas are located, extractive companies cannot simply pick up and leave when community relations are poor, which motivates them to promote good community relations through CSR.[68] In fragile states characterized by instability and violent conflict, companies must attend to the need to secure their employees and fixed assets, which requires the cooperation of local communities. Under these conditions, the incentive structure is in place for profit-making firms to serve as the "functional equivalent of the state."[69]

This is true regardless of the home country where the extractive companies are headquartered. In his recent book *The New Kings of Crude*, Luke Patey demonstrates that the targeting of oilfields as part of military strategy created incentives for Indian and Chinese companies to adopt CSR.[70] While the general perception in the West is that Chinese and Indian MNCs are irresponsible, Patey's account reveals that the China National Petroleum Corporation had to change its ways after the 2008 kidnapping and murder of five of its employees. Where previously it had been aloof, the company realized it had to actively seek out community engagement.[71]

In the case of the equally inauspicious setting of the Democratic Republic of the Congo (DRC), Hönke and Börzel found that major mining companies in Katanga province were among the first to apply and further develop the Voluntary Principles on Security and Human Rights.[72] The Voluntary Principles require that companies train both private and public security providers to ensure that human rights abuses are avoided in the delivery of security. These findings are significant because they suggest that, even in the face of widespread and widely reported evidence of extractive companies' association with increased insecurity and human rights abuses, there are nevertheless "instances of localized success in areas of severe failure."[73]

The fact that extractive companies need to engage with local communities does not automatically translate into effective CSR strategies. As Hönke and Börzel demonstrate in their research on CSR initiatives in the DRC, it is possible for companies to work effectively with local communities to provide services where the government cannot or will not.[74] Only under specific conditions, however, will CSR be effective in terms of having a positive impact on local communities. For example, Anvil Mining's effort to train state security personnel in keeping with the Voluntary Principles failed because state authorities considered that activity to be the prerogative of the state.[75] On the other hand, Anvil was able to institute a highly effective training program for its in-house private security provider, whose success was a function of the company's well-established internal policies, monitoring, and sanctioning systems.[76]

What this brief vignette suggests is that individual extractive companies can and do undertake CSR initiatives, even in the most inauspicious settings. Civil war does not necessarily preclude CSR adoption, while the relatively ideal conditions in a country such as Ghana do not guarantee that companies will behave responsibly. As important as institutional context is, internal dynamics within individual companies are also an important predictor of effective CSR.[77]

Conclusion

This short exploration of the scope of CSR practices in resource-rich fragile and stable states suggests several positive conclusions about CSR's potential in addressing state fragility. Private sector support for CSR initiatives represents an important departure for extractive industries usually associated in the fragile state context with human rights abuses and violent conflict. Given the critical role of major extractive companies in the development of a country's natural resources, the private sector has a critical role to play in both fragile and stable state settings.[78]

It is clear, too, that institutional context (developed/developing; fragile/stable) exerts an important influence on the likelihood that CSR will be practised, on the type of CSR initiatives undertaken, and on the likelihood of their success. Even in areas of extreme state fragility with minimal, if any, governmental oversight, profit-seeking companies are motivated to provide public goods normally delivered by the state. The focus of their CSR, however, tends to be on local communities, because good community relations provide a degree of insurance against costly and sometimes violent disruptions to their operations. The more fragile and violent-prone the setting, the more localized the CSR initiatives.

To be effective and sustainable, community-level CSR projects need to be integrated with national development priorities and support state capacity building at the local and national levels, so as not to undermine the government's role in the delivery of social services and infrastructure. CSR initiatives that partner with NGOs are most appropriate because profit-oriented companies typically lack the competency to design initiatives conducive to development. As seen in the DRC, companies must also have internal systems and monitoring mechanisms in place to ensure the effectiveness of their CSR work. States characterized by extreme fragility, such as South Sudan, are not the most auspicious settings for effective CSR, but the fixed nature of their investments means that oil-and-gas companies have an incentive to promote strong community relations. This has been demonstrated to be the case for Indian and Chinese companies, even though such companies typically have a very poor record in terms of labour and other human rights, and environmental protection.

An important caveat is that community-level CSR initiatives, however well intended, can exacerbate pre-existing tensions within communities, or create new conflicts. Since extractive companies tend to focus their CSR on their immediate catchment areas, their initiatives can increase conflict with nearby communities not in the immediate vicinity of their operations and can thereby heighten the insecurity of already vulnerable populations.[79] Ultimately, the strengthening of the global normative framework as it pertains to global companies is a necessary complement to effective CSR on the part of individual companies.

Notes

1. Hany Besada, ed., *From Civil Strife to Peacebuilding: Examining Private Sector Involvement in West African Reconstruction* (Waterloo, ON: Centre for International Governance Innovation and Wilfrid Laurier University Press, 2009), 8; Paul Collier and Anke Hoeffler, "Greed and Grievance in Civil War," *Oxford Economic Papers* 56, no. 4 (August 2004): 563–64.

2. Ian Smillie, *Diamonds* (Hoboken, NJ: John Wiley and Sons, 2014), and Ian Smillie, Lansana Gberie, and Ralph Hazleton, *The Heart of the Matter: Sierra Leone, Diamonds and Human Security* (Ottawa: Partnership Africa Canada, 2000).

3. Hevina S. Dashwood, *The Rise of Global Corporate Social Responsibility: Mining and the Spread of Global Norms* (Cambridge:

Cambridge University Press, 2012), 9.

4   Roy Culpeper and Gail Whiteman, "The Corporate Stake in Social Responsibility," in *Canadian Corporations and Social Responsibility*, ed. Michelle Hibler and Rowena Beamish (Ottawa: The North-South Institute, 1998), 24.

5   Dashwood, *The Rise of Global Corporate Social Responsibility*, 17; Hevina S. Dashwood, "Sustainable Development and Industry Self-Regulation: Developments in the Global Mining Sector," *Business and Society*, 53, no. 4 (2014): 555–56.

6   Canada, House of Commons, *Driving Inclusive Economic Growth: The Role of the Private Sector in International Development* (Ottawa: Standing Committee on Foreign Affairs and International Development, 2012), 36–37.

7   Canada, Department of Foreign Affairs, Trade and Development (DFATD), *Building the Canadian Advantage: A Corporate Social Responsibility (CSR) Strategy for the Canadian Extractive Sector*, March 2009, http://www.international.gc.ca/trade-agreements-accords-commerciaux/topics-domaines/other-autre/csr-strat-rse.aspx (accessed 1 August 2014).

8   Canada, Department of Foreign Affairs, Trade and Development, "START in Sudan and South Sudan," http://www.international.gc.ca/start-gtsr/sudan-soudan.aspx (accessed 1 August 2014).

9   Ibid.

10 Gavin Hilson, "Championing the Rhetoric? 'Corporate Social Responsibility' in Ghana's Mining Sector," *Greener Management International* (2007): 43–56; Gavin Hilson and S. M. Banchirigah, "Are Alternative Livelihood Projects Alleviating Poverty in Mining Communities? Experiences from Ghana," *Journal of Development Studies* 45, no. 2 (2009): 172–96.

11 For a detailed account of concerns raised about CIRDI, see the student-initiated coalition of civil society organizations at Stop the Institute: http://stoptheinstitute.ca/ (accessed June 16, 2015).

12 Canada, "Doing Business the Canadian Way: A Strategy to Advance Corporate Social Responsibility in Canada's Extractive Sector Abroad," announced in the news release "Canada's Enhanced Corporate Social Responsibility Strategy to Strengthen Canada's Extractive Sector Abroad," November 14, 2014, http://www.international.gc.ca/trade-agreements-accords-commerciaux/topics-domaines/other-autre/csr-strat-rse.aspx?lang=eng (accessed June 12, 2015).

13 Harker Commission Report, *Human Security in Sudan: The Report of a Canadian Assessment Mission*, prepared for the Minister of Foreign Affairs (Ottawa: DFAIT, January 2000).

14 Robert O. Matthews, "Sudan's Humanitarian Disaster: Will Canada Live Up to Its Responsibility to Protect?," *International Journal* 60, no. 4 (Autumn 2005): 1050–55.

15 Luke Patey, "State Rules: Oil Companies and Armed Conflict in Sudan," *Third World Quarterly* 28, no. 5 (2007): 998.

16 Canada, House of Commons, *Mining in Developing Countries and CSR*, Report of the Standing Committee on Foreign Affairs and International Trade (SCFAIT), 2005.

17 Parliament of Canada, *Government Response to the Fourteenth Report of the Standing Committee on Foreign Affairs and International Trade*, October 2005.

18 Canada, Department of Foreign Affairs and International Trade, *Building the Canadian Advantage: A Corporate Social Responsibility (CSR) Strategy for the Canadian Extractive Sector*, March 2009.

19 Noteworthy in this regard is Liberal Member of Parliament John McKay's private member's bill, C-300.

20 Dashwood, *The Rise of Global Corporate Social Responsibility*, 78–82.

21 Hevina S. Dashwood, "Global Private Governance: Explaining Initiatives in the Global Mining Sector," in *The Handbook of Global Companies*, ed. John Mikler (West Sussex, UK: John Wiley and Sons, 2013), 457.

22 John Gerard Ruggie, *Guiding Principles on Business and Human Rights: Implementing the United Nations "Protect, Respect and Remedy" Framework*, UN Doc., PJ HRC/17/31 (2011).

23 Ibid.

24 John Gerard Ruggie, *Protect, Respect and Remedy: A Framework for Business and Human Rights*, UN Doc., A/HRC/8/5 (2008).

25 Ibid., 17.

26 Ibid.

27 Ibid., 18–19.

28 See Abiodun Alao, *Natural Resources and Conflict in Africa: The Tragedy of Endowment* (New York: University of Rochester Press, 2007); Richard M. Auty, "Natural Resources, Capital Accumulation and the Resource Curse," *Ecological Economics* 61, no. 4 (2007): 627–34; Alan. H. Gelb, *Oil Windfalls: Blessing or Curse?* (New York: Oxford UP, 1988); Jeffrey D. Sachs and Andrew M. Warner, "Natural Resource Abundance and Economic Growth," Working Paper 5398 (1995).

29 See Jonathan Di John, "Is There Really a Resource Curse? A Critical Survey of Theory and Evidence," *Global Governance: A Review of Multilateralism and International Organizations* 17, no. 2 (2011): 167–84; Terry Lynn Karl, *The Paradox of Plenty: Oil Booms and Petro-States* (Berkeley: University of California, 1997); Mick Moore, "Revenues, State Formation, and the Quality of Governance in Developing Countries," *International Political Science Review* 25, no. 3 (2004): 297–319; Michael Ross, "Does Oil Hinder Democracy?" *World Politics* 53, no. 3 (2001): 325–61.

30 See Paul Collier and Anke Hoeffler, "Greed and Grievance in Civil War," *Oxford Economic Papers* 56, no. 4 (August 2004): 563–95; Macartan Humphreys, Jeffrey Sachs, and Joseph E. Stiglitz, *Escaping the Resource Curse* (New York: Columbia University Press, 2007); Michael Ross, "How Do Natural Resources Influence Civil War? Evidence from 13 Cases,"

31 See, for example, Philippe Le Billion, "Angola's Political Economy of War: The Role of Oil and Diamonds, 1975–2000," *African Affairs* 100, no. 398 (2001): 55–80.

32 Collier and Hoeffler, "Greed and Grievance in Civil War," 563, 580–81.

33 Besada, *From Civil Strife to Peacebuilding*, 1–16.

34 Uwafiokun Idemudia, "Business and Peacemaking in the Context of Limited Statehood: Lessons from Nigeria," paper presented at the annual conference of the International Studies Association, San Francisco, 2–6 April 2013.

35 Hany Besada, "Doing Business in Fragile States: The Private Sector, Natural Resources and Conflict in Africa," Background research paper submitted to the High-Level Panel on the Post-2015 Development Agenda, May 2013.

36 OECD, *Busan Partnership for Effective Development Co-operation*, Fourth High Level Forum on Aid Effectiveness, Busan, Republic of Korea, 29 November–1 December 2011.

37 Canada, House of Commons, *Driving Inclusive Economic Growth: The Role of the Private Sector in International Development*, Standing Committee on Foreign Affairs and International Development (2012): 3–12.

38 Besada, "Doing Business in Fragile States," 10; Hevina S. Dashwood and Uwafiokun Idemudia, "Global Natural Resource Governance Initiatives and Local Adoption: The Example of the Extractive Industry Transparency Initiative (EITI) in Ghana and Nigeria," paper presented at the annual meeting of the Canadian Political Science Association (CPSA), Brock University, 29 May 2014.

39 See, for example, Steve Coll, *Private Empire: Exxon Mobil and American Power* (New York: Penguin Press, 2012), 93–121; Luke Patey, *The New Kings of Crude: China, India, and the Global Struggle for Oil in Sudan and South Sudan* (London: Hurst, 2014), 68–70.

40 Tanja A. Börzel and Thomas Risse, "Governance without a State—Can it Work?", *Regulation and Governance* 4, no. 2 (2010): 20–21.

41 Thomas Donaldson and Lee E. Preston, "The Stakeholder Theory of Corporations: Concepts, Evidence and Implications," *Academy of Management Review* 20, no. 1 (1995): 65–91; David Jacobs and Kathleen Getz, "Dialogue on the Stakeholder Theory of the Corporation: Concepts, Evidence, and Implications," *The Academy of Management Review* 20, no. 4 (1995): 793–95; David Wheeler, Barry Colbert, and R. Edward Freeman, "Focusing on Value: Reconciling Corporate Social Responsibility, Sustainability and a Stakeholder Approach in a Network World," *Journal of General Management* 28, no. 3 (2003): 1–28.

42 Frederick Bird, "Ethical Reflections on the Challenges Facing International Businesses in Developing Areas," in *International Businesses and*

(International Organization 58, no. 1 (2004): 35–68.)

Challenges of Poverty in the Developing World: Case Studies on Global Responsibilities and Practices, ed. Frederick Bird and W. Stewart (New York: Palgrave Macmillan, 2004), 14–33; Daniel Ofori, "Social Responsibility and Ethics in Ghana: Stakeholders' Expectations and Challenges," in *Management and Economic Development in Sub-Saharan Africa: Theoretical and Applied Perspectives,* ed. J. Okpara (London: Adonis and Abbey, 2007), 67.

43 Bird, "Ethical Reflections on the Challenges Facing International Businesses in Developing Areas," 16–20.

44 Besada, "Doing Business in Fragile States," 16.

45 Hevina S. Dashwood and Bill Buenar Puplampu, "Corporate Social Responsibility and Canadian Mining Companies in the Developing World: The Role of Organizational Leadership and Learning," *Canadian Journal of Development Studies* 30, no. 1–2 (2010): 181–82.

46 Julia Sagebien and Nicole Marie Lindsay, eds., *Corporate Social Responsibility and Governance Ecosystems: Emerging Patterns in the Stakeholder Relationships of Canadian Mining Companies Operating in Latin America* (New York: Palgrave-Macmillan, 2011), 12–30.

47 Bird, "Ethical Reflections on the Challenges Facing International Businesses in Developing Areas," 22–23.

48 Besada, "Doing Business in Fragile States," 21.

49 The World Bank, "World Development Indicators: Ghana," http://databank.worldbank.org/data/views/reports/tableview.aspx (accessed 1 August 2014).

50 Besada, *From Civil Strife to Peacebuilding,* 15–20; Patey, "State Rules: Oil Companies and Armed Conflict in Sudan," 76–78.

51 See Dashwood and Puplampu, "Corporate Social Responsibility and Canadian Mining Companies in the Developing World."

52 Commission on Human Rights and Administrative Justice, *The State of Human Rights in Mining Communities in Ghana* (Accra: CHRAJ, 2008), 3–10. Also see Thomas Akabzaa, *Boom and Dislocation: The Environmental and Social Impacts of Mining in the Wassa West District of Ghana* (Accra: Third World Network, 2000), 39–93; Daniel Ayine, "The Human Rights Dimension to Corporate Mining in Ghana: The Case of Tarkwa District," in *Mining, Development and Social Conflicts in Africa* (Accra: Third World Network, 2001), 85–101; Theresa Garvin et al., "Community-Company Relations in Gold Mining in Ghana," *Journal of Environmental Management* 90 (2009): 571; Gavin Hilson, "Championing the Rhetoric? 'Corporate Social Responsibility' in Ghana's Mining Sector," *Greener Management International* (2007): 43–56; Gavin Hilson, "Harvesting Mineral Riches: 1000 Years of Gold Mining in Ghana," *Resources Policy* 28 (2002): 13–26.

53 Hevina Dashwood, and B. B. Puplampu, "Case Study of Golden Star Resources in Ghana: A Multi-Perspective Approach," prepared for Canada's Department of Foreign

Affairs and International Trade (as part of larger collaborative research project), http://www.ryerson.ca/csrinstitute/current_projects/Dfait_ch3_GSR_Ghana.pdf.

54 Gavin Hilson and Mohammed Banchirigah Sadia, "Are Alternative Livelihood Projects Alleviating Poverty in Mining Communities? Experience from Ghana," *Journal of Development Studies* 45, no. 2 (2009): 172–96.

55 Dashwood and Puplampu, "Case Study of Golden Star Resources in Ghana: A Multi-Perspective Approach."

56 This term was originally coined by James Cooney in the late 1990s in his capacity as senior executive responsible for CSR at Placer Dome Inc., a Canadian company later taken over by Barrick Gold in 2006.

57 Hevina S. Dashwood and Bill Buenar Puplampu, "Multistakeholder Partnerships in Mining in Ghana: From Engagement to Development," in *New Approaches to the Governance of Natural Resources: Insights from Africa*, ed. Andrew Grant and Tim Shaw (London: Palgrave-Macmillan, 2015), 131–53.

58 Ibid.

59 The partnerships included Barrick Gold and World Vision in Peru, Plan Canada and IAMGOLD in Burkina Faso, and Rio Tinto Alcan and WUSC in Ghana.

60 For critical perspectives, see Catherine Coumans, "Whose Development? Mining, Local Resistance, and Development Agendas," in *Governance Ecosystems: CSR in the Latin American Mining Sector*, ed. Julia Sagebien and Nicole Marie Lindsay (London: Palgrave, 2011), 114–32; Elizabeth Blackwood and Veronika Stewart, "CIDA and the Mining Sector: Extractive Industries as an Overseas Development Strategy," in Stephen Brown, *Struggling for Effectiveness: CIDA and Canadian Foreign Aid* (Montreal: McGill-Queen's University Press, 2012), 217–45.

61 Besada, "Doing Business in Fragile States," 13.

62 Idemudia, "Business and Peacemaking in the Context of Limited Statehood: Lessons from Nigeria."

63 Anthea Pitt, "The Bitter Legacy," *Petroleum Economist* (July 1, 2014), 1.

64 Besada, "Doing Business in Fragile States," 25.

65 Tanja A. Börzel, Jana Hönke, and Christian Thauer, "How Much State Does it Take? Corporate Responsibility, Multinational Corporations, and Limited Statehood in South Africa," *Business and Politics* 14, no. 3 (2012): 1–34; Jana Hönke and Christian Thauer, "Multinational Corporations and Service Provision in Sub-Saharan Africa: Legitimacy and Institutionalization Matter," *Governance: An International Journal of Policy, Administration and Institutions* (2014): 1–20; Jana Hönke and Tanja Börzel, "Multinational Companies and the Quality of Local Governance in Sub-Saharan Africa: The Challenges of Limited and Restrained Statehood," paper presented at the annual meeting of the International Studies

66 Dashwood and Puplampu, "Corporate Social Responsibility and Canadian Mining Companies in the Developing World," 186–87.

67 Hönke and Börzel, "Multinational Companies and the Quality of Local Governance in Sub-Saharan Africa," 10.

68 Dashwood, *The Rise of Global Corporate Social Responsibility*, 84–86.

69 Börzel and Risse, "Governance without a State—Can it Work?," 120–21.

70 Patey, *The New Kings of Crude*, 197–205.

71 Dashwood, *The Rise of Global Corporate Social Responsibility*, 17–18.

72 Hönke and Börzel, "Multinational Companies and the Quality of Local Governance in Sub-Saharan Africa," 13.

73 Ibid.

74 Ibid.

75 Jana Hönke and Christian Thauer, "Multinational Corporations and Service Provision in Sub-Saharan Africa: Legitimacy and Institutionalization Matter," 8. Anvil Mining was a Canadian company until taken over by China's Minmetal Corp. in 2012.

76 Ibid., 13.

77 Dashwood, *The Rise of Global Corporate Social Responsibility*, 49–63; Bill Buenar Puplampu and Hevina S. Dashwood, "Investigating the Organizational Antecedents of a Mining Firm's Efforts to Reinvent Its CSR: The Case of Golden Star Resources in Ghana," *Business and Society Review* 116, no. 4 (2011): 472–78.

78 Besada, "Doing Business in Fragile States," 2–4.

79 Jana Hönke with Esther Thomas, "Governance for Whom? Capturing the Inclusiveness and Unintended Effects of Governance," SFB Working Paper Series 31 (Berlin: Freie Universität Berlin, 2012), 9–12.

Association, San Francisco, 2–6 April 2013.

CHAPTER 11

CONCLUSION

Darren Brunk

In time and space, Kinshasa and Kandahar are worlds apart. More than five decades and almost 7,000 kilometres stand between Canada's abortive mission to reform the Armée Nationale Congolaise (ANC) in the early 1960s and the withdrawal of the last Canadian soldiers engaged in the reform of the Afghan National Army (ANA). Canada has travelled a circuitous route from one to the other—through Biafra and Bosnia, Timor Leste, Haiti, Colombia, Pakistan, and points in between. Since winding down its mission in Afghanistan, Canada has undertaken whole-of-government responses to conflict-driven crises in Libya, Ukraine, Mali, Sudan and South Sudan, and currently Iraq, to say nothing of the significant outlays of development, humanitarian, and peacebuilding assistance that it has contributed to multilateral efforts in many more countries.

So surely, after all this time and experience, it can be said with confidence that Canada does fragile states engagement well? Sadly, the all too frequent answer is "not yet."

While the reasons for failure—or lack of success—have varied from context to context, Canada's efforts have not led to sustainable changes in the metrics of what constitutes a functional liberal state. In 1960s Congo, the UN mission in which Canada participated was successful in achieving its mandate, but Canada, when repeatedly asked, did not finish the essential work of reforming the Congolese military. Canada thus must share some of the blame for the Congo's predictable slide into Joseph Mobutu's long, authoritarian, and kleptocratic reign.

A similar story might be told of Canada's much later engagements in Bosnia and Afghanistan. In each instance, while Canada may point to its particular successes within the confines of a broader multilateral mission—in Bosnia as part of UNPROFOR and in Afghanistan as the ISAF lead in Kandahar—these Canadian successes cannot paper over the ultimate failures of the larger effort. In Duane Bratt's chapter on Bosnia, UNPROFOR may have carried out important aspects of its mandate to relieve the suffering of populations within the Bosnian conflict, but the mandate was never sufficient to end the conflict itself. Similarly, Stephen Saideman demonstrates that even the best whole-of-government efforts could not prevent Canada's eventual failure in Kandahar when domestic political calculations forced the premature end of Canadian engagement.

And in Biafra, Canada scarcely showed up at all. Popular humanitarian impulses were superseded by the Canadian government's more proximate concerns—notably the Quebec sovereignty issue. The government's non-interventionist position was hardened by the strident commentary of French officials. Ardent supporters of the separatist Biafrans and Quebecois, they equated the Canadian government's denial of Quebecois separatist claims to those of Nigeria in Biafra. On the balance sheet between Biafran suffering, on the one hand, and a maligned and introspective Canada, on the other, the Biafrans never stood a chance. As parliamentarians David MacDonald and Andrew Brewin reported succinctly in 1970, "there is an attitude of caution and . . . of weighing the views of our allies rather than the merits of the issue."[1]

MacDonald and Brewin might well have used the same language to describe Canada's belated support for the legitimate independence claims of East Timor. Whether as a conscious rhetorical device or a sincere informed assessment, the presumption of East Timor's claims to statehood—either as a lost cause or certain failure—made it far too easy for Canada to favour its interests in Indonesia over the merits of East Timor's case. In Haiti, Canada can point to a long history of on-again, off-again engagement. But in a country in which external shocks—economic or natural—are significant drivers of fragility, Canada has failed to recognize its place amongst these external forces. When Canada uses Haiti's internal fragility dynamics—weak institutions, corruption, poor governance—as a reason to circumvent the state in its development efforts rather than as a reason to engage with it, Ottawa inadvertently reinforces the country's fragility. As David Webster succinctly explains, describing a similar dynamic in Canada's bilateral relationship with East Timor, why put your faith in the government of East Timor (or Haiti, or Afghanistan) when aid is branded with logos from Oxfam or USC Canada?

Based on these perspectives, success for Canada in its fragile state engagements has been elusive. There is a thread of failure running at least 7,000 kilometres through Canada's engagements in fragile states from Afghanistan to the Democratic Republic of the Congo (DRC) and beyond. But are these the only lessons and interpretations that we should draw from this collection? Is the story of some of Canada's most significant efforts across many different contexts really as bleak as all this?

The Limits of the Evidence: Defining "Failure" and Measuring "Success" in Fragile Situations

The value of a comparative collection is that it allows us to look at Canada's experience across contexts and to compare trends, dynamics, and conclusions drawn from one context to the next. One trend across these case studies is clear: Canada's interventions have been incomplete. Canadian efforts have not, on their own or in the confines of larger missions, resolved the underlying root causes of the fragile situations with which they were engaged. However, this broad trend does not tell the whole story. As we scan across the different analyses, one notes that there are important distinctions between how authors interpret Canada's "failure" from one context to the next. When we interrogate these differences in interpretations, a more complex story of Canada's experiences emerges.

So, what has Canadian failure looked like? At one, very negative extreme, a failed engagement might mean doing "more harm than good" in an already fractious context. Given such a definition, Talisman's complicity in Sudanese war crimes might be a case in point, or, drawing on Andrew Thompson's analysis, Canada's post-Aristide engagement in Haiti. In East Timor and Biafra, Canada "failed" in part through inaction, but even this does not tell the whole story. In Biafra, the eventual humanitarian response by Canadian civil society may in fact have contributed to the prolongation of the conflict and human suffering by maintaining supply lines through aid convoys that allowed Biafran separatists to carry on their struggle long after their defeat on the battlefield. In East Timor, Canada wasn't just a passive bystander to the suffering of the East Timorese; successive Canadian governments advocated against East Timor's independence claims and were close partners with Indonesia's Suharto regime—a partnership that included Canadian arms exports. In each case, the portrait painted of Canada's engagement is one of failure defined by Canadian actions that may have exacerbated the conditions of fragility—that is, failure by doing "more harm than good."

Alternately, "failure" might also be shorthand for suboptimal outcomes in situations where "we could have done more"; where an intervention in an already dire situation prevented the worst possible scenario from occurring, but where a more concerted or earlier intervention could have potentially resulted in more substantive, positive change. Such a definition of failure could apply in the DRC, Bosnia, and Afghanistan. In each instance, Canada mitigated some of the worst effects of a pre-existing crisis. But each time, the effort in which Canada participated was either too small in size or too narrow in scope to bring a sustainable end to the crisis by tackling deeper root and proximate causes.

Yet, if Canada should share responsibility for its "failure to do better," does this failure negate Canada's success in arresting or preventing the worst possible outcome? However we answer this question, it is clear that in even providing the space to ask the question, there is a qualitative difference between "failure to do better" and the far more absolute "more harm than good." "Failure to do better" is a distinct type of failure that is tinged with success, and in that respect is a very different result than doing "more harm than good."

When discussing fragile or failed states, these distinctions are more than semantics. Indeed, in many of today's most complex environments, it is hard to envision what, exactly, a successful Canadian engagement might look like. Could even an unlimited outlay of Canadian blood and treasure hope to achieve anything but a sub-optimal outcome in the face of expansive crises in Syria, Ukraine, Somalia, or present-day DRC? Even in such situations, however, action may still be warranted, justified by the sheer scale of human suffering, or as a sub-optimal stopgap to protect Canada's domestic security or commercial interests. In these situations of foreseeable failure, Canada can still choose to act. In such situations, external actors can still aspire to limit or reduce the worst possible outcomes, even if these best efforts are never likely to resolve—or even come close to tackling—root and proximate causes. In such instances where a sub-optimal outcome is acceptable, understanding the degree of failure we are willing to accept as "good enough" becomes an important policy question.[2]

In fragile and failed states, international efforts can expect to be hampered by the effects of war or an otherwise broken social contract. There is often a flood of weapons and armed groups with entrenched hatreds and grievances, or powerful commercial and political interests; there are other informal power brokers and economic actors happy to work outside the regulatory structure of the state; there are psychologically and physically damaged individuals in divided and dislocated communities; and there are frequently external state or non-state actors with their own stake in ensuring that state sovereignty in neighbouring territories remains weak. Across this arduous terrain, a fledgling state must somehow outcompete these rival sites of power, authority, and legitimacy. In such environments, is a functioning state a level of success toward which outside actors should aspire, or to which they can be fairly held to account? If this maximalist state-building objective is not a realistic standard in the most complex environments, what, then, should be the ultimate benchmark for success?

Moreover, as the chapters of this collection illustrate, the particular conditions of "fragility" and "failure" vary widely from one context to the next. As David Webster and Tom Keating remind us, the invocation of the terms "failure" and "fragility" can all too often be used as a politically expedient rhetorical tool, used variously to legitimize Canadian policy decisions both for and against intervention. For Keating, in the post–Cold War era, the concept of "state failure" is an echo of the nineteenth-century "Standard of Civilization," evoking the right and responsibility of Western states to intervene in the sovereign affairs of states failing to live up to the dominant liberal-democratic state standards. In quite a different rhetorical role, in East Timor, the power of the term was used to reinforce a policy of inaction by framing East Timor as a context predestined for failure. When and why these terms are invoked always requires a healthy dose of critical reflection.

Even where fragility and failure may have some resonance in describing very real dynamics, the concepts do not always apply in the same way in all contexts. In Pakistan and Colombia, fragility, to the extent that it exists, appears as a localized mistrust in the legitimacy and representativeness of state institutions. It is manifested through marginalized regions and populations alienated by how and for whom the state chooses to project its power, rather than a concern with its lack of capacity. For instance, as Julian Schofield contends, "Pakistan is not a failed state... but a state with a feeble developmental priority, in which there is a general unwillingness to provide a social-political framework in which citizens can meet their basic needs." In Bosnia and East Timor, however, the state may enjoy fairly wide legitimacy, but the fragility challenge lies in building and extending the state's weak capacity. In Nigeria, Afghanistan, the DRC, and Haiti, the challenge is more likely a mixture of both.

If indeed the concept of fragility exists on a spectrum that requires a degree of tailoring in terms of its applicability from one context to the next, notions of failed or successful engagements should also exist along a correlated spectrum. The question of success is intrinsically linked to the concept of failure and fragility; we cannot know what constitutes an appropriate dosage of the cure if we cannot agree on the nature or extent of the ailment. In this respect, Keating is right when he argues that we must be conscious of the biases of what we consider to be the "state ideal" at the "successful" pole of the state fragility spectrum. The ideal type of the functional state at one end of the spectrum is as flawed as the ideal type of failure at the other end. Our ideal types of "success" and "failure" along this spectrum should be equally dynamic and critically reflective.

The Next 7,000 Kilometres: Where Does Canada Go from Here?

Though the conditions of fragility that Canada is likely to meet in its next overseas challenge may differ from the experiences found in the past, what lessons can this collection offer to help improve on future engagements? Three recurrent themes in particular stand out across the cases explored.

First, it is necessary to take the "state" out of "fragile states." It is entirely unhelpful and unreflective of reality to speak of fragile states; in our theoretical understanding and real-world engagements with fragility, we need to decouple the concept of "fragility" from the state. Traditional notes of state sovereignty have negatively influenced our ability to understand and effectively address fragile situations. For example, the states of Colombia and Pakistan may be resilient and quite strong in some aspects of their governance and legitimacy, and in specific geographic regions. Moreover, questions of whether or not the state itself is failed or fragile are indeed vital insofar as they help us determine the extent to which the state should be a focus of our responses to fragile situations. However, policymakers must be careful not to allow a focus on the durability and stability of the state *itself* to distract them from considering how to best respond to situations of fragility, however localized, within the boundaries of a particular state.

The economic, social, and political drivers, and dynamics of instability in Pakistan's Swat region, or the ongoing prevalence of armed criminal gangs in many of Colombia's provinces and cities, do pose significant threats to regional and international peace and security. But as Schofield argues, the complex origins of these localized crises require more than disconnected and disjointed development or military responses; they require an integrated approach drawing on the full range of political, civilian, and military security, and development tools essential for any fragile state engagement. This being the case, whether the state of Pakistan is itself at risk is secondary to the far more fundamental threat posed by fragility to significant populations within the country, and potentially to Canada's external interests. However important an actor and stakeholder is in addressing drivers of fragility, our tendency to treat the state as the principal referent object of fragility or failure is often misplaced.

Second, the collection emphasizes the vital role that Canadian national interests—be they electoral calculations, federalist tensions, or commercial and other domestic interests—play in influencing Canada's policies around engagements in fragile states and in helping to determine the depth and durability of Canada's commitment to those engagements. Traditional realist commercial and foreign policy calculations may have been at play in dissuading Canadian action in the face of compelling moral claims by the East Timorese. Geopolitical worries over relations with an emerging group of decolonizing states inhibited Canadian willingness to operate outside the confines of a UN mandate in the DRC. Fears that the success of secessionist movements abroad might encourage Quebec separatist claims at home led Canada to privilege approaches that reinforced the integrity of the central state—for example, in Nigeria. And electoral calculations clearly shaped Canada's engagement strategy in Afghanistan.

Though in each case the decisive Canadian "interest" varied, the trend apparent across the chapters is that domestic preoccupations are important determinants in how governments define the objectives, scope, and timelines for Canadian engagement. Though the influence of domestic interests may seem obvious in principle, Canadian fragile state policymaking has done little to date to account for this domestic dynamic in practice. Effective fragile state policymaking must better account for the permissive environment in Canada that underpins its sustainability.

Canadians were moved by scenes of human suffering in Biafra, Bosnia, East Timor, and Haiti. Moreover, in these instances, Canadians mobilized to act—either through government or their own collective action. Canadians were particularly aggrieved to see their own companies—especially in the extractive sector—doing "more harm than good" in Sudan, the Americas, and elsewhere. As Hevina Dashwood explains, an entire segment of Canadian civil society has emerged to hold Canadian companies accountable for their actions overseas, notably in fragile situations. Clearly, Canadians have the will to see their government and civil society engage. Yet public discourse has rarely examined the depth of Canadians' collective will to do fragile states engagement "right." This conscious shift in public discourse must occur if we are to improve the results of our engagements in fragile states.

Canadian policy discussion and development around fragile states must be more honest about the political appetite for intervention. Such a policy shift necessarily requires a much more frank debate within government and in public about the sacrifices Canadians are prepared to make if Canada is to move beyond the minimalist realm of "we could have done more" toward more expensive, maximalist "successful" fragile state engagement. This is the fundamental challenge that Tom Keating raises when he writes, "Canadian policy has demonstrated ongoing support for favouring international interventions to rescue failed states; yet . . . in practice this has often meant selectively supporting a minimal degree of international intervention at little real cost over the long term." Canada has the knowledge and resources to improve on its fragile state engagements; Keating's challenge underlines the other essential, often overlooked aspect of the equation: can Canada muster the necessary collective *will* to see engagements through to the tough standards of success that have proved so elusive in the past?

Long-term projects, at least, offer a skeptical Canadian public the promise of an unambiguously laudable outcome. Mobilizing political will becomes infinitely harder, however, when Canadians are asked to lend their support to morally ambiguous standards of success. No one knows this more than former Supreme Court justice Louise Arbour, who has also served as chief prosecutor for the International Criminal Tribunals for Rwanda and the former Yugoslavia, as well as UN high commissioner for human rights. For over two decades, she has been at the heart of pioneering efforts to bring justice to victims of conflict in fragile states around the world. Yet she has recently questioned the maximalist standards often used to assess success for interventionist efforts. "There is a basic flaw in the international effort to simultaneously pursue justice, peace and human rights," she recently said in an interview. "The negotiation of a lasting peace often requires a delaying, or forgiving, of justice.... What I'm trying to promote, maybe as a way out of this, is the idea of a kind of political empathy as a strategic advantage. Not as a sentimental, do-gooder virtue ... but something that is sustained and has a capacity to genuinely try to understand what an issue looks like from an opponent's or from another party's point of view—a blueprint for understanding before you act, as opposed to rushing into things."[3]

Even if we find the alchemy to conjure a stronger political will, Canadian engagements might still founder on the divisive rocks of domestic national interest. As Carleton University historian Norman Hillmer reminds us, "the national interest is a slippery beast."[4] It is always hard to reconcile diverse Canadian foreign policy and national interests around a particular fragile state engagement. In the DRC, Ottawa's desire to bolster such multilateral security fora as the UN and its interest in positioning Canada favourably among the newly decolonized states provided just enough political will to justify Canada's initial commitment to the ONUC. But this same rationale—fear of upsetting the decolonized block of countries at the UN and undermining the UN as an effective multilateral body—was later used to dissuade Canada from engaging in ANC reform outside a UN-sanctioned mission. Even with strong domestic political will, Canadian fragile state engagements will not automatically improve. It will be more important and tougher to untangle the web of interconnected interests that enable and constrain the form of an engagement, even within the perfect permissive environment.

Third and finally, lest we believe that the prognosis for engagement in fragile states is all doom and gloom, there are also more positive conclusions to be drawn from this collection. In particular, Canada has shown a capacity and willingness to change and adapt its practice over time. The MacDonald-Brewin report, the Harker Commission, and the Canadian-initiated International Commission on Intervention and State Sovereignty (ICISS) all led to important policy discussions and, frequently, significant changes in how the government of Canada approached subsequent engagements in fragile states. Contrast, for example, the limited military mission Canada undertook as part of the UN Operation in the Congo to the multifaceted "comprehensive approach" Canada adopted as part of the NATO-ISAF mission in Afghanistan. In Kandahar, Canada was present on the ground with a much broader array of tools and practices than could ever have been conceived in 1960s Congo. Embedded in the Kandahar Provincial Reconstruction Team, Canada's Afghan mission included a significant military presence to train and assist the ANA; political expertise to build government institutions and to navigate the thorny political challenge of bringing together divergent actors within a shared state framework; civilian policing expertise to build local security capacity; and a sizable development program building the foundations for Afghanistan to carry out its own state-building project.

Moreover, far from being a static mission, Canada altered its techniques in Afghanistan as it went. As Saideman rightly notes, the "comprehensive approach" adopted in Afghanistan between 2005 and 2011 was not without its serious challenges. Recognizing these shortcomings, the government made significant efforts to review its failures and develop solutions. The Manley Report was one important effort in this respect. As the report concluded, many of these operational shortcomings exhibited in the "comprehensive" approach made it clear that in order for "whole of government" approaches to work in practice, it was also essential to embed a stronger culture and infrastructure of interdepartmental cooperation and coordination in Ottawa, where it could inform government strategy before separate ministries and departments arrived in the field. Nowhere was the learning curve in Afghanistan steeper than in the Department of Foreign Affairs and International Trade (DFAIT), which, as Saideman points out, "had little experience in mounting expeditions of this kind and facilitating governance." Acknowledging the need to develop these critical abilities, DFAIT established a dedicated centre of policy, program, deployment, and coordination expertise, specifically designed to improve Canada's engagements in fragile and conflict-affected states—the Stabilization and Reconstruction Task Force (START). DFAIT was a pioneer in developing these new fragile state–specific tools.

Of course, Canada is not learning on its own. There is a much-improved global understanding of how Western nations have collectively failed in the past and of the basic principles that must guide engagements in the future. One of the first notable achievements in this regard came in 2004, when major donor states within the OECD Development Assistance Committee (OECD-DAC) formed the International Network on Conflict and Fragility (INCAF), a donor initiative established so that contributors can monitor and assess their engagements in fragile and conflict-affected states. To date, INCAF has helped inform the international community's first best-practice standard for effective peacebuilding, articulated in the 2007 ten Principles for Good International Engagement in Fragile States and Situations (Fragile States Principles).[5]

Since the founding of INCAF, a growing range of stakeholders—including fragile state and non-traditional donor governments—have added their voices to these learning exercises, most notably through such policy and advocacy bodies as the International Dialogue on Peacebuilding and Statebuilding ("the Dialogue") and the g7+ group of fragile state governments. Together, the members of the Dialogue and the g7+ crafted the "New Deal" for engagement in fragile states, which outlines a series of best-practice commitments to be undertaken by both fragile state governments *and* their international partners. Like the Fragile States Principles, the New Deal re-emphasizes the twin pillars of local context and coherence of effort. However, as a set of "best practice" commitments drafted in part by fragile states themselves, the New Deal exemplifies—just as it adds a layer of detail and operational relevance to—the commitments to context and coherence outlined in the Fragile State Principles. This emerging body of knowledge and consensus around fragile state good practice raises the prospect that Canada's next significant engagement will be better than the last, and that Canadians and the international community will be much better equipped to challenge the Canadian approach where it fails to live up to clearly defined standards.[6]

Seven thousand kilometres stretch between Kinshasa and Kandahar. And yet, when one looks at the record of Canadian engagements in fragile states along the road from one to the next, it's hard to know—just how far have we travelled? Both the DRC and Afghanistan would be strong candidates today for Canada's next fragile states engagement. In that important respect, perhaps the distance is not as far as we'd like to think. No doubt, looking at the historical record, Canada's efforts have not, as a general rule, resulted in sustainable, resilient, and peaceful countries. At times, Canadian engagement may well have worsened conflict, instability, and human rights conditions in already fragile situations. And yet, while our successes may not have been fully realized, neither have our failures always been so complete. In notable cases, Canadian actions have contributed to the alleviation of suffering, a reduction in armed conflict, and the strengthening of weak institutions. All too frequently, Canada has left its important work incomplete or unfinished.

Though results to date have been imperfect, there is still good reason to believe that, under the right conditions, Canada can make a positive contribution through its fragile states engagements. If this statement is true, then it prompts the critical question: what *are* the right conditions? This collection points toward some possible answers. Establishing the right conditions for engagement begins at home, in Canada. The process starts by assessing, as part of the public discourse, whether Canadians are prepared to see a particular commitment through, based on clear, results-based benchmarks for when Canada can and should consider the job done. What benchmarks are Canadians prepared to accept as the standard of success? Is it enough to carry on as has been done in the past, accepting that we "failed to do more," but at the very least having avoided the worst possible outcome? Or is the "Canadian standard" for fragile states engagement going to be something more—a standard that aims at a fundamental change in the political, economic, and social conditions of a state or region, where Canadians can say "fragility is no more"? If Canadians, as a result of this discussion around a prospective engagement, cannot be confident of achieving this high standard of success, what then? When is it enough to accept the minimalist "could have done more" alternative?

This collection does not provide ready answers to these tough questions, but it clearly demonstrates the need for the discussion. Canada has long engaged fragile states and will doubtless continue to do so. Let us start the discussion now, using the evidence and lessons from this volume as a point of departure. For, tomorrow or the next day, we will surely see new crises and conflicts that will trouble our collective conscience. Canadians will write to their public officials to learn what Canada intends to do. Policymakers will gather to consider what Canada can do. Government ministers will weigh the gravity of the situation against Canada's interests and the appetite of the Canadian voter before deciding what we will do. Before we engage in the next fragile situation, let us be confident that throughout this decision-making process we are, all of us, sharing a discussion around hard questions over what Canada should do. We need to get this conversation right. Seven thousand kilometres is a long way to travel for nothing.

Notes

1. Andrew Brewin and David MacDonald, *Canada and the Biafran Tragedy* (Toronto: James Lorimer, 1970), 135.

2. For a fuller exploration of the debate around the distinctions of success and failure in fragile and failed states, see, for example, Charles Call and Vanessa Wyeth, eds., *Building States to Build Peace* (Boulder: Lynne Rienner, 2008).

3. Doug Saunders, "Why Louise Arbour is thinking twice," *Globe and Mail*, 28 March 2015.

4. Norman Hillmer, "National Independence and the National Interest: O. D. Skelton's Department of External Affairs in the 1920s," in Greg Donaghy and Michael K. Carroll, *In the National Interest: Canadian Foreign Policy and the Department of Foreign Affairs and International Trade, 1909–2009* (Calgary: University of Calgary Press, 2010), 11.

5. OECD-INCAF, "Principles for Good International Engagement in Fragile States and Situations," http://www.oecd.org/development/conflictandfragility/effectiveengagementinfragilestates.htm (accessed 7 November 2012).

Note: The Fragile State Principles are: 1) Take context as the starting point; 2) Do no harm; 3) Focus on state building as the central objective; 4) Prioritize prevention; 5) Recognize the links between political, security and development objectives; 6) Promote non-discrimination as a basis for inclusive and stable societies;

7) Align with local priorities in different ways in different contexts; 8) Agree on practical coordination mechanisms between international actors; 9) Act fast ... but stay engaged long enough to give success a chance; and 10) Avoid pockets of exclusion.

6   World Bank, *World Development Report 2011: Conflict, Security and Development*, 185, http://go.worldbank.org (accessed 7 November 2012).

CONTRIBUTORS

STEPHANIE BANGARTH is an Associate Professor of History at King's University College at Western University.

DUANE BRATT is Chair and Professor in the Department of Economics, Justice, and Policy Studies at Mount Royal University.

DARREN BRUNK is a senior peacebuilding specialist at Global Affairs Canada. He is currently a Visiting Lecturer at Victoria University of Wellington in New Zealand.

MICHAEL K. CARROLL is an Associate Professor of History at MacEwan University.

HEVINA S. DASHWOOD is Chair and Professor in the Global Affairs Canada.

JEAN DAUDELIN is an Associate Professor at the Norman Paterson School of International Affairs at Carleton University.

GREG DONAGHY is Head of the Historical Section at Global Affairs Canada, and General Editor of its series, *Documents on Canadian External Relations*.

TOM KEATING is Professor Emeritus of Political Science at the University of Alberta.

Stephen M. Saideman is Professor at the Norman Paterson School of International Affairs and holds the Paterson Chair in International Affairs at Carleton University.

Julian Schofield is an Associate Professor in the Department of Political Science at Concordia University.

Kevin A. Spooner is an Associate Professor of North American Studies and History at Wilfrid Laurier University.

Andrew S. Thompson is a Senior Fellow at the Centre for International Governance Innovation, an Adjunct Assistant Professor of Political Science at the University of Waterloo, and Program Officer, Global Governance Programs at the Balsillie School of International Affairs.

David Webster is an Associate Professor of History at Bishop's University.

BIBLIOGRAPHY

Archival Sources

Diefenbaker Canada Centre
John G. Diefenbaker Papers

Library and Archives Canada
Andrew Brewin Papers
Department of External Affairs Records
Department of National Defence Records

Private Collection—Toronto
East Timor Alert Network Papers

University of British Columbia Archives
British Columbia Civil Liberties Association Papers

Newspapers and Periodicals
American Forces Press Service
Catholic New Times
CBC News

The Economist
Embassy
Financial Times
Globe and Mail
Independent
Leader-Post (Regina)
Montreal Star
The National
National Post
Newsday
New York Times
Pakistan Observer
Postmedia News
Reuters
The Strategist
Sydney Morning Herald
Toronto Star
Victoria Colonist

Government and Institutional Publications

Australia

Australia. Documents on Australian Foreign Policy: Australia and the Indonesian Incorporation of East Timor, 1974–1976. Melbourne: Melbourne University Press, 2000.

Canada

Canada. Canadian International Development Agency. *Annual Aid Review*. Ottawa: Government of Canada, 1974.

———. *Annual Report, 1974–75*. Ottawa: Government of Canada, 1975.

———. *Annual Report, 1975–76*. Ottawa: Government of Canada, 1976.

———. *Annual Report, 1977–78*. Ottawa: Government of Canada, 1978.

———. *Canada and the Developing World.* Ottawa: Queen's Printer, 1970.

———. *Canada's Statistical Report on International Assistance—Fiscal Year 2006–2007.* Gatineau, QC: CIDA, 2009.

———. "Canadian Cooperation with Haiti: Reflecting on a Decade of 'Difficult Partnership.'" Ottawa: Government of Canada, 2004.

———. "News Releases," 1981, 1986, 1987, 1988, 1989, 1990.

———. *On the Road to Recovery: Breaking the Cycle of Poverty and Fragility: Guidelines for Effective Development Cooperation in Fragile States.* November 2005.

———. *Statistical Report on International Assistance, 2009–2010.* Ottawa: CIDA, 2011.

———. *Statistical Report on Official Development Assistance 1998–1999.* Ottawa: CIDA, 2000.

———. *Statistical Report on Official Development Assistance 1999–2000.* Ottawa: CIDA, 2001.

———. *Statistical Report on Official Development Assistance 2000–2001.* Ottawa: CIDA, 2002.

———. *Statistical Report on Official Development Assistance 2003–2004.* Ottawa: CIDA, 2005.

Canada. Department of External Affairs. *A Report on Canada's External Aid Programs 1965–66.* Ottawa: External Aid Office, 1966.

———. *Foreign Policy for Canadians*, Pacific Booklet. Ottawa: Queen's Printer, 1970.

Canada. Department of Foreign Affairs and International Trade. *Building the Canadian Advantage: A Corporate Social Responsibility (CSR) Strategy for the Canadian Extractive Sector.* March 2009. http://www.international.gc.ca/trade-agreements-accords-commerciaux/topics-domaines/other-autre/csr-strat-rse.aspx.

———. *Canada's International Policy Statement: A Role of Pride and Influence in the World—Diplomacy.* 2005. http://publications.gc.ca/collections/Collection/FR4-4-2005E.pdf.

———. *Indonesia: A Guide for Canadian Business, 1995–96.* Ottawa: Queen's Printer, 1995.

Canada. Department of Foreign Affairs, Trade and Development. "CIDA's Strategic Overview." http://www.acdi-cida.gc.ca/acdi-cida/acdi-cida.nsf/eng/NAT-911133132-NK9.

———. *Canada's Enhanced Corporate Social Responsibility Strategy to Strengthen Canada's Extractive Sector Abroad*. 14 November 2014. http://www.international.gc.ca/trade-agreements-accords-commerciaux/topics-domaines/other-autre/csr-strat-rse.aspx?lang=eng

———. *Canada Updates List of Development Countries of Focus*. June 2014. http://www.international.gc.ca/media/dev/news-communiques/2014/06/27abg.aspx?lang=eng.

———. *Government Response to the Fourteenth Report of the Standing Committee on Foreign Affairs and International Trade*. October 2005.

———. "START in Sudan and South Sudan." http://www.international.gc.ca/start-gtsr/sudan-soudan.aspx.

Canada. Department of National Defence. "1994 Defence White Paper." Ottawa: Queen's Printer, 1994.

Canada. House of Commons. "Canada's International Policy Put to the Test in Haiti." Report of the Standing Committee on Foreign Affairs and International Development. December 2006.

———. *Debates*. 27th Parliament, 18 January 1966–23 April 1968.

———. *Hansard*. 1987, 1988, 1991.

———. "Government Response to the Eighth Report of the Standing Committee on Foreign Affairs and International Development. A Focus on Democracy Support." 2 November 2007.

———. *Minutes of Proceedings and Evidence*. Standing Committee on External Affairs and National Defence, 10 October 1968.

Canada. House of Commons. Standing Committee on Foreign Affairs and International Development. "Advancing Canada's Role in International Support for Democratic Development." Ottawa: Government of Canada, July 2007.

———. "Canada's International Policy Put to the Test in Haiti." Ottawa: December 2006.

———. *Driving Inclusive Economic Growth: The Role of the Private Sector in International Development*. Ottawa: Government of Canada, 2012.

———. *Mining in Developing Countries and CSR*. Ottawa: Government of Canada, 2005.

Canada. Office of the Prime Minister. "Notes for an address by Prime Minister Brian Mulroney on the occasion of the centennial anniversary convocation." Stanford University, 29 September 1991.

Donaghy, Greg, ed. *Documents on Canadian External Relations, Volume 17: 1951.* Ottawa: Canadian Government Publishing, 1996.

Harker Commission Report. *Human Security in Sudan: The Report of a Canadian Assessment Mission.* Prepared for the Minister of Foreign Affairs. Ottawa: DFAIT, January 2000.

European Commission

European Commission. Directorate-General for Trade. "European Union, Trade in Goods with Pakistan." 2012.

Organisation for Economic Co-operation and Development (OECD)

OECD. *Busan Partnership for Effective Development Co-operation.* Fourth High Level Forum on Aid Effectiveness, Busan, Republic of Korea, 29 November–1 December 2011.

———. *Fragile States: Resource Flows and Trends.* Paris: OECD, 2013.

———. *The Paris Declaration on Aid Effectiveness and the Accra Agenda for Action.* 2005/2008.

———. *Whole of Government Approaches to Fragile States.* Paris: OECD, 2006.

Pakistan

Pakistan. Finance Division. *Poverty Reduction Strategy Paper II.* 2010.

United Nations

Boutros-Ghali, Boutros. *An Agenda for Peace: Preventive Diplomacy, Peacemaking and Peace-keeping.* New York: United Nations Department of Public Information, 31 January 1992.

Cordier, Andrew W., and Wilder Foote, eds. *Public Papers of the Secretaries-General of the United Nations, vol. 5, Dag Hammarskjöld 1960–61.* New York: Columbia University Press, 1975.

Ruggie, John Gerard. Guiding Principles on Business and Human Rights: Implementing the United Nations "Protect, Respect and Remedy" Framework. 2011. UN Doc. PJ HRC/17/31.

———. Protect, Respect and Remedy: A Framework for Business and Human Rights. 2008. UN Doc. A/HRC/8/5.

United Nations. *The Blue Helmets: A Review of United Nations Peace-keeping*, 3rd edition. UN Department of Public Information: New York, 1996.

United Nations. Transcript of Press Conference by Secretary-General Kofi Annan at United Nations Headquarters, 21 March 2005. United Nations Information Service—Vienna.

United Nations. *Yearbook of the United Nations 1963*. New York: Office of Public Information, United Nations, 1963.

United Nations Department of Public Information. The United Nations and the Situation in the Former Yugoslavia. May 1993.

United Nations Development Program. "Human Development Reports."

———. "Human Development Report for Latin America 2013–2014. Citizen Security with a Human Face: Evidence and proposals for Latin America." New York: United Nations Development Program, 2013.

United Nations Economic and Social Council (ECOSOC). Resolutions.

United Nations General Assembly (UNGA). Resolutions.

United Nations High Commissioner for Refugees. Information Notes on the Former Yugoslavia. July 1994.

United Nations Security Council (UNSC) Resolutions.

United States

Public Papers of the Presidents of the United States: George Bush. Washington, DC: GPO, 1992.

Public Papers of the Presidents of the United States: Jimmy Carter. Washington, DC: GPO, 1981.

Public Papers of the Presidents of the United States: Ronald Reagan. Washington, DC: GPO, 1983.

United States. Department of Defense. "Quadrennial Defense Review, 2014." http://archives.defense.gov/pubs/2014_Quadrennial_Defense_Review.pdf.

United States. Department of State. *Foreign Relations of the United States (FRUS), 1961–1963, Vol. 20: Congo Crisis.* Washington: GPO, 1995.

———. "The National Security Strategy of the United States of America." September 2002. http://www.state.gov/documents/organization/63562.pdf.

USAID. Congressional Presentation, Fiscal Year 1975, Annex III: Latin America and the Caribbean. Washington, DC: GPO, 1976.

———. Congressional Presentation, Fiscal Year 1978, Annex III: Latin America and the Caribbean. Washington, DC: GPO, 1979.

———. Congressional Presentation, Fiscal Year 1987, Annex III: Latin America and the Caribbean. Washington, DC: GPO, 1987.

———. Congressional Presentation, Fiscal Year 1988, Annex III: Latin America and the Caribbean. Washington, DC: GPO, 1988.

———. Congressional Presentation, Fiscal Year 1989, Annex III: Latin America and the Caribbean. Washington, D.C.: GPO, 1989.

———. Congressional Presentation, Fiscal Year 1991, Annex III: Latin America and the Caribbean. Washington, DC: GPO, 1991.

———. "Getting to Zero: A Discussion Paper on Ending Extreme Poverty." 21 November 2013.

World Bank

Crime and Violence in Central America: A Development Challenge. Washington, DC: The World Bank, 2011.

World Development Indicators: Ghana. http://databank.worldbank.org/data/views/reports/tableview.aspx.

Non-Governmental Organizations

Americas Watch. "Haiti: Human Rights Under Hereditary Dictatorship." New York: Americas Watch in conjunction with the Lawyer's Committee for International Human Rights, October 1985.

———. "Haiti: Report of a Human Rights Mission, June 26–29, 1983." New York: Americas Watch in conjunction with the Lawyer's Committee for International Human Rights, August 1983.

Amnesty International. "Amnesty Hints at Haiti's 'Cynicism and Deception' Over Political Prisoners." London: Amnesty International Publications, 1 March 1973.

———. "Haiti: After the Earthquake—Initial Mission Findings, March 2010." London: Amnesty International, March 2010.

———. "Haiti: Current Concerns." London: Amnesty International Publications, November 1988.

———. "Haiti: Human Rights Violations, October 1980 to October 1981." London: Amnesty International Publications, November 1981.

———. "Haiti: Human Rights Violations in the Aftermath of the Coup D'état, October 1991." London: Amnesty International Publications, October 1991.

———. "Haiti: The Human Rights Tragedy—Human Rights Violations Since the Coup." London: Amnesty International Publications, January 1992.

———. "News Release." London: Amnesty International Publications, 9 January 1977.

———. "Report on the Situation of Political Prisoners in Haiti, 1973." London: Amnesty International Publications, 1973.

———. "USA/Haiti: The Price of Rejection—Human Rights Consequences for Rejected Haitian Asylum-Seekers." London: Amnesty International Publications, May 1994.

Commission on Human Rights and Administrative Justice. "The State of Human Rights in Mining Communities in Ghana." Accra, Ghana: CHRAJ, 2008.

Fund for Peace. "2014 Fragile State Index." http://fsi.fundforpeace.org/rankings-2014.

Fund for Peace. "2013 Failed States Index." http://fsi.fundforpeace.org/rankings-2013-sortable.

Global Humanitarian Assistance. Briefing Paper: Pakistan: Country Aid Factsheet. Somerset: August 2010.

Helsinki Watch. *War Crimes in Bosnia-Hercegovina*. Vols. 1–2. New York: Human Rights Watch, 1992.

International Rights Women's Action Watch. "Democratic Republic of the Congo." December 1999.

National Labor Committee. "Sweatshop Development." *In The Haiti Files: Decoding the Crisis*, edited by James Ridgeway. Washington, DC: Essential Books, 1994.

North-South Institute. *Fragile States or Failing Development: Canadian Development Report 2008.* Ottawa: Renouf Publishing, 2008.

Saferworld. "Conflict Sensitivity in South Sudan: Ensuring economic development supports peace." 30 August 2013. http://www.saferworld.org.uk/news-and-views/comment/103?utm_source=smartmail&utm_medium=email&utm_campaign=2013+September+e-news.

UK Save the Children. "Unlocking Progress in Fragile States: Optimising High-Impact Maternal and Child Survival Interventions." London: Save the Children UK, 2010.

Washington Office on Haiti. "Action Alert." Washington, DC: Washington Office on Haiti, July 1987.

———. "Democratic Process in Jeopardy in Haiti." Washington, DC: Washington Office on Haiti, 3 November 1987.

Books and Articles

"CIDA's Key Role in Haiti's 2004 Coup d'État: Funding Regime Change, Dictatorship and Human Rights Atrocities, One Haitian NGO at a Time." *Press for Conversion* 61 (September 2007).

Ahmad, Junaid. "Pakistan-Canada Economic Relations." MBA thesis, Concordia University, 1976.

Akabzaa, Thomas. *Boom and Dislocation: The Environmental and Social Impacts of Mining in the Wassa West District of Ghana.* Accra: Third World Network, 2000.

Alao, Abiodun. *Natural Resources and Conflict in Africa: The Tragedy of Endowment.* New York: University of Rochester Press, 2007.

Andreas, Peter. *Blue Helmets and Black Markets: The Business of Survival in the Siege of Sarajevo.* Ithaca: Cornell University Press, 2008.

Autesserre, Séverine. *Peaceland: Conflict Resolution and the Everyday Politics of International Intervention.* Cambridge: Cambridge University Press, 2014.

Auty, Richard M. "Natural Resources, Capital Accumulation and the Resource Curse." *Ecological Economics* 61, no. 4 (2007): 627–34.

Ayine, Daniel. "The human rights dimension to corporate mining in Ghana: The case of Tarkwa District." In *Mining, Development and Social Conflicts in Africa*, 85–101. Accra: Third World Network, 2001.

Baranyi, Stephen. "Le Canada, Haïti et les dilemmes de l'intervention dans les 'États fragiles.'" Ébauche présentée au Congrès de LASA à Montréal, 5–8 septembre 2007.

Barbara, Julien. "Nation Building and the Role of the Private Sector as a Political Peace-Builder." *Conflict Security and Development* 6 (2006): 581–94.

Barry, Donald. "Interest Groups and the Foreign Policy Process: The Case of Biafra." In *Pressure Group Behaviour in Canadian Politics*, edited by A. Paul Pross, 117–47. Toronto: McGraw-Hill Ryerson, 1975.

Bercuson, David J., and J. L. Granatstein, with Nancy Pearson Mackie. *Lessons Learned? What Canada Should Learn from Afghanistan*. Calgary: CDFAI, 2011.

Berry-Shaw, Nikolas, and Dru Oja Jay. *Paved with Good Intentions: Canada's Development NGOS from Idealism to Imperialism*. Halifax: Fernwood, 2012.

Besada, Hany. "Doing Business in Fragile States: The Private Sector, Natural Resources and Conflict in Africa." Background research paper submitted to the High-Level Panel on the Post-2015 Development Agenda, May 2013.

Besada, Hany, ed. *From Civil Strife to Peacebuilding: Examining Private Sector Involvement in West African Reconstruction*. Waterloo, ON: Centre for International Governance Innovation and Wilfrid Laurier University Press, 2009.

Bird, Frederick. "Ethical Reflections on the Challenges Facing International Businesses in Developing Areas." In *International Businesses and Challenges of Poverty in the Developing World: Case studies on global responsibilities and practices*, edited by Frederick Bird and W. Stewart, 14–33. New York: Palgrave Macmillan, 2004.

Bonney, Richard, Tridivesh Singh Maini, and Tahir Malik, eds. *Warriors after War*. Oxford: Peter Lang, 2011.

Börzel, Tanja A., Jana Hönke and Christian Thauer. "How Much State Does it Take? Corporate Responsibility, Multinational Corporations, and Limited Statehood in South Africa." *Business and Politics* 14, no. 3 (2012): 1–34.

Börzel, Tanja A., and Thomas Risse. "Governance without a State—Can It Work?" *Regulation and Governance* 4, no. 2 (2010): 1–22.

Bothwell, Robert. *Alliance and Illusion: Canada and the World, 1945–1984.* Vancouver: UBC Press, 2007.

Bratt, Duane. "Assessing the Success of UN Peacekeeping Operations," *International Peacekeeping* 3, no. 4 (Winter 1996): 64–81.

———. *The Politics of Candu Exports.* Toronto: University of Toronto Press, 2006.

———. "Tools and Levers: Energy as an Instrument of Canadian Foreign Policy." In *Canada Among Nations 2008*, edited by Robert Bothwell and Jean Daudelin. Montreal: McGill-Queen's University Press, 2009.

Bratt, Duane, and Christopher Kukucha, eds. *Readings in Canadian Foreign Policy.* Don Mills: Oxford University Press, 2011.

Braune, Johannes. "Pakistan's Security Today and Tomorrow." A conference of the Canadian Security Intelligence Service jointly sponsored by Canada's departments of Foreign Affairs and International Trade, National Defence and Public Safety/CSIS. 22–23 January 2009. http://www.csis-scrs.gc.ca/pblctns/wrld-wtch/2009/PAKISTAN_ENGLISH_REPORT_2013.pdf.

Brewin, Andrew, and David MacDonald. *Canada and the Biafran Tragedy.* Toronto: James Lorimer, 1970.

Brewster, Murray, ed. *The Savage War: The Untold Battles of Afghanistan.* Mississauga, ON: Wiley, 2011.

Brinkerhoff, Derick W., ed. *Governance in Post-Conflict Societies: Rebuilding Fragile States.* London: Routledge, 2007.

Brock, Lothar, Hans-Henrik Holm, George Sørensen, and Michael Stohl. *Fragile States: Violence and the Failure of Intervention.* Cambridge, UK: Polity Press, 2012.

Brouwer, Ruth Compton. "When Missions Become Development: Ironies of 'NGOization' in Mainstream Canadian Churches in the 1960s." *Canadian Historical Review* 91, no. 4 (December 2010): 661–93.

Brown, J. C. Gordon. *Blazes Along a Diplomatic Trail: A Memoir of Four Posts in the Canadian Foreign Service.* Victoria: Trafford Publishing, 2000.

Brown, Stephen, ed. *Struggling for Effectiveness: CIDA and Canadian Foreign Aid.* Montreal: McGill-Queen's University Press, 2012.

Burney, Derek. *Getting It Done: A Memoir.* Montreal: McGill-Queen's University Press, 2005.

Call, Charles, and Vanessa Wyeth, eds. *Building States to Build Peace.* Boulder: Lynne Rienner, 2008.

Carey, Peter. "To struggle for freedom: Indonesia yesterday, East Timor today." *Inside Indonesia* 49 (January–March 1997): 26–27.

Carin, Barry. *Reinventing CIDA—One Year Later*. Calgary: Canadian Defence and Foreign Affairs Institute, 2011.

Carment, David. "Effective Defence Policy for Responding to Failed and Failing States." Prepared for the Canadian Defence and Foreign Affairs Institute's "Research Paper Series." Calgary: CDFAI, June 2005.

Carment, David, S. Prest, J. Gazo, T. Bell, and S. Houghton. "Assessing the Circumstances and Forms of Canada's Involvement in Fragile States: Towards a Methodology of Relevance and Impact." Ottawa: NPSIA, December 2006.

Carment, David, Stewart Prest, and Yiagadeesen Samy. *Security, Development and the Fragile State: Bridging the Gap Between Theory and Policy*. New York: Routledge, 2009.

Carment, David, and Y. Samy. "Engaging Fragile States: Closing the Gap between Theory and Policy." *Global Dialogue* 13, no. 1 (2011): 1–11.

Cassar, Anis. *European Aid to Pakistan: Steadily on the Rise*. Paris: European Institute for Security Studies, December 2009.

Chandrasekaran, Rajiv. *Little America: The War Within the War for Afghanistan*. New York: Alfred A. Knopf, 2012.

Chin, Gregory. "Shifting Purpose—Asia's Rise and Canada's Foreign Aid." *International Journal* 64, no. 4 (Autumn 2009): 989–1009.

Chopra, Jarat. "Building State Failure in East Timor." *Development and Change* 33 (2002): 979–1000.

Coll, Steve. *Private Empire: Exxon Mobil and American Power*. New York: Penguin Press, 2012.

Collier, Paul, and Anke Hoeffler. "Greed and Grievance in Civil War." *Oxford Economic Papers* 56, no. 4 (August 2004): 563–95.

Cotton, James. "Timor-Leste and the discourse of state failure," *Australian Journal of International Affairs* 61, no. 4 (2007): 455–70.

Cousens, Elizabeth M., and Chetan Kumar, with Karin Wermester, eds. *Peacebuilding as Politics: Cultivating Peace in Fragile Societies*. Boulder: Lynne Rienner Publishers, 2001.

Crnobrnja, Mihailo. *The Yugoslav Drama*. Montreal: McGill-Queen's University Press, 1994.

Culpeper, Roy, and Gail Whiteman. "The Corporate Stake in Social Responsibility." In *Canadian Corporations and Social Responsibility*, edited by Michelle Hibler and Rowena Beamish. Ottawa: North-South Institute, 1998.

Dagg, Chris. "Linking Aid to Human Rights in Indonesia: A Canadian Perspective." *Issues* 7, no. 1 (Winter 1993): 3-12.

Damrosch, Lori Fisler, ed. *Enforcing Restraint: Collective Intervention in Internal Conflicts*. New York: Council on Foreign Relations, 1993.

Dashwood, Hevina S. "Global Private Governance: Explaining Initiatives in the Global Mining Sector." In *The Handbook of Global Companies*, edited by John Mikler, 456–73. West Sussex, UK: John Wiley and Sons, 2013.

———. *The Rise of Global Corporate Social Responsibility: Mining and the Spread of Global Norms*. Cambridge: Cambridge University Press, 2012.

———. "Sustainable Development and Industry Self-Regulation: Developments in the Global Mining Sector." *Business and Society* 53, no. 4 (2014): 551–82.

Dashwood, Hevina S., and Bill Buenar Puplampu. "Corporate Social Responsibility and Canadian Mining Companies in the Developing World: The Role of Organizational Leadership and Learning." *Canadian Journal of Development Studies* 30, nos. 1–2 (2010): 175–96.

———. "Multistakeholder Partnerships in Mining in Ghana: From Engagement to Development." In *New Approaches to the Governance of Natural Resources: Insights from Africa*, edited by Andrew Grant and Tim Shaw. New York: Palgrave-Macmillan, 2014.

Dashwood, Hevina S., and Uwafiokun Idemudia. "Global Natural Resource Governance Initiatives and Local Adoption: The example of the Extractive Industry Transparency Initiative (EITI) in Ghana and Nigeria." Paper presented at the annual meeting of the Canadian Political Science Association (CPSA), Brock University, 29 May 2014.

Daudelin, Jean. "A New Drug Warrior?" In *The State and Security in Mexico: Transformation and Crisis in Regional Perspective*. New York: Routledge, 2012.

Daudelin, Jean, and Yiagadeesen Samy. *In Praise of Taxes? Fiscal Pacts, Development Policy and Conflict Risk*. CSDS Working Paper 07. Ottawa: Centre for Security and Defence Studies, 2008.

Daudelin, Jean, and Daniel Schwanen, eds. *Canada Among Nations 2007: What Room for Manoeuvre?* Montreal: McGill-Queen's University Press, 2008.

Delvoie, Louis. "Taming the South Asian Nuclear Tiger: Causes and Consequences, and Canadian Responses." In *A Big League Player?*, edited by Fen Osler Hampson, Martin Rudner, and Michael Hart, 233–52. Oxford: Oxford University Press, 1999.

Demombynes, Gabriel. *Drug trafficking and violence in Central America and beyond*. Washington, DC: World Bank, 2011.

Di John, Jonathan. "Is There Really a Resource Curse? A Critical Survey of Theory and Evidence." *Global Governance: A Review of Multilateralism and International Organizations* 17, no. 2 (2011): 167–84.

———. "The Concept, Causes and Consequences of Failed States: A Critical Review of the Literature and Agenda for Research with Specific Reference to Sub-Saharan Africa." *European Journal of Development Research* 22, no. 1 (2010): 10–30.

Diamond, Jared. *Collapse: How Societies Choose to Fail or Succeed*. New York: Viking, 2005.

Diehl, Paul F. *Evaluating Peace Operations*. Boulder: Lynne Rienner Publishers, 2010.

Djankov, Simeon, Jose G. Montalvo, and Marta Reynal-Querol. "The curse of aid." *Journal of Economic Growth* 13, no. 3 (2008): 169–94.

Donaghy, Greg. "All God's Children: Lloyd Axworthy, Human Security, and Canadian Foreign Policy, 1996–2000." *Canadian Foreign Policy*, 10, no. 2 (Winter 2003): 39–58.

Donaghy, Greg, and Michael K. Carroll. *In the National Interest: Canadian Foreign Policy and the Department of Foreign Affairs and International Trade, 1909–2009*. Calgary: University of Calgary Press, 2010.

Donaldson, Thomas, and Lee E. Preston. "The Stakeholder Theory of Corporations: Concepts, Evidence and Implications." *Academy of Management Review* 20, no. 1 (1995): 65–91.

Dorronsoro, Gilles. *Revolution Unending: Afghanistan, 1979 to the Present*. New York: Columbia University Press, 2013.

Durch, William J., ed. *The Evolution of UN Peacekeeping: Case Studies and Comparative Analysis*. Washington: Henry L. Stimson Center: 1993.

Ellul, Jacques. *L'illusion politique*. Paris: Robert Laffont, 1965.

Emizet, Kisangani N. F. "Explaining the Rise and Fall of Military Regimes: Civil-Military Relations in the Congo." *Armed Forces and Society* 26, no. 2 (2000): 203–27.

English, John. *Just Watch Me: The Life of Pierre Elliott Trudeau, 1968–2000.* Toronto: Knopf Canada, 2009.

Ezrow, Natasha M., and Erica Frantz. *Failed States and Institutional Decay: Understanding Instability and Poverty in the Developing World.* New York: Bloomsbury, 2013.

Faruqui, Ahmad, and Julian Schofield. "Pakistan: The Political Economy of Militarism." *Journal of Conflict, Security and Development* 2, no. 2 (2003): 5–23.

Fatton, Robert, Jr. *Haiti's Predatory Republic: The Unending Transition to Democracy.* Boulder: Lynne Rienner Publishers, 2002.

Fernandes, Clinton. *Reluctant Savior: Australia, Indonesia and the Independence of East Timor.* Melbourne: Scribe Publications, 2004.

Fitch, Robert, and Mary Oppenheimer. "Biafra: Let them Eat Oil." *Ramparts* (7 September 1967): 34-38.

Forsythe, David. "International Humanitarianism in the Contemporary World: Forms and Issues." In *Multilateralism Under Challenge: Power, International Order and Structural Change*, edited by Edward Neuman, Ramesh Thakur, and John Tirman. Washington: Brookings Institution Press, 2006.

Gammer, Nicholas. *From Peacekeeping to Peacemaking: Canada's Response to the Yugoslav Crisis.* Montreal: McGill-Queen's University Press, 2001.

Garvin, Theresa, Tara K. McGee, Karen E. Smoyer-Tomic, and Emmanuel Ato Aubynn. "Community-company relations in gold mining in Ghana." *Journal of Environmental Management* 90 (2009): 571–86.

Gauthier, Alexandre, and Simon Lapointe. *Canadian Trade and Investment Activity: Canada-Pakistan.* Ottawa: Parliamentary and Information Service, 2010.

Gelb, Alan. H. *Oil Windfalls: Blessing or Curse?* New York: Oxford University Press, 1988.

Gendron, Robin S. "PT Inco and the Culture of Business in Indonesia: The case of Tjendra v. Jessup." Paper presented to the Canadian Association of Asian Studies, Waterloo, ON, November 2008.

Goldstone, Jack A., et al. *State Failure Task Force Report: Phase III Findings.* McLean, VA: Science Applications International Corporation, 2000.

Gong, Gerrit W. *The Standard of Civilization in International Society.* Oxford: Oxford University Press, 1984.

Granatstein, J. L., and Robert Bothwell. *Pirouette: Pierre Trudeau and Canadian Foreign Policy*. Toronto: University of Toronto Press, 1991.

Grono, Nick. "Fragile States, Searching for Effective Approaches and the Right Mix of Instruments." 29 January 2007. http://www.crisisgroup.org/en/publication-type/speeches/2007/grono-fragile-states-searching-for-effective-approaches-and-the-right-mix-of-instruments.aspx.

Gros, Jean-Germain. *State Failure, Underdevelopment, and Foreign Intervention in Haiti*. New York: Routledge, 2012.

Gutman, Roy. *A Witness to Genocide*. MacMillan: New York, 1993.

Hampson, Fen Osler, and Paul Heinbecker, eds. *Canada Among Nations 2009–2010*. Montreal: McGill-Queen's University Press, 2010.

Hawes, Michael K., and Joel J. Sokolsky, eds. *North American Perspectives on European Security*. Lewiston, NY: Edwin Mellen Press, 1990.

Head, Ivan, and Pierre Trudeau. *The Canadian Way: Shaping Canada's Foreign Policy, 1968–1984*. Toronto: McClelland and Stewart, 1995.

Heine, Jorge, and Andrew S. Thompson, eds. *Fixing Haiti: MINUSTAH and Beyond*. Tokyo: United Nations University Press, 2011.

Helman, Gerald B., and Steven R. Ratner. "Saving Failed States." *Foreign Policy* 89 (Winter 1992–93): 3–20.

Higgins, Rosalyn. *United Nations Peacekeeping, 1946–1967: Documents and Commentary*. Vol. 3. Oxford: Oxford University Press, 1980.

Hillier, Rick. *A Soldier First: Bullets, Bureaucrats and the Politics of War*. Toronto: HarperCollins, 2010.

Hilson, Gavin. "Championing the Rhetoric? 'Corporate Social Responsibility' in Ghana's Mining Sector." *Greener Management International* 53 (2007): 43–56.

———. "Harvesting Mineral Riches: 1000 Years of Gold Mining in Ghana." *Resources Policy* 28 (2002):13–26.

Hilson, Gavin, and Mohammed Banchirigah Sadia. "Are Alternative Livelihood Projects Alleviating Poverty in Mining Communities? Experience from Ghana." *Journal of Development Studies* 45, no. 2 (2009): 172–96.

Hochschild, Adam. *King Leopold's Ghost: A Story of Greed, Terror, and Heroism in Colonial Africa*. New York: Houghton Mifflin, 1998.

Holland, Kenneth. "The Canadian Provincial Reconstruction Team: The Arm of Development in Kandahar Province." *American Review of Canadian Studies* 40, no. 2 (2010): 276–91.

Holmes, John W. "Le Canada dans le monde." *Politique étrangère* 33, no. 4 (1968): 293–314.

Hönke, Jana. "Multinationals and Security Governance in the Community. Participation, discipline and indirect rule." *Journal of Intervention and Statebuilding* 6, no. 1 (2012): 89–105.

Hönke, Jana, and Tanja Börzel. "Multinational Companies and the Quality of Local Governance in Sub-Saharan Africa: The Challenges of Limited and Restrained Statehood." Paper presented at the annual meeting of the International Studies Association, San Francisco, 2–6 April 2013.

Hönke, Jana, and Christian Thauer. "Multinational Corporations and Service Provision in Sub-Saharan Africa: Legitimacy and Institutionalization Matter." *Governance: An International Journal of Policy, Administration and Institutions* 27, no. 4 (2014): 697-716.

Hönke, Jana, with Esther Thomas. "Governance for Whom? Capturing the inclusiveness and unintended effects of governance." SFB Working Paper Series 31. Berlin: Freie Universität Berlin, 2012.

Horn, Bernd. *No lack of courage: Operation Medusa, Afghanistan.* Toronto: Dundurn Press, 2010.

Hoskyns, Catherine. *The Congo since Independence.* London: Oxford University Press, 1965.

Huebert, Rob. "Failed and Failing States: The Core Threat to Canadian Security." In *In The Canadian Interest? Assessing Canada's International Policy Statement.* Calgary: CDFAI, 2006.

Humphreys, Macartan, Jeffrey Sachs, and Joseph. E. Stiglitz. *Escaping the Resource Curse.* New York: Columbia University Press, 2007.

Idemudia, Uwafiokun. "Business and Peacemaking in the Context of Limited Statehood: Lessons from Nigeria." Paper presented at the annual conference of the International Studies Association, San Francisco, 2–6 April 2013.

Iriye, Akira, and Robert David Johnson, eds. *Asia Pacific in an Age of Globalization.* Basingstoke, UK: Palgrave Macmillan, 2015.

Jackson, R. H. "Morality, Democracy and Foreign Policy." In *Canada Among Nations, 1995: Democracy and Foreign Policy*, edited by M. A. Cameron and M. A. Molot. Ottawa: Carleton University Press, 1995.

———. *Quasi-States: Sovereignty, International Relations and the Third World*. Cambridge: Cambridge University Press, 1990.

———. "Surrogate Sovereignty? Great Power Responsibility and 'Failed States.'" Working Paper No. 25. Institute of International Relations, University of British Columbia, November 1998.

Jacobs, David, and Kathleen Getz. "Dialogue on the Stakeholder Theory of the Corporation: Concepts, Evidence, and Implications." *The Academy of Management Review* 20, no. 4 (1995): 793–95.

Jamali, Dima, and Ramez Mirshak. "Business-Conflict Linkages: Revisiting MNCs, CSR and Conflict." *Journal of Business Ethics* 93 (2010): 443–64.

Johnston, Peter. *Cooper's Snoopers and Other Follies: Fragments of a Life*. Victoria: Trafford, 2002.

Jones, Dorothy. *Code of Peace: Ethics and Security in a World of Warlord States*. Chicago: University of Chicago Press, 1991.

Kaplan, Seth D. *Fixing Fragile States: A New Paradigm for Development*. Westport, CT: Praeger Security International, 2008.

Karl, Terry Lynn. *The Paradox of Plenty: Oil Booms and Petro-States*. Berkeley: University of California Press, 1997.

Keating, Tom, and Nick Gammer. "The 'New Look' in Canadian Foreign Policy." *International Journal* 48, no. 4 (Autumn 1993): 720–48.

Keck, Margaret E., and Kathryn Sikkink. *Activists Beyond Borders: Advocacy Networks in International Politics*. Ithaca: Cornell University Press, 1998.

Kelegama, Saman. *EU Trade Policy and Democracy Building in South Asia*. Colombo: Institute of Policy Studies of Sri Lanka, 2010.

Kirton, John. *Canadian Foreign Policy in a Changing World*. Toronto: Thompson Nelson, 2007.

Klassen, Jerome, and Greg Albo, eds. *Empire's Ally: Canada and the War in Afghanistan*. Toronto: University of Toronto Press, 2013.

Kronstadt, K. Alan. *Direct Overt U.S. Aid and Military Reimbursements to Pakistan, FY2002-FY2011*. Prepared for the Congressional Research Service using sources from the DoS, DoD, DoA, and USAID, 16 February 2010.

Laguerre, Michel S. *The Military and Society in Haiti*. Knoxville: University of Tennessee Press, 1993.

Le Billion, Philippe. "Angola's Political Economy of War: The Role of Oil and Diamonds, 1975–2000." *African Affairs* 100, no. 398 (2001): 55–80.

Leadbeater, Marie. *Negligent Neighbour: New Zealand's Complicity in the Invasion and Occupation of Timor-Leste*. Nelson, New Zealand: Craig Potton Publishing, 2006.

Lewis, Stephen. *Journey to Biafra*. Don Mills, ON: Thistle Printing, 1968.

MacKenzie, Major-General (Retired) Lewis. *Peacekeeper: The Road to Sarajevo*. Vancouver: Douglas and McIntyre, 1993.

Manley, Hon. John, Derek H. Burney, Hon. Jake Epp, Hon. Paul Tellier, and Pamela Wallin. *Independent Panel on Canada's Future Role in Afghanistan*. Ottawa: Minister of Public Works and Government Services, 2008.

Marten, Kimberly. "From Kabul to Kandahar: The Canadian Forces and Change." *American Review of Canadian Studies* 40, no. 2 (2010): 214–36.

Martin, Ian. "Timor-Leste was not a failed state, it was a young state!" 10 Anos da Independência, http://10anosindependencia.blogs.sapo.tl/12695.html

Massie, Justin, and Stephane Roussel. "Preventing, Substituting, or Complementing the Use of Force? Development Assistance in Canadian Strategic Culture." Paper presented at the annual meeting of the Canadian Political Science Association (CPSA), 2011.

Matthews, Robert O. "Sudan's Humanitarian Disaster: Will Canada Live up to its Responsibility to Protect?" *International Journal* 60, no. 4 (Autumn 2005): 1049–64.

McCallum, Hugh. "Remembering the Nightmare of Biafra." *Presbyterian Record* (September 2004).

McKercher, Asa. "The Centre Cannot Hold: Canada, Colonialism and the 'Afro-Asian Bloc' at the United Nations, 1960–62." *Journal of Imperial and Commonwealth History* 42, no. 2 (2014): 329–49.

Meehan, John, and David Webster. "From King to Kandahar: Canada, Multilateralism and Conflict in the Pacific, 1909–2009." In *Canada Among Nations 2008*, edited by Robert Bothwell and Jean Daudelin. Montreal: McGill-Queen's University Press, 2009.

Meren, David. "An Atmosphere of *Liberation*: The Role of Decolonization in the France-Quebec Rapprochement of the 1960s." *Canadian Historical Review* 92, no. 2 (June 2012): 263–94.

Miall, Hugh. *The Peacemakers: Peaceful Settlement of Disputes since 1945*. New York: Palgrave Macmillan, 1992.

Milam, William. *Bangladesh and Pakistan: Flirting with Failure in South Asia*. London: Hurst, 2009.

Miller, Paul D. *Armed State Building: Confronting State Failure 1898–2012*. Ithaca: Cornell University Press, 2013.

Mills, Sean. "Quebec, Haiti, and the Deportation Crisis of 1974." *Canadian Historical Review* 94, no. 3 (September 2013): 405–35.

Moore, Mick. "Revenues, State Formation, and the Quality of Governance in Developing Countries." *International Political Science Review* 25, no. 3 (2004): 297–319.

Morley, J. W., ed. *Driven by Growth: Political Change in the Asia-Pacific Region*. Armonk NY: M. E. Sharpe, 1999.

Myers, Tamara. "Blistered and Bleeding, Tired and Determined: Visual Representations of Children and Youth in the Miles for Millions Walkathon." *Journal of the Canadian Historical Association* 22, no. 1 (2011): 245–75.

Narasimhan, Madhu. "The World's Youngest Failed State: Letter From East Timor." *Foreign Affairs*, 12 August 2014.

Naudé, Wim, Amelia U. Santos-Paulino, and Mark McGillivray, eds. *Fragile States: Causes, Costs, and Responses*. Oxford: Oxford University Press, 2011.

Newman, Peter C. *Here Be Dragons: Telling Tales of People, Passion, and Power*. Toronto: McClelland and Stewart, 2004.

Oetzel, Jennifer, and Kathleen A. Getz. "Why and how might firms respond strategically to violent conflict?" *Journal of International Business Studies* 43 (2012): 166–86.

Oetzel, Jennifer, Michelle Westermann-Behaylo, Charles Koerber, Timothy L. Fort, and Jorge Rivera. "Business and Peace: Sketching the Terrain." *Journal of Business Ethics* 89 (2010): 351–73.

Off, Carol. *The Lion, the Fox, and the Eagle: a story of generals and justice in Rwanda and Yugoslavia*. Toronto: Vintage, 2000.

Ofori, Daniel. "Social Responsibility and Ethics in Ghana: Stakeholders' Expectations and Challenges." In *Management and Economic Development in Sub-Saharan Africa: Theoretical and Applied Perspectives*, edited by J. Okpara, 63–97. London: Adonis and Abbey, 2007.

Okonta, Ike, and Kate Meagher, "Introduction—Legacies of Biafra: Violence, Identity and Citizenship in Nigeria." *Africa Development* 34, no. 1 (2009): 1–7.

Painchaud, Paul, ed. *From Mackenzie King to Pierre Trudeau*. Québec: Les Presses de L'Universite de Laval, 1989.

Patey, Luke. *The New Kings of Crude: China, India, and the Global Struggle for Oil in Sudan and South Sudan*. London: Hurst, 2014.

———. "State Rules: Oil Companies and Armed Conflict in Sudan." *Third World Quarterly* 28, no. 5 (2007): 997–1016.

Pelcovits, N. A., and Kevin L. Kramer. "Local Conflicts and UN Peacekeeping: The Uses of Computerized Data." *International Studies Quarterly* 20, no. 4 (December 1976): 533–52.

Pereira, Agio. "Timor-Leste Success: Why It Won't Be the Next Failed State." *Foreign Affairs*, 26 August 2014.

Perusse, Roland I. *Haitian Democracy Restored, 1991–1995*. New York: University Press of America, 1995.

Pinker, Steven. *The Better Angels of Our Nature: Why Violence Has Declined*. New York: Viking Books, 2011.

Pitt, Anthea. "The Bitter Legacy." *Petroleum Economist* (1 July 2014): 1–2.

Pratt, Cranford, ed. *Canadian International Development Assistance Policies: An Appraisal*. Montreal: McGill-Queen's University Press, 1994.

Puplampu, Bill Buenar, and Hevina S. Dashwood. "Investigating the Organizational Antecedents of a Mining Firm's Efforts to Reinvent its CSR: The Case of Golden Star Resources in Ghana." *Business and Society Review* 116, no. 4 (2011): 467–507.

Raziullah Azmi, M. *Pakistan-Canada Relations 1947–1982*. Islamabad: Quaid-i-Azam University, 1982.

Roberts, Chris. "Canadian Foreign Policy and African State Formation: Responsibilities, Silences, Culpabilities." Paper presented at the annual meeting of the Canadian Political Science Association (CPSA), Victoria, BC, 2013.

Rotberg, R. I., ed. *When States Fail: Causes and Consequences*. Princeton: Princeton University Press, 2004.

Rubin, Barnett R. *The Fragmentation Of Afghanistan: State Formation And Collapse In The International System*. New Haven: Yale University Press, 2002.

Sachs, Jeffrey D., and Andrew M. Warner. "Natural Resource Abundance and Economic Growth." Working Paper 5398. 1995.

Sagebien, Julia, and Nicole Marie Lindsay, eds. *Corporate Social Responsibility and Governance Ecosystems: Emerging Patterns in the Stakeholder Relationships of Canadian Mining Companies Operating in Latin America*. New York: Palgrave-Macmillan, 2011.

Saideman, Stephen. "Canadian Forces in Afghanistan: Generational Change While Under Fire." In *Military Adaptation and War in Afghanistan*, edited by Theo Farrell, Frans Osinga, and James Russell, 219–241. Palo Alto: Stanford University Press, 2013.

Sattar, Abdul. *Pakistan's Foreign Policy*. Karachi: Oxford University Press, 2007.

Schlegel, John P. *The Deceptive Ash: Bilingualism and Canadian Policy in Africa, 1957–1971*. Washington, DC: University Press of America, 1978.

Schmitz, Gerald. *Canadian Policy Toward Afghanistan to 2011 and Beyond: Issues, Prospects and Options*. Ottawa: Reference and Strategic Analysis Division, Parliamentary Information and Research Division, 2010.

Schofield, Clive. "A 'Fair Go' for East Timor? Sharing the Resources of the Timor Sea." *Contemporary Southeast Asia* 27, no. 2 (August 2005): 255–80.

Schofield, Julian. "Arms Races and War in the Indo-Pakistan Rivalry, 1947–1971." *Journal of South Asian and Middle Eastern Studies* 26, no. 3 (Spring 2003): 33–49.

———. "Diversionary Wars: Pashtun Unrest and the Sources of the Pakistan-Afghan Confrontation." *Canadian Foreign Policy Journal* 17, no. 1 (March 2011): 38–49.

———. "Pakistan's Counter-Insurgency Doctrine." In *Routledge Handbook of Insurgency and Counterinsurgency*, edited by Paul Rich and Isabelle Duyvesteyn. London: Routledge, 2012.

———. "Pakistan's Strategic Trade with Afghanistan." *Sicherheit und Frieden* (Security and Peace) 4 (2010): 251–56.

———. "The Prospect of a Populist Islamist Takeover of Pakistan." In *Escaping Quagmire: Strategy, Security and the Future of Pakistan*, edited by Usama Butt and N. Elahi, 215–32. New York: Continuum, 2010.

Schofield, Julian, Brent Gerchicoff, and Jose Saramago. "Afghan Development Through Regional Trade." In *Afghanistan in the Balance: Counterinsurgency, Comprehensive Approach and Political Order*, edited by Hans-Georg Ehrhart, 141–55. Montreal: McGill-Queen's University Press, 2011.

Schofield, Julian, and Jose Saramago. "Pakistani Interests in NATO's Afghanistan." In *Adaptation of NATO*, edited by Natalie Mychajlyszyn, 129–46. University of Manitoba Bison Papers Series 11. Winnipeg: University of Manitoba Centre for Defence and Security Studies, 2008.

Schofield, Julian, and Michael Zekulin. "Appraising the Threat of an Islamist Military Coup in Post-OBL Pakistan." *Defense and Security Analysis* 27, no. 4 (December 2011): 181–92.

Scott, David. *Last Flight out of Dili: Memoirs of an Accidental Activist in the Triumph of East Timor*. North Melbourne: Pluto Press Australia, 2005.

Shamsie, Yasmine, and Andrew S. Thompson, eds. *Haiti: Hope for a Fragile State*. Waterloo, ON: Wilfrid Laurier University Press and Centre for International Governance Innovation, 2006.

Simons, Penelope, and Audrey Macklin. *The Governance Gap: Extractive Industries, Human Rights, and the Home State Advantage*. New York: Routledge, 2014.

Smillie, Ian. *Diamonds*. Hoboken, NJ: John Wiley and Sons, 2014.

Smilie, Ian, Lansana Gberie, and Ralph Hazleton. *The Heart of the Matter: Sierra Leone, Diamonds and Human Security*. Ottawa: Partnership Africa Canada, 2000.

Spicer, Keith. *A Samaritan State? External Aid in Canada's Foreign Policy*. Toronto: University of Toronto Press, 1966.

Simpson, Bradley. "'Illegally and Beautifully': The United States, the Indonesian Invasion of East Timor and the International Community." *Cold War History* 5, no. 3 (August 2005): 281–315.

Simpson, Erin. "Who Failed the World's 'Failed States'?" *Peace Magazine* (April–June 2007): 6.

Singh, Swaran. "Sino-Pak Defence Co-operation: Joint Ventures and Weapons Procurement." *Peace Initiatives* 5, nos. 3–4 (May–December 1999): 1–15.

Southard, Malia. *Southard, Looking the Other Way: The Indonesian Bond, Partnership or Plunder?* Victoria: South Pacific Peoples Foundation of Canada, 1997.

Spooner, Kevin A. *Canada, the Congo Crisis, and UN Peacekeeping, 1960–64.* Vancouver: UBC Press, 2009.

Stein, Janice Gross, and J. Eugene Lang. *The Unexpected War: Canada in Kandahar.* Toronto: Viking Canada, 2007.

Stewart, Walter. *Trudeau in Power.* New York: Outerbridge and Dienstfry, 1971.

Thaler, Kai. "Timor-Leste and the g7+: A new approach to the security and development aid nexus." *IPRIS Lusophone Countries Bulletin* 18 (2011): 4–7.

Thompson, Dale C., and Roger F. Swanson. *Canadian Foreign Policy: Options and Perspectives.* Toronto: McGraw-Hill Ryerson, 1971.

Thorardson, Bruce. *Trudeau and Foreign Policy: A Study in Decision Making.* Toronto: Oxford University Press, 1972.

Tomlin, Brian, Norman Hillmer, and Fen Osler Hampson. *Canada's International Policies.* Oxford: Oxford University Press, 2008.

Trouillot, Michel-Rolph. *Haiti: State Against Nation.* New York: Monthly Press Review, 1990.

Waal, Alex de. *Famine Crimes: Politics and the Disaster Relief Industry in Africa.* Bloomington: Indiana University Press, 1997.

Walzer, Michael. *Just and Unjust Wars: A Moral Argument with Historical Illustrations.* New York: Basic Books, 1977.

Warnock, John. *Creating a Failed State: The US and Canada in Afghanistan.* Halifax: Fernwood, 2008.

Weber, Max. *Economy and Society.* Berkeley: University of California Press, 1978.

Webster, David. *Fire and the Full Moon: Canada and Indonesia in a Decolonizing World.* Vancouver: UBC Press, 2009.

———. "Languages of Human Rights in Timor-Leste." *Asia Pacific Perspectives* 11, no. 1 (August 2013): 5-21.

———. "Human Rights: Across the Pacific Both Ways." In *Asia Pacific in an Age of Globalization*, edited by Akira Iriye and Robert David Johnson, 111-121. Basingstoke, UK: Palgrave Macmillan, 2015.

———. "Self-fulfilling prophecies and human rights in Canada's foreign policy: the case of East Timor." *International Journal* 65, no. 3 (2010): 739–50.

Welsh, Jennifer M. *At Home in the World: Canada's Global Vision for the 21st Century.* Toronto: HarperCollins, 2004.

Welsh, Jennifer, and Ngaire Woods, eds. *Exporting Good Governance: Temptations and Challenges in Canada's Aid Program*. Waterloo, ON: Wilfrid Laurier University Press, 2007.

Wesley, Michael. "Blue Berets or Blindfolds? Peacekeeping and the Hostage Effect." *International Peacekeeping* 2, no. 4 (Winter 1995): 457–82.

Wheeler, David, Barry Colbert, and R. Edward Freeman. "Focusing on Value: Reconciling Corporate Social Responsibility, Sustainability and a Stakeholder Approach in a Network World." *Journal of General Management* 28, no. 3 (2003): 1–28.

Willis, Matthew. "An Unexpected War, A Not-Unexpected Mission: The Origins of Kandahar 2005." January 2013. http://opencanada.org/features/the-think-tank/essays/an-unexpected-war-a-not-unexpected-mission/.

Wilner, A. "Making the World Safe for Canada: Canadian Security Policy in a World of Failed States." Halifax: Atlantic Institute for Market Studies, 2008.

Wolf, Klaus Dieter, Nicole Dietelhoff, and Stefan Engert. "Corporate Security Responsibility: Towards a Conceptual Framework for a Comparative Research Agenda." *Cooperation and Conflict* 42, no. 3 (2007): 294–320.

Wolfe, Robert, ed. *Diplomatic Missions*. Kingston, ON: Queen's University School of Policy Studies, 1998.

Woodward, Susan L. "Soft intervention and the puzzling neglect of economic actors." In *Strengthening Peace in Post-Civil War States: Transforming Spoilers into Stakeholders*, edited by Matthew Hoodie and Caroline A. Hartzell. Chicago: University of Chicago Press, 2010.

Zametica, John. *The Yugoslav Conflict*. Adelphi Paper 270. London: International Institute for Strategic Studies, Summer 1992.

Zartman, I. William, ed. *Collapsed States: The Disintegration and Restoration of Legitimate Authority*. Boulder: Lynne Rienner Publishers, 1995.

Ziaja, Sebastian, and Javier Fabra Mata. *State fragility indices: potentials, messages and limitations*. Bonn: Deutsches Institut für Entwicklungspolitik, 2010.

INDEX

A

Abbas, Mekki, 40
Acheson, Dean, 33
Adoula, Cyrille, 34, 43, 44, 45, 47
Afghanistan, 2, 3, 5, 6, 10, 25, 27, 28, 74,
    122, 126, 127, 130, 131, 135, 161, 162,
    165–82, 188, 200, 237, 238, 239, 240,
    242, 244, 246, 247, 248
    Afghan National Army (ANA), 171,
        172, 237, 246
    Afghan National Police (ANP), 171, 172
    Afghan National Security Forces, 168
    Dahla dam, 173, 175, 176, 181
    Helmand Province, 168, 171
    Kabul, 126, 127, 167, 174, 180
    Kandahar, 5, 165–82, 238, 246
    Operation Medusa, 171
    Provincial Reconstruction Teams
        (PRT), 25, 169, 170, 173, 246
    school construction, 173, 175, 180, 181
    Taliban, 167, 168, 169, 171, 181
African Union, 220
Alatas, Ali, 83, 86
Alexander, Boniface, 109
Amnesty International, 83, 104, 105, 107,
    116n14
Angle, H. H., 133
Angola, 73, 160, 208
Annan, Kofi, 55
Anvil Mining, 228
Arbour, Louise, 7, 245

Argentina, 193
Aristide, Jean-Bertrand, 103, 104, 105, 107,
    108, 109, 111, 201
Asanko Gold, 220
Asia Pacific Economic Cooperation
    (APEC), 85, 86–87
Asia Partnership for Human Development,
    83
Association of Southeast Asian Nations
    (ASEAN), 78, 80
Australia, 76, 77, 78, 79, 80, 81, 82, 88, 89, 90
Avril, Prosper, 103
Axworthy, Lloyd, 2, 7, 22, 85, 86, 87, 211,
    212

B

Bahamas, 196, 201
Balkans, 5, 155
Bangladesh, 123, 124, 127, 159
Baranyi, Stephen, 110, 113
Barbados, 201
Barnes, Michael, 65
Barry, Donald, 57, 63, 69n5
Barton, William, 42
Belgium, 33, 37, 43, 45
Belize, 191, 196
Belo, Carlos Ximenes, 75, 76, 83
Bermuda, 201

279

Bernier, Maxime, 110, 174
Berry, Glyn, 173
Besada, Hany, 225
Biafra, 5, 15, 53–69, 159, 237, 238, 239, 240, 244
Blair, Tony, 215
Boban, Mate, 149
Boko Haram, 69
Börzel, Tanja, 226, 227
Bosniacs, 148, 149, 150, 152, 153, 154, 155, 157
Bosnia, 5, 143–62, 168, 237, 238, 240, 242, 244. *See also* Sarajevo
    ethnic cleansing, 143, 147, 148, 150, 155, 160
    Sarajevo airport, 144, 145, 151, 152, 154, 156, 159
    Srebrenica Massacre, 154, 155, 157
Bothwell, Robert, 60, 66
Botswana, 217
Bouchard, Lucien, 158
Boutros-Ghali, Boutros, 151–52, 160
Brazil, 187, 188, 190, 191, 193, 194, 202
Brewin, Andrew, 5, 54, 56, 58, 61, 62–64, 65, 66, 67, 68, 71n18, 238, 246
Brewster, Murray, 177
Britain. *See under* United Kingdom
Brown, J. C. Gordon, 47
Bunche, Ralph, 42–43
Burke, Samuel Martin, 129
Burney, Derek, 80
Burns, E. L. M., 42
Busan Declaration, 217
Bush, George H. W., 105
Bush, George W., 167

C

Cambodia, 73, 80, 159, 160
Canada
    and Afghanistan, 3, 5, 25, 26, 27, 28, 126, 127, 130, 135, 161, 162, 165–82, 237, 238, 239, 240, 244, 246, 247, 248
    Afghanistan Task Force, 177, 179
    alliances, 23, 24–25, 28
    and Americas, 185–205
    and Biafra, 53–69, 237, 238, 239, 244
    Bloc Québécois, 158, 178
    and Bosnia, 147, 156–57, 237, 238, 240, 242, 244
    Canadian Forces, 48, 132, 157, 169, 170–72, 173, 175, 176, 178, 179, 180, 181
    and Congo, Democratic Republic of, 4, 5, 6, 16, 33–49, 101, 237, 239, 240, 242, 244, 245, 246, 248
    Constitution, 18, 158
    Corporate Social Responsibility, 209, 211–13, 244
    Corrections Canada, 169, 173, 181
    Department of External Affairs, 39, 40, 41, 43, 44, 64, 80, 81, 84, 162
    Department of Foreign Affairs and International Trade (DFAIT), 2, 111, 126, 127, 132, 169, 173–74, 177, 179, 180, 181, 197–98, 247
    Department of Foreign Affairs, Trade and Development (DFATD), 209, 211
    Department of National Defence (DND), 39, 40, 41, 44, 162, 197, 198–99, 201
    development assistance, 14, 15, 17, 18, 28, 58, 99, 110, 111, 127, 128–31, 194–97, 198, 202, 208, 209, 220
    Elections Canada, 103
    failed/fragile states, 1–7, 11–29, 33, 47, 55, 68, 73, 74, 98, 110, 126, 130–31, 134, 146, 158, 160, 161, 165, 166, 167, 177, 178, 181, 185–86, 187, 190, 194–95, 196, 197, 198, 199, 203, 221, 237–49
    and Haiti, 4–5, 6, 25, 28, 74, 97–114, 186, 194–95, 196, 198, 200, 201, 202, 203, 237, 238–39, 244
    House of Commons, *See under* Canada, Parliament
    International Policy Statement, 2, 20
    and Kosovo, 9, 19, 27, 161, 162

and Libya, 10, 27, 161, 162, 237
Meech Lake Accord, 158
multilateralism, 4, 17, 20, 24, 28, 38, 39, 44, 45, 48, 49, 144, 194, 197, 237, 238, 245
North Atlantic Treaty Organization (NATO), 4, 5, 6, 9–10, 15, 19, 20, 23, 24, 28, 44, 126, 162, 169, 171, 172, 179
Opération des Nations Unies au Congo (ONUC), 38, 40, 42, 43, 45, 46–47, 49, 237, 245, 246
and Pakistan, 35, 121, 122, 126–35, 140n75, 237, 242
Parliament, 26, 56, 59, 60, 62, 63, 65, 66, 67, 82, 102, 104, 110, 111, 179, 180, 212, 217–18
Parti Québécois, 158
peacekeeping, 15, 33, 46, 55, 88, 121, 132, 133, 143–44, 151, 152, 156–57, 159, 160, 161, 160, 171, 237, 244
Prime Minister's Office (PMO), 126, 162
Privy Council Office (PCO), 126, 177, 184n36
Quebec, 17, 55, 61, 62, 63–64, 68, 145, 158, 238, 244
Representative of Canada in Kandahar (RoCK), 173, 177, 179, 181
Royal Canadian Mounted Police (RCMP), 197, 198, 201
Stabilization and Reconstruction Task Force (START), 2, 181, 209, 247
Standing Committee on External Affairs and National Defence, 63
Standing Committee on Foreign Affairs and International Development, 110, 111, 218
Standing Committee on Foreign Affairs and International Trade, 212, 213
and Syria, 28, 240
and Timor-Leste, 73–91, 237, 238, 239, 240, 241, 242, 243, 244
Treasury Board, 126

and United Nations, 2, 4, 5, 9–10, 15, 16, 17, 20, 23, 24, 28, 33, 40, 41, 42, 43, 44, 45, 46, 47, 48–49, 54, 59, 61–62, 63, 64, 65, 68, 81–82, 104–5, 121, 128, 132, 143–44, 156–57, 159, 160–61, 162, 245
and United States, 4, 5, 25, 28, 41, 98, 109, 121, 202
White Paper on Defence (1994), 19
Whole of Government approach, 25, 169–70, 177–78, 179, 237, 238, 246
Canada Haiti Action Network, 109
Canadian Broadcasting Corporation (CBC), 63, 84
Canadian Catholic Organization for Development and Peace (CCODP), 83, 85
Canadian International Council, 2
Canadian International Development Agency (CIDA), 12, 58, 68, 78, 85, 99, 101, 102, 103, 110, 111, 126, 127, 131, 169, 173, 175–77, 178, 179, 181, 194, 197, 198, 201, 225
  Office for Democratic Governance, 110
Canadian International Resources and Development Institute (CIRDI), 211, 230n11
Canadian Serbian League, 9
Canadian University Service Overseas (CUSO), 57, 61, 68
Canairelief, 53, 54, 59–60, 61, 63, 67
Caribbean, 5, 100, 127, 186, 192, 194, 196, 197, 200, 201, 202, 203
Carment, David, 8n10, 24, 25, 187
Carter, Jimmy, 18, 81, 108
Castro, Fidel, 80
Cayman Islands, 201
Cédras, Raoul, 104, 105, 106, 107, 108
Central African Republic, 109
Central America, 5, 186, 192, 194, 196,197, 198, 200, 201, 202, 203
Central Intelligence Agency, 174
Chamblain, Louis-Jodel, 108
Chavez, Hugo, 193
Chile, 109

China, 14, 82, 122, 126, 133, 134, 221, 226, 227, 229
Chrétien, Jean, 2, 22, 85, 86, 131, 162, 211
Ciric, Dragan, 9
Clark, Joe, 84, 161
Claude, Sylvio, 102
Clinton, William J., 108
Cold War, 1, 2, 10, 14, 17, 18, 33, 79, 84, 122, 127, 128, 158, 160
Collier, Paul, 216
Colombia, 3, 188, 190, 191, 193, 194, 237, 242, 243
Colombo Plan, 4, 14, 59, 127, 128
Commission on Human Rights and Administrative Justice, 222
Commonwealth, 4, 14, 15, 16, 56, 59, 63, 84, 128
communism, 1, 3, 4, 14, 22, 28, 44, 77, 79, 80, 127, 128, 134
Conference on Security and Co-operation in Europe, 17
Congo, Democratic Republic of, 4, 5, 6, 15, 16, 33–51, 187, 227, 229, 239, 240, 242, 245, 248
    Armée nationale congolaise (ANC), 34, 35, 37, 38, 39, 40, 41–43, 44–45, 47–48, 237, 245
    Katanga, 37, 41, 42, 43, 227
Corporate Social Responsibility (CSR), 6, 207–29
Costa Rica, 193
Croatia, 146, 147, 148, 149, 150, 151, 152, 155, 158, 160
Croatian Defence Council, 149
Cuba, 80, 192, 193
Cyprus, 15, 71n16

D

Darfur, 220
Davidson, Jeffrey, 210
Dayton Agreement, 154
decolonization 13, 15, 16, 57, 73, 79, 244, 245
democracy, 18, 26, 34, 84, 97, 101, 102, 103, 104, 105, 110, 134, 220
de Gaulle, Charles, 61, 71n16
Delworth, W. T., 78
Dickinson, Lawrence, 83, 85
Diefenbaker, John, 38, 41, 42–43, 122, 127, 129
Dominican Republic, 101, 107
drugs, 1, 127, 186, 188, 190, 196, 202, 203
Duvalier, François "Papa Doc," 98–99,
Duvalier, Jean-Claude "Baby Doc," 99–100, 101
    Jean-Claudism, 99

E

Eagleburger, Lawrence, 150
East Pakistan. See Bangladesh
East Timor. See under Timor-Leste, Democratic Republic of
East Timor Alert Network (ETAN), 83, 84, 86
Ebola, 1
Economist, 121
El Salvador, 160, 186, 188, 191, 196, 197, 200, 201, 202
Ethiopia, 44
ethnic cleansing, 143, 147, 148, 150, 155, 160
English, John, 59, 61, 70n5
Epp, Jake, 179
European Community, 147
European Union, 109, 130, 132, 134, 135
Evans, Gareth, 20
Extractive Industries Transparency Initiative (EITI), 214, 215

F

failed states, 10–11, 13, 19, 22, 23, 26, 29n2, 34, 55, 74–75, 90
Failed States Index, 69, 89, 188
Fast, Ed, 210
Fatton, Robert, Jr., 99
federalism, 55, 63, 64, 68
Foreign Affairs, 91
Foreign Policy, 143
Forestier, Michel, 145
Forsythe, David P., 67
fragile states, 1–7, 11–29, 34, 47, 48, 55, 74, 78–79, 89, 90–91, 97, 98, 111, 174, 177, 181, 185–86, 188, 190, 192, 195, 196, 199, 200, 201, 202, 207, 208, 209, 210, 216, 217, 225, 227, 228, 241, 247, 249n2
Fragile States Index, 69, 89
France, 15, 40, 53, 56, 59, 61, 66, 88, 99, 100, 106, 109, 150, 152, 156, 238
Francophonie, La, 78, 84, 101
Friends of Haiti, 106
Front pour L'Avancement et le Preogrès Haitien (FRAPH), 104, 108
Fund for Peace, 3, 8n10, 69

G

g7+, 91, 247
Gabon, 63
Galhos, Bella, 83
Gandhi, Indira, 122
Garang, John, 225
Gauvin, Michel, 40–41, 43, 44, 47, 101
Gee, Marcus, 76, 77, 88–89
genocide, 19, 55, 56, 57, 64–65, 68, 73, 148, 150
Germany, 88, 158, 171
Ghana, 38–39, 207, 208, 209, 210, 211, 217, 220–25, 226, 228
    Environmental Protection Agency, 223
Global Peace and Security Fund, 2
Global Reporting Initiative (GRI), 214
Global South, 1, 12, 14, 15, 68, 89, 207, 214

Globe and Mail, 56, 62, 74, 76, 88
Golberg, Elissa, 173, 181
Golden Star Resources, 220, 222, 223–24
Governors Island Agreement, 106, 107–8
Gowon, Yakubu, 67
Granatstein, J. L., 66
Green, Howard, 16, 40, 42, 49
Greene, Michael, 43
Greene Plan, 43, 44
Grono, Nick, 3
Guatemala, 186, 196, 198, 200, 201, 202
Guinea-Bissau, 73
Gulf War, 161
Gusmão, Xanana, 87
Guyana, 192, 196

H

Habibie, B. J., 87, 88
Haiti, 3, 4–5, 6, 10, 17, 25, 26, 28, 74, 97–114, 160, 186, 188, 192, 193, 194–95, 196, 197, 198, 200, 201, 202, 203, 237, 238–39, 242, 244
    Cannibal Army, 108
    Conseil National de Gouvernement (CNG), 101, 102
    earthquake, 97, 112–14, 201
    Hurricane Allen, 100
    Interim Cooperation Framework, 109
    Interim Development Program, 101
    Interim Haiti Recovery Commission, 113
    Tontons Macoutes, 99, 100, 101, 115n2
Halifax Initiative, 212
Hall, Ingrid, 84
Hammarskjöld, Dag, 35, 39, 40, 41
Harker, John, 211, 246
Harkness, Douglas, 42–43
Harman, Gary, 45
Harper, Stephen, 28, 109, 110, 162, 178, 180, 213
Head, Ivan, 57–58, 67, 69n5
Helman, Gerald, 2, 143
Helsinki Watch, 148
Hillier, Rick, 169

Hillmer, Norman, 245
Hochschild, Adam, 35
Hoeffler, Anke, 216
Holbrooke, Richard, 154
Honduras, 91, 186, 191, 192, 196, 200, 201, 202
Hönke, Jana, 226, 227
Huebert, Rob, 21
Human Development Index, 91 124
human rights, 7, 12, 18, 19, 20, 22, 55, 65, 76, 77, 81, 82, 83, 84, 85, 86, 87, 89, 90, 97, 101, 102, 103, 104, 105, 107, 109, 110, 116n14, 128, 130, 135, 159, 160, 209, 210, 211, 212, 214, 215, 218, 220, 221, 222, 223, 227, 228, 229, 245, 248
human security, 2, 19, 22, 85, 110, 162, 193

I

Idemudia, Uwafiokun, 226
Inco, 78
India, 63, 121, 122, 124, 125, 126, 127, 128, 129, 132, 134, 135, 221, 226, 227, 229
Indonesia, 73–91, 148, 238, 240
Inter-American Development Bank, 99
Interim Haiti Recovery Commission, 113
Interim Swine Repopulation Project, 100
International Commission of Control and Supervision in Vietnam, 78
International Commission on Intervention and State Sovereignty (ICISS), 19–20, 246
International Council on Mining and Metals, 214
International Criminal Tribunal for the Former Yugoslavia, 157
International Dialogue on Peacebuilding and Statebuilding, 247
International Donors' Conference for the Economic and Social Development of Haiti, 109–10, 113
International Military Observer Team (IMOT), 59, 64
International Monetary Fund, 221

International Network on Conflict and Fragility (INCAF), 247
International Policy Statement, 2, 20
Iran, 126
Iraq, 10, 150, 161, 172, 237
Ismaili Agha Khan Foundation, 132
Israel, 43, 61
Italy, 43, 45, 163n14
Izetbegović, Alija, 148

J

Jackson, Robert, 11, 24
Jaffer, Rahim, 132
Jamaica, 191, 196, 198
Janssens, Emile, 37
Japan, 12, 77, 78, 88, 130, 134
Jean, Michaëlle, 113
Johnson, Ted, 53–54, 59, 60, 61, 63, 68
Joint Church Aid, 68
Jonaissant, Emile, 108
Jones, Michel, 156
The Journal (TV program), 84

K

Karachi Nuclear Power Plant (KANUPP), 128–29
Karadžić, Radovan, 149, 152
Karzai, Ahmed Wali, 168, 174, 182n6
Karzai, Hamid, 167, 168, 173, 174
Kasavubu, Joseph, 37
Kashmir, 121, 122, 132, 133, 134, 135
Keck, Margaret, 82
Kennedy, Edward, 65
Kennedy, John F., 34, 40, 45, 47
Khalid, Asadullah, 174
Khan, Wajid, 132
Khmer Rouge, 73
Kiir, Salva, 225
Kinross, 220
Korea, Republic of, 78, 128, 161
Kosovo, 9–10, 19, 27, 146, 161, 162, 163n14
Kuwait, 150, 161

L

La Francophonie. *See* Francophonie
Laguerre, Michel S., 98, 103
Landry, Monique, 101
Laos, 80
Latin America, 69, 74, 127, 201, 203
Latortue, Gérard, 109
Leopold II, 35
Lewis, Stephen, 56, 62, 64–65
Liberia, 160, 217
Libya, 10, 27, 161, 162, 237
Lopes da Cruz, Francisco, 87
Lopes, Martinho da Costa, 83
Lumumba, Patrice, 36, 37, 38, 40

M

MacDonald, David, 5, 54, 56, 58, 61, 62–67, 68, 238, 246
Macdonald Laurier Institute, 20
MacEachen, Allan, 80
Macedonia, 146, 160
Machar, Rick, 225
MacKenzie, Lewis, 144, 145, 152, 156, 157, 159–60
Maduro, Nicolás, 193
Malary, François-Guy, 107
Malaysia, 63, 71n16, 82
Mali, 237
Manigat, Leslie, 102, 103
Manley, John, 179
Manley Panel, 177, 178–80, 181, 246
Marshall Plan, 14
Martin, Ian, 91
Martin, Paul Jr., 2, 20, 21, 110, 162, 169, 178, 213
McCallum, Hugh, 66–67
McDougall, Barbara, 84, 104–5, 157, 159, 161
McGill University, 103
McLean, Walter, 54, 61, 70n7, 70n7, 70–71n14
Meagher, Kate, 55
Mengesha, Iyassu, 41

Mexico, 191, 193, 194
Milam, William, 122
Miller, Frank R., 41
Milošević, Slobodan, 146, 149
Mining Watch Canada, 212, 221
Mitterrand, Francois, 152
Mladić, Ratko, 157
Mobutu, Joseph-Desiré, 34, 35, 37, 39–41, 43, 44, 45, 47, 49, 49n1, 238
Mojekwu, Christopher Chukwuemeka, 63
Montenegro, 146
Mozambique, 73, 160
Muggah, Robert, 111–12
Mulroney, Brian, 2, 17, 18, 69, 84–85, 102, 104, 158, 159, 160, 162
Mulroney, David, 179, 184n33

N

Namphy, Henri, 101, 102, 103
napalm, 81–82
National Labor Committee (NLC), 105
natural resources,
　gas, 6, 208, 209, 211, 217, 224, 227, 229
　minerals, 6, 188, 208, 209, 211, 215, 217, 221, 226, 227
　oil, 6, 53, 66, 67, 78–79, 90, 188, 192, 193, 208, 209, 211, 217, 225–26, 227, 229
Netherlands, 80, 85, 88, 154, 157, 171
Neves, Guteriano, 91
Newman, Peter C., 61
New Zealand, 79
Nicaragua, 160, 198
niche diplomacy, 85–86
Nigeria, 5, 15, 17, 44, 53–69, 217, 226, 238, 242, 244
　Civil War, 5, 53
　Federal Military Government, 5, 59, 62, 67
　First Republic, 56
Nigeria/Biafra Relief Fund of Canada, 59
9/11. *See under* terrorism
Nkrumah, Kwame, 38
Noel-Baker, Philip, 65

non-governmental organizations (NGOs), 5, 54, 55, 68, 83, 86, 102, 130, 211, 212, 213, 214, 215, 221, 223, 224, 225, 229
Non-Proliferation Treaty (NPT), 126–27, 134
North Atlantic Treaty Organization (NATO), 4, 5, 6, 9–10, 15, 17, 19, 20, 23, 28, 44, 126, 143, 154, 155, 159
  and Afghanistan, 126, 130, 131, 167, 168, 169, 171, 172, 179, 180, 246
  Implementation Force (IFOR), 153, 161
  Operation Deliberate Force, 153
Norway, 43, 45, 177
Nunn, Sam, 108
Nystrom, Lorne, 71n18

O

Obama, Barack, 179
Ojukwu, Odumegwu, 67
Okonta Ike, 55
Organisation for Economic Co-operation and Development (OECD), 111, 215, 247
  Busan Declaration, 217
Organization of African Unity (OAU), 59, 63
Organization of American States (OAS), 17, 104, 108
Organization of the Petroleum Exporting Countries (OPEC), 193
Ouellet, André, 85
Oxfam, 59, 67, 239

P

Pakistan, 3, 5, 63, 121–35, 168, 237, 242, 243
  coup d'état, 122–23
  military, 123, 132–34
  Taliban, 123
Panama, 108
Pan American Health Organization (PAHO), 99, 103
Pascal-Trouillot, Ertha, 103–4

Patey, Luke, 227,
peacekeeping, 15, 35, 49, 88, 89, 106, 107, 108, 121, 143–44, 145, 151, 152–53, 154, 155, 156, 159, 160, 161, 171, 220
Pearson, Lester B., 4, 14, 46, 56, 122
Pereira, Agio, 91
Peren, Roger, 79
Pertamina, 78–79
Philippe, Guy, 108
Philippines, 212
Portugal, 15, 56, 61, 73, 77, 79, 88
Powell, Colin, 108, 109
Presbyterian Church of Canada, 57, 59
Press, Stewart, 187
Préval, René, 108, 109, 111, 112

Q

Quebec, 17, 55, 61, 62, 63–64, 68, 145, 158, 238, 244

R

Ramos-Horta, José, 75, 76
Ratner, Steven, 2, 143
Reagan, Ronald, 100
Rechner, Patrick, 160
Red Cross, International Committee of the, 64, 68
Regina Leader-Post, 66
resource curse, 216–18, 226
Responsibility to Protect (R2P), 2, 7, 20, 24, 29, 68, 162
Rhodesia, 63, 71n16
Rio Tinto Alcan, 224
Robinson, Randall, 107
Roman Catholic Church, 53, 59
Rossillon, Philippe, 66
Ruggie, John Gerard, 215
Rumsfeld, Donald, 167
Russo-Japanese War, 12

S

Sadli, Mohammad, 78,
Sahnoun, Mohamed, 20
Salutin, Rick, 74,
Samy, Yiagadeesen, 187
Sanger, Clyde, 56,
Sarajevo, 144, 145, 148, 150–51, 152, 153, 154, 155, 156, 157, 159
Saudi Arabia, 122, 126, 134
Schlegel, John, 70n5
Serbia, 9, 10, 19, 146, 147, 149, 150, 151
Serbian Democratic Party, 149
Sharp, Mitchell, 53, 60, 63, 68
Sierra Leone, 208, 217
Sikkink, Kathryn, 82
Simpson, Erin, 2
Singapore, 71n16, 82
Slovenia, 146, 147, 158
Smillie, Ian, 68, 208
Soares, Abé Barreto, 83
Somalia, 10, 17, 89, 145, 160, 161, 168, 169, 240
South Africa, 69
South Korea. See under Korea, Republic of
South Sudan, 91, 207, 208, 209, 218, 220–21, 225–26, 229, 237
    Comprehensive Peace Agreement (2005), 226
    Sudanese People's Liberation Army, 225
sovereignty, 2, 11, 12, 13, 17, 18, 20, 22, 24, 27, 29, 48–49, 55, 159, 160, 161, 241, 243, 246
    Canada, 17, 48
    Haiti, 26
    International Commission on Intervention and State Sovereignty (ICISS), 19–20, 246
    Quebec, 158, 238
    Yugoslavia, 10
Soviet Union. See under Union of Soviet Socialist Republics
Stairs, Denis, 26, 27
state fragility. See under fragile states
St. Laurent, Louis, 3, 134

Stanfield, Robert, 63
Stewart, Ralph, 71n18
Sudan, 211–12, 220–21, 226, 237, 239, 244
Suharto, 76, 77, 78, 79, 80, 84, 86, 87, 240
Suriname, 192, 196
Swanson, Roger, 69n5
Sweden, 59
Switzerland, 42
Syria, 28, 240

T

Taliban, 122, 123, 167, 168, 169, 171, 181
Talisman Energy Incorporated, 211–12, 216, 220, 221, 239
Taylor, Charles, 56, 62
Tet Ansanm, 101
terrorism, 2, 10, 21, 22
    9/11, 2, 10, 20, 122, 126, 130, 134
Timor-Leste, Democratic Republic of, 3, 73–91, 237, 238, 239, 240, 241, 242, 243, 244,
    lost cause, 75, 76, 77, 81, 82, 87, 88, 90, 91, 241
Thauer, Christian, 226
Third World Network, 223
Thompson, Dale, 69n5
Thompson, Denis, 171
Thornberry, Cedric, 152
Tito, Josip Broz, 146
Toronto Daily Star, 53, 62
Toronto Dominion Bank, 78
TransAfrica, 107
Tremblay, Paul, 44
Trinidad and Tobago, 196
Trudeau, Pierre Elliott, 5, 17, 18, 53, 54, 55, 57–58, 59, 60, 61–62, 66, 68, 69–70n5, 77–78, 81, 115–16n11, 122
Tudman, Franjo, 148, 149
Tunisia, 44,
TVI Pacific, 212

U

Ukraine, 188, 237, 240
Union of Soviet Socialist Republics (USSR), 1, 3, 14, 44, 56, 59, 66, 81, 160
   and Afghanistan, 127, 167
United Arab Emirates, 134
United Kingdom, 15, 53, 56, 59, 62, 65, 66, 88, 127, 134, 150, 156, 171
United Nations, 4, 5, 6, 9–10, 15, 17, 20, 23, 28, 39, 40, 41, 42, 43, 44, 45, 46, 47, 48, 49, 54, 59, 61–62, 63, 65, 67, 68, 73, 80, 82, 88, 103, 105, 107, 108, 109, 113, 143, 145, 147, 150–51, 156
   Congo Advisory Committee, 42, 44–45, 48
   Charter, 151, 159
   Civilian Mission in Haiti (MICIVIH), 106, 107, 160
   Disaster Relief Office, 68
   Framework for Business and Human Rights, 215
   General Assembly, 12, 35, 39, 68, 80, 104, 161
   GA Resolution 1514, 12, 15, 16, 20
   Human Development Index, 91, 124
   Human Rights Commission, 101
   Human Right Council, 103
   Military Observer Group in India and Pakistan (UNMOGIP), 121, 132, 133
   Mission in Haiti (UNMIH), 106, 160, 202
   Mission in the Republic of South Sudan (UNMISS), 220
   Multinational Interim Force (MIF), 109
   Office on Drugs and Crime (UNDOC), 188
   Opération des Nations Unies au Congo (ONUC), 33, 35, 37, 38, 40, 42, 43, 45, 46, 47, 49, 237, 245, 246
   Protection Force (UNPROFOR), 144, 148, 150–57, 159, 160, 161, 238
   Security Council, 19, 35–37, 40, 45, 87, 102, 104, 107, 109, 151, 152, 153, 156, 160
   Stabilization Mission in Haiti (MINUSTAH), 109, 113, 160
   United Nations Emergency Force (UNEF), 42
United States Agency for International Development (USAID), 99–100, 102, 103, 117n41
United States, 1, 2, 4–5, 9, 10, 14, 20, 34, 40, 43, 45, 47, 80, 81, 84, 88, 90, 98, 100, 103, 108, 109, 122, 127, 147, 160, 161, 202, 212
   and Afghanistan, 25, 130, 167, 172, 178, 179
   and Bosnia, 147, 150, 154
   Coast Guard, 100, 105
   Congressional Black Caucus, 107
   and Haiti, 5, 25, 99, 100–101, 102, 103, 105, 106, 107, 108, 109, 114, 202
   National Security Strategy (2003), 20
   and Pakistan, 122, 127, 128, 129, 130, 132, 133, 134
Universal Declaration of Human Rights, 159
U Thant, 41, 42–43, 44, 45

V

Vance, Jonathan, 176, 178
Venezuela, 106, 186, 191, 192, 193, 196, 197, 203
Versailles, Treaty of, 12
Victoria Colonist, 49
Vietnam, 15, 56, 78, 80, 83, 122
Voluntary Principles on Security and Human Rights, 214, 215, 227, 228

W

Walker, James E., 61
Walzer, Michael, 161
Washington Office on Haiti, 101
Wassa Association of Communities Affected by Mining, 223
Weber, Max, 187, 206n4
Wesley, Michael, 155
West Indies, 63, 186, 192, 196, 197, 200, 201–2, 203
Whitlam, Gough, 80
Williams, G. Mennen, 45
Wilner, Alex, 20, 24, 26
Wood, William, 39
Woodward, Susan, 225
Woolcott, Richard, 89
World Bank, 111, 188, 208, 221
World Health Organization, 103
World University Service Canada (WUSC), 224, 234n59
Wright, Jim, 24

Y

Yugoslavia, 10, 17, 143, 146, 147, 157, 158, 161, 245
Yugoslav National Army (JNA), 147–48

Z

Zaire, 49n1
Zimbabwe, 84

www.ingramcontent.com/pod-product-compliance
Lightning Source LLC
Chambersburg PA
CBHW070754230426
43665CB00017B/2355